LIFE
of a
SALESMAN

R. ALEX JACKSON

EDITED AND COMPILED BY COLLEEN AND FELICIA KETCHESON

Life of a Salesman
Copyright © 2021 by Colleen and Felicia Ketcheson

Tellwell Talent
www.tellwell.ca

ISBN
978-0-2288-5996-3 (Paperback)
978-0-2288-5997-0 (eBook)

CONTENTS

FOREWORD

My grandpa was a storyteller. I have many fond memories of the family sitting around the dinner table listening to him tell stories from his childhood and young adulthood. They were always interesting and entertaining.

My grandpa was also a writer. In 1999, he gave his three children each a collection of his stories. He wrote letters to all his grandchildren, starting with my brother and I in 1997. I was his most frequent correspondent, and we wrote letters to each other approximately once per month during the last four years of his life. Over the years, he also published several magazine articles, newspaper articles, and letters to the editor. However, he never published his stories.

A few hours after his death, I had a sudden idea. My grandpa had so many entertaining and interesting stories to tell – why don't I share them with the world? Immediately, I knew it was the perfect project for my mom and me. A few days after his death, I broached the subject with her, and she thought it was a terrific idea. We started going through his files, knowing there'd be documents that could contribute to the book. Not only did we find the stories he wrote for his children, but numerous other stories, letters he wrote, sermons and devotions he gave for church, and 25 pages of a historical religion book he started writing 16 years earlier.

The purpose of this book is to do for my grandpa what he never did himself. We are certain he would have wanted to publish his stories, so they can be enjoyed by others as we have enjoyed them. In addition to his writings, this book contains his biography. As you'll see, he led a very full and interesting life and was a prolific volunteer. When he passed away, he was a board member of the Riverview Park and Zoo, located in Peterborough, Ontario. As my grandpa loved the zoo, we knew it was fitting for the proceeds from the sale of this book to be donated to the Riverview Park and Zoo in his name.

Grandpa also had a lot of great wisdom to share, and so we hope you also enjoy his quotes throughout, as they speak to his philosophical outlook, personality, and interests. Unless otherwise stated, these quotes are from the letters he wrote to me. Finally, we obtained memories and stories from numerous people who knew him to fully underscore who he was.

We hope you enjoy,

— Felicia Ketcheson

ACKNOWLEDGEMENTS

As this book is considerably longer than initially anticipated, compiling it took longer than we expected. However, it has been more rewarding than we thought it would. We have learned more about our dad and grandpa while doing for him what he never did for himself: publish his stories.

Many of the memories provided by others would never have made it into this book if not for the help of Sam Jackson. He was able to obtain memories from people living in Peterborough and recommend other people we should track down.

Thank you to Shirley Jackson, our mom and grandma, for providing dates and pictures, and confirming information. As always, your ability to remember such facts is astonishing.

While having a book containing stories dad/grandpa wrote is wonderful, we knew that including stories and memories from those who knew him would be even better. We are grateful to everyone who contributed memories. We were not sure how open people would be to such an endeavour; however, everyone was eager to contribute. And contribute you did!

To our dad/grandpa's immediate family members (Shirley, Steve and Sam Jackson and Edward Ketcheson), thank you for reading a draft and providing your comments and suggestions prior to publication.

This section would not be complete without also thanking Alex/ dad/grandpa. You provided us with wisdom and inspiration. We have countless fond memories of your entertaining us with stories. This compilation is a window into who you were. We cannot thank you enough for all you have done for us.

– Colleen and Felicia Ketcheson

QUOTES ABOUT ALEX'S PAST

I have spent a bunch of my life in fancy hotels and dining rooms so I can do without it now. Some people really enjoy it, but I would prefer a walk in the woods with a picnic basket. (2000)

Regarding having grown up without email or internet: HOW DID WE EVER SURVIVE WHEN I WAS A KID??? (2000)

I never enjoyed school much. I got good marks, in grade school anyway, but there were too many bullies, and it was a Catholic School, so they spent a lot of time learning about the church, going to confession, and having visits from the priest. I guess they still do that, but I don't know. High school was much different, but not sure I liked it much either. Anyway, my like or dislike was more to do with home life and where I lived than what the school was like. Ya gotta be there so you may as well like it and learn all you can. (2001)

I think grade eight was my best year. As I recall, it was very easy, and I did not have to write any exams, and I won the speaking contest at the end of the year. Perhaps grade eight is not as easy now though, and the curriculum certainly has changed. (2002)

Sure glad I'm not in school. When spring came, and the sun streamed through the window and hit me in the face, I wanted out. Don't you do this, but when that happened in grade eight, I did not bother to return to class after lunch. A friend and I got on our bikes and went fishing for the afternoon. I was the best student in the class, nice, polite, marks in the nineties and was bored. After a couple of times the teacher (a nun) did not even ask for an explanation or a note. Not that I was that smart, just the rest of the kids were a bunch of yahoos and the subjects were easy. (2003)

School was never my forte, although I like to read and learn stuff, I found it boring and too slow. (2005)

"Danny Boy" for some weird reason is one of my favourite [songs]. When I hear it, I think of my mother, so maybe that is why I am smitten with it. Too bad you did not know her.... To me she was a saint and hardly a day passes that I do not recall some memory of her. Weird eh! Age nor time do not diminish [sorrow] or love, the passing of time simply makes both more understandable and bearable. (2005)

My only school trip was in grade 8 when a friend and I skipped school one spring day. (2005, to Edward)

A year after Felicia got her driver's license: Do you like to drive, or is it scary and just a way to get where you want to go? Some kids don't care at all about driving, or care about cars, and then there are the Uncle Sam types. I guess I was sort of like them. I always liked cars and always wanted to drive. I got my license when I was 15. Piece of cake then; no written stuff, just get a thirty-day permit, five bucks probably, or maybe even two, and then take a driving test, the same day if you were capable. That's what I did. We drove around a few blocks, parallel parked, answered a few questions, paid ten dollars, I think, and drove away with a license. There were no 400 series roads to worry about then so we could just drive whenever and wherever. (2006)

After the Yukon and the Northwest Territories, I will have seen most of Canada right up to the top of Newfoundland and Labrador; been to Moosonee, visited all the Atlantic provinces and criss-crossed the prairies numerous times, and been from Alberta to British Columbia via every pass in the Rockies, been to just about every city and small town in Ontario from Windsor to Goderich, Thunder Bay to Timmins, etc. Not a world traveller but really want to explore my own country before I venture too far afield, after all it is larger than all of Europe, has unrivalled scenery, sunny beaches, snowy mountains, and everything in between, and we are kind to each other and usually civilized. Can't think of a better place to live or visit. (2015)

QUOTES ABOUT GROWING UP

Most kids like some of their classmates, but not all. Some are different, or have different ideas because of their home life, or addiction to TV, or all kinds of reasons that we cannot fathom. It is important to associate with those kids that have the same values and interests that you do. You know though, you can be a positive influence. Even if those you do not like or associate with are a bit rough there is usually something to like about them and even being nice to them when they are jerks, not accepting their antics, but just being you and treating them like any other human being can affect their lives. It does not happen that day or the next, and you may not even know about the change, but in years to come you may read, hear, or meet them and find that they actually turned out to be human beings. Your treatment of them as a kid may have been an influence on that. (1999)

Glad you like being a kid. Stay that way as long as you can. We all grow up soon enough and are not always happy with the things that confront us. (2001)

Actually, if you are thinking of a career in any field related to computers, or any branch of science, that math stuff is almost a necessity. People really do use it. Ask your Uncle Steve. His head is like a math textbook. Me, I still prefer colouring books, although when I was in the computer business, I did know, and use, some of that complicated math gooble-de-gook. I think that most of what I did know has evaporated through my grey, or white, hair. Hair that colour will do that, you know. Perhaps I should wear a hat so the knowledge will not escape! (2002)

A week before Felicia started grade 8: Getting close, eh? Only one more week of sleeping in and bumming around. I bet once you get there you will like it. Just think, five more years and you will be ready for university, or college, or travel! Scary eh! You know, every year, every age, has its own particular blessings and lessons, but on reflection, most people think of their childhood years as the most carefree and fun. Enjoy yours and don't be in a panic to become an adult. Grade eight through high school can be trying times because of the growing changes to our bodies, peer pressure to be like the rest of the gang, the desire to be grown up without the experience to handle it, and just the daily stuff life throws at us. But you know that period can also be the most fun, the most rewarding, the most memorable of our lives, and I am sure you will handle it just fine. (2002)

By the time you get this you will have [been] back in the halls of learning for a week, or almost. Hope you like your new class and the subjects are interesting. Learn the stuff anyway. You know, as you go through life, people can take all kinds of things from us, but one thing no one can take away is knowledge. Absorb everything your little brain can hold, whether it seems important or not. You just never know when you might need that little fact or bit of history. (2002)

The next thing I know you will be off to university somewhere. Do you know what you want to do when you are out of the education system? Most of us spend our whole lives and are not sure, so if you cannot decide, don't feel bad, no matter what the system tells you that you need to decide now. We all need goals to strive for, but I think the biggest goal is to live one's life in love and not fear. That may not make much sense now, but someday it will. (2003)

Like you, I was an outsider when I started high school, but it did not take long before I had my group of friends and knew all the others too. Kids are cruel, you know. Sometimes they are just made that way, sometimes they are brought up that way because their parents have no idea how to raise kids, but mostly kids just don't realize. Kids do not have the experience to realize what they are doing and how they make others feel. But even the biggest jerks, when someone explains their actions to them, turn into human beings. Part of growing up. Not a nice part sometimes, but just another step in the process to become a functioning human being. (2003)

You know, from your age until eighteen or so, are touted as the happiest and best years of your life. Not sure where that philosophy originated, but I could explain the rationale behind it if you wish. In retrospect it may be true, but not so when you are actually going through it. As you age, you realize that every day is the best time of your life. Everything is new. Every experience is new and different, and presents an opportunity to learn something, to see the magic of nature as the colours change, and the seasons come and go with their own personality. Friendly, cold, warm, sunny, or drizzly hail and just plain yucky, people come in all brands, just like the weather. We seem to look at yesterday many years ago as being great and forget that today could be great also if we just let it. So that's my philosophy lesson for today. (2003)

Honest, I was a kid in high school once, and I can almost remember the anticipation, or not, of seeing last year's buddies. High school is the kind of environment that can cement a lifelong friendship and believe me, lifelong friendships are not very common, and something to be cherished. (2004)

Working for a living is not always fun, but you have to have money to eat and buy cars, so what are you going to do. I am sure in not too many years you will find out too. Stay a kid as long as you can. (2004)

High schools are full of kids, but it can be a lonely place as teenagers are such a messed-up part of humanity. I proposed banning them from the age of thirteen until twenty, to the north pole or a similar location. However, we were all part of that transition, and dippy to one degree or another, but magically adulthood emerges, well for most anyway, just like cytolysis takes place for a butterfly. Like a cocoon splitting open, one day a wingy kid wakes up and becomes a human being. Not all go through that transition or are affected similarly, and some never become adults, and some are always adults. I bet if you think about your friends, you can slot them into those categories pretty easily. (2005)

Do you have an idea where you want to go and what you want to take [in university]? Tough decisions when one does not have the experience nor lifetime of knowledge to call on. Try not to make your choices based on what and where your friends are taking and going. That kind of decision only leads to a bunch of wasted money and usually no education. (2005)

School can be a real pain, well not school, but the kids who attend. It is hard not to be concerned as one feels left out, inferior, or whatever, as the others hang out in their little cliques. But you know most are jerks, and the best one can do is feel sorry for them, as they are the ones with no self-esteem, usually do to with their home life, or lack there off. Guess the best I can say is do not sacrifice your values or principles to be part of the gang. I know you would not do that. No one respects anyone who does that, not even the gang members. Better to stand your ground, be yourself, treat everyone with respect, even the jerks, and as the saying goes, you rise above the crowd. When I was a teenager working at the bowling alley, almost all the other kids knew and used every swear word you can imagine, and probably you hear at school. Using foul and obscene language does not make you an adult, nor smart, it just makes one sound stupid and uneducated. My boss commented on the fact that I was the only kid who did not swear, and the other kids, even the bad ones, respected me for it. Unfortunately, we live in the present, especially teenagers, and I know how hard it is to be on the outside and not be in that circle. Too bad we cannot jump ahead ten years or so and look back and see how insignificant and unimportant it was that for a very few months we felt sort of isolated and out of the loop. It is only when one gets through the teenage years, reads a bit, learns a bit, that we understand the trauma of being a teenager. I would not go through it again for anything, although they can be some of the most fun and memorable years of one's life. So just continue to be Felicia, and perhaps one day those other characters will grow up too. (2005)

Ya know what, school is just about over for another year. May starts next week and I bet a month after that you will be all done?? Are you excited, and looking forward to summer, and then your last year of school? What a time in your life. It is exciting, scary, and amongst all life experiences, a time that seems to stick in one's memory forever. Savour the time, the friends, the experiences and enjoy every moment. No other time in your life will be quite the same as it is, like a long doorway from childhood to adulthood, and you are stuck in the middle, no longer a kid, but not quite able to participate as an adult. In some ways a lousy period in one's journey through this thing called life, but in retrospect, for most people, the most carefree, and certainly the most memorable. (2006)

You know though that most of us go through our whole lives and are not sure what we want as a career. (2006)

Just do the best you can, and don't be concerned with those people who tell you that you should know what you are going to do with the rest of your life. (2006)

Regarding finishing high school: When people take a different direction in life the close friendships seem to fade as those things one had in common are gone and no common bond exists. I have friends though that are in business, some are professionals, some are labourers or factory workers, but they are all people, and if one works at it and wants to, you can stay friends. (2007)

INTRODUCTION

Our dad/grandpa would tell stories to his family about his childhood, youth and working days, usually after a great meal. We were all enthralled with his wonderful way of capturing our attention. Alex was a born storyteller, and no matter how many times we had heard a particular story, we were hooked. On December 25, 1999, he put most of those stories in a booklet for each of his three children. This book contains those stories as well as those found in letters or elsewhere after his death; those not included in the original booklet are marked with an asterisk (*).

The stories are roughly in chronological order, to the best of our knowledge, the exception of which being most of the vacation and bike stories being grouped together, despite him being various ages. The stories are as he wrote them in his unique voice plus the added headings within the stories, minor editing, and changes to some names. His way of talking and writing was so different that in 2017 his grandchildren read an article in *Our Canada,* not knowing it was written by their grandpa, and commented that it sounded just like him.

– Colleen and Felicia Ketcheson

ALEX'S STORIES

Preface to the Booklet by Alex in 1999

I have been fiddling with this for a year or so. Every once in a while, I sit at the computer and doodle away. Once I started down memory lane, incidences come into my head like a flood, and I have to stop and grab a piece of paper to write them down, lest they slip away.

Do not think that I just found out about some fatal illness that will take me away shortly, or that I have a premonition of a car fatality, or any such thing. I heard some very moving talks by a few people a while ago, and ever since I have been thinking of doing this. Their words or thoughts were the catalyst to get me to commit to paper.

Guess what I really want to say is what a wonderful journey the last sixty-four years have been. I remember the time when I did not know anyone that old, or so I thought. Anyway, I have been around those many years, good and bad, and when I look back it has been a hoot and will continue to be so for as long as God allows.

I really want to tell you, Sam, Colleen, and Steven, that you share a great deal of responsibility for making it so. Many parents, and I know lots who unload their tale of woes about their kids, had they even *one* like you guys they would be ecstatic. When kids are little, parents daily tell them, "I love you." As the kids age, the "I love you" often disappears, perhaps more so with fathers and sons. Not manly, I guess. I think that showing it in your actions, your teachings, and your example, through how you live and treat others, is more important than saying it. But I know it is very comforting to hear that you are valued and loved. Your actions and daily lives are a comfort to me. It seems to me that your mother and I did our most important job in life properly. You, however, will be the final judge.

I say that I am doing this for you. For you, so you will have a glimpse of another time, a time when growing up was so completely different and foreign from your early years, that it probably will seem very strange, and perhaps almost not believable. Not everything will be accurate. Memory is not always perfect, but I am trying to record things as accurately as possible. I am recording only the happy times because that is what I mostly remember. Memory is a great gift. It seems to have the ability to turf out the bad stuff, unless of course there were some really bad things, like abuse. I did not experience that.

I never had the desire to be a writer, at least not to make a living at it, but when I get started it is hard to leave the keys and attend to the things that I must do. I just want to put down on paper, or the screen, all these memories that are invading my poor head. Sign of getting old? I don't really know, but I do know that while I want you to have this so you can say, "boy, he was crazy, or that must have been fun, or how did they survive like that," I think I am really doing it for me. Something inside is just bursting to record this stuff.

I wish that I had kept a diary. So many things I remember, and don't remember, that shaped my destiny, that kids would like to know when it is too late, and there is no one left with the answers. I regret many times not asking my mother things I would like to know now. Dad was not one to discuss things with kids. He was a father, I guess, but not a dad. He did not have time for kids, but once an adult you could sort of talk to him. I did not have the nerve for many years and when I did, I did not ask, and now obviously it is too late.

Please do not hesitate to ask. Unlike my dad, but like my mom I think, you may have noticed that I like little kids. I think they are great characters. Innocent of the world's problems, full of questions, trusting, and eager to learn. Adults have such an awesome responsibility towards kids, and most of us don't realize until it is too late. I don't know why I threw that in, but the fingers just would not stop.

Hope you enjoy the stories.

My Pig

One dark evening a knock came to the door. It was Charlie Warnock. I did not call him Charlie. I was about three and a half years old. Mr. Warnock was the local butcher and a friend of dad's. He was a big, round, jolly guy. I don't think he was married, so he had no kids, and always had candy or something for me on his frequent visits. This evening he had a large cardboard box. He set it on the floor in the kitchen, and said it was a present for me. I do not know what nationality he was, but he had a decided accent. I thought he sounded funny, but I liked him, and was anxious to see what was in the box. The flaps were opened, but the box was too high for me to see inside. With some help I grabbed the top, hoisted myself up and promptly tumbled inside, to keep company with a very small, squealing pig.

I guess it was not a pig, but just a piglet. I thought he was pretty cute, and we took to one another immediately; maybe because he was my size and vice versa. I have no idea why the local butcher would give a kid a pig for a present, but I accepted. The piglet lived in the box for the rest of the night. We fed him with a bottle for a while, and then he was moved to a little pen outside. We had pigs in a pigpen, but my little friend got the run of the backyard when I was outside. He did not have to go near the pigpen or the barnyard for some time.

We chased each other around the yard, but unlike the goat that came later, he was not worth a hoot at jumping or climbing. He could dig, though. He got bigger very rapidly. I fed him all the vegetables that I could safely forage from the garden, along with daily rations of chop. All pigs got fed chop. Wheat, oats, not sure but maybe both, were taken to the mill in town and ground up. The result looked like flour and was called chop. The chop was mixed with water and poured into a trough for the pigs. It was not very appetizing looking, and slopped all over, especially when the pigs discovered it. You have probably heard the term, *slopping the hogs*. This would not happen today. Pigs now eat very well. Anyway, my pig got his share of slop.

We had fun but never really bonded like Muggs (Gordon's dog), or even my juvenile delinquent, the goat. Pigs get very big fast and

13

are considered only good for one purpose on a farm. One day, not my decision, and I don't think I was even consulted, my pig was transformed into bacon, head cheese, pork hocks and roasts. Pretty traumatic for a kid, but let's face it, even kids have to eat.

Potato Bugs

Do you know what potato bugs are? They are little reddish guys that seem to like to eat the leaves of potato plants. No leaves left on the plants, no potatoes under the ground. You can now buy a powder to sprinkle on the plants to kill the bugs. Whether it was available or not when I was a kid, I do not know, but we had a lot of potato plants, and a lot of potato bugs.

Neither Marlene nor I were old enough to go to school. We each had a honey pail and went to the garden, and one plant and one bug at a time, flicked the potato bugs into our honey pails. I remember going into the kitchen with my little pail full of bugs, and saying to my mother, "we brought lunch, can you fry these for us?" Not sure why I thought you could eat potato bugs, but I guess it looked like enough for a meal, since we each had a small pail full. I don't think she cooked them.

King and Jigs

Dad had a team of horses to do the farm work. They were called King and Jigs. I think King and Jigs were the names of two cartoon characters. The horses were Clydesdales, and unlike a cartoon character they were big. Dad and Ed were breaking corn in a field by the creek. The horses pulled the wagon and dad, and Ed were breaking off the ears and throwing them into the wagon.

It would be autumn and probably cold outside. I was four or five years old and was sitting on the seat in the front of the wagon, where you would sit to drive the horses. This team of farm horses was very well trained, and really did not need a driver in the wagon. You could walk beside and tell them which way to turn, go, or stop, and they would obey. I guess I thought they needed some guidance, or maybe I was cold from sitting and doing nothing, so I picked up the reins and hollered for them to go. The pace for breaking corn is slow for a four-year-old. King and Jigs obeyed my commands, until father roared at them as they headed towards the bank into the creek. I don't think I ever got my horse driving license!

King and Jigs did a lot of work around the farm and they seemed to enjoy it. One would go to the granary and shovel wheat into bags that held about seventy-five pounds. The bags, fifty or more, were then loaded onto the wagon, and King and Jigs pulled it into town to the mill to be ground up into chop for the pigs.

One day I was allowed to go along. It was great to sit on top of the bags on the wagon, as it trundled along the highway into town. You sat up high so you could see stuff, and it was just a nice feeling to sit on the bags high up in the air, to smell the wheat and fresh air, and watch the horses trotting along. I have no recollection of the mill. Perhaps I slept during the chop making process. I just recall the ride. I also think it is unfortunate that most kids will not get the opportunity to have such an experience. Maybe my dad was really a dad then because I do recall these and other times when I was very little, following him around when he did chores and work on the farm.

Thrashing March

Thrashings were fun. Great fun if you were four years old and did not have to help. Guess I saw my job as being an annoyance. I was great at it. Someone owned a large thrashing machine and took it around to all the farms in turn, as the wheat or oats were ready. The thrasher was pulled by a large smoke and steam belching, iron-wheeled tractor. The tractor also powered the thrasher once it arrived and was set up. The area farmers followed the thrasher with their horses and wagons. Everyone pitched in to help each other. Did any money change hands? I have no idea.

Our turn came and they descended like a family reunion. Horses and wagons, and of course the smoking monster with his large attachment. You may not have seen a thrasher work, but I am sure you have seen them sitting outside museums or other places. Some are not too large, but most were huge. The thrasher took bundles of wheat in one end, shook the heck out of it, spit the wheat out a spout into a waiting receptacle, (usually a wagon with all four sides boxed in) and the straw went out the other end.

The thrasher would be placed where the farmer wanted the straw stack to be. The straw was used for bedding for horses and cattle, so it was usually close to the barn. Sometimes if there were lots, and still some left over from last year, the straw stack would be in the corner of a field, away from the barn. That way it could be burnt if not wanted, and not burn down the whole place. Straw stacks were used to provide bedding for the animals, and I can recall one year when there was a massive pile and it was not needed, I guess, as my dad set it on fire. It was the biggest fire I ever remember. Dry straw burns so fast you can hardly imagine, and a stack that large sure makes one big fire. Straw stacks can go fifteen or twenty feet high, and be much bigger around, and burns like gasoline. I was four or five at the time but can still picture that huge mound of straw all aflame.

For the thrashing I am talking about though, the machine and its giant steam gadget that powered it were right in the barnyard. It is quite a remarkable thing to see a bare spot, a large bare spot in the farmyard, and by evening it is covered by a great mound of straw. Great place for kids to jump into. Just don't drop a needle if you want it back. The tractor is parked about twenty or more feet from the thrasher, and a large belt is run from the tractor to the thrasher. It does not go that fast, but one still does not want to get too close. Sometimes they jump off. Belts that size don't recognize anything as puny as arms or legs, or even heads.

The steam engine hisses and and makes all kinds of neat sounds, if you appreciate machinery like this. The owner must constantly feed it, making one think that all such contraptions are teenagers, since they are always in need of more food and water. The thrasher makes lots of loud clanging noises, so that if you are right beside it, it is like being in the front row at a rock concert. I think the noise is just so it can let you know that it is doing something.

The farmers with their wagons would traverse the fields and load up with sheaves of wheat and bring them to the hungry mouth of the thrasher. The sheaves would be tossed in using a pitchfork, and when the wagon was empty another would take its place, and it would head back out for another load. How long this took depended on how many acres of wheat there were, how many wagons, and how far the field was from where the thrasher was parked. Usually, a long day would do. Some larger farms would carry on the next day.

The farm where all the activity was taking place, was also the local feed mill for the dozen or more workers. The wives all arrived at various times during the day. They brought food, although the host provided the meat and main items. All pitched in to make pies, lots of different kinds of pies. That many men working that hard were hungry, both for lunch and supper. Everything was cooked on the wood stove and the men washed up outside using the pump. Not sure about other facilities, but I suspect the outhouse took a beating that day too. Of course, the horses all had to be fed and watered. I recall it being very hot, and inside probably worse, with the wood stove going full tilt most of the day. Except for all the hard work it was more like a picnic. Everyone should experience a thrashing, especially as a kid.

Eunice, the Goat, and the Piano Box

The straw stack stood next to the barn. The grain had been shovelled into the granary, and the smoke and steam belching monster towed its charge across the road to Stacey's farm. I was four years old I think and wanted to help. I was not allowed around the real action with the men, so I helped my mother. I say helped but I think my mother would have a different version. I don't remember Gordon or Marlene being around at all, but I guess they must have been. Edward would be out working with the thrashing gang.

She and some other ladies baked pies at our house and took them over to the Staceys. I wanted to carry one and I remember the reluctance but must have whined sufficiently that I got to carry one, accompanied by my mother and helpers. I don't remember what kind, but I do remember that just about in the middle of the road, that darn pie slipped from my grasp and splattered on the asphalt. Not sure what was said, but I doubt that they were pleased.

When we got to the Stacey's kitchen, I suspect I was just a bit underfoot. I guess to get me out of the way, but to still make me think I was doing something, Eunice and I went to get wood. Eunice was a nice lady as I remember, but I have no idea how old she was. There was a sort of shed attached to the back of the house. You went out the back door, and to your left a few feet was the door to the shed.

The shed housed the wood, along with lots of other interesting items, including a piano box. Pianos were shipped I guess in large wooden crates. Picture a piano and imagine the box for it. This box was open at the top and the side facing out was closed in, to about the height of the keyboard. The rest was open at the front. It was just the right size for storing wood for the kitchen stove. The ladies had been using it up at a good rate, so only one corner and part of the bottom of the box had any wood left.

Eunice reached the wood and gave me a couple of pieces, and then loaded her arms up. We were about to leave for the kitchen with our load when we heard a bumping noise. There in the doorway, trying to get his horns through so he could get in, was a large goat. Alex Stacey, the grandfather (because of me everyone referred to him as old Alex and me as little Alex), had some sheep, and this one nasty ram. Rams are not happy characters and like to try out their horns on anything in their way. At this time that would be Eunice and me.

He was doing a good job of twisting his head to get through, and we were not a happy pair of wood getters. She hollered at him, but he only seemed concerned about getting at us. She dropped the armload of wood and lifted me into the piano box. Since I could hardly see over the edge it seemed like a safe spot. Eunice then hoisted her skirt and scrambled in with me. I recall that it was not an easy task, so I doubt that she was that young and spry. She made it into the piano box with seconds to spare, as the ram finally wiggled through the door, and came over to torment the occupants of the piano box.

Eunice hollered, thinking someone in the kitchen would come to our rescue. I probably hollered too but I don't remember. I just remember watching that ram from the back of the box. We could just about look one another in the eye, but he was taller than me. He just stood there seemingly defying us to try to get out. We were yelling in vain, and I do remember her comforting me, and telling me that we really would not have to spend the rest of our lives as captives in a piano box. But I have to go pee! It seemed like an eternity, and probably was fifteen minutes or more.

The kitchen staff really did not need the wood in a hurry and were probably glad to not have me under foot for a while. Their supply did finally get low, and someone was dispatched to find out why we had not returned with the wood. She, whoever it was, stuck her head in the door and immediately retreated for the kitchen. Old Alex was around somewhere. He was too old then to work with the thrashing gang. A few more minutes and he appeared in the doorway, and with a few whacks of his cane on the rump of the ram, it decided to leave. We were rescued from the piano box. The story of Eunice, little Alex, the goat, and piano box did the rounds at thrashings for a long time after that.

Bus to Katie's

Mother and I took the bus to Windsor. I was four and all dressed up. I do not remember the time of year, but it was warm, but not summertime hot. The bus stopped at our laneway. Check out the picture of a bus running around in the middle of the depression, and you will know what it looked like. I was impressed and a bit scared. I do not remember being on a bus before, and Windsor seemed a long way away.

We got off at the bus station and walked around downtown. My mother had worked in Windsor and really did not like the farm, so I imagine this was a treat for her, and a trip back to nostalgia. I was fascinated by the big stores and amazed at the people and cars. Tons of houses all jammed together. Where were the fields? We saw a kid's pedal car in the window of a department store, and I thought it would be just the thing for me to navigate the farm lanes. No number of pleadings helped. I imagine there were people during the depression with sufficient funds to buy their kids a pedal car, but my mother was not one of them. We kept walking. We were going to visit Katie.

Katie was a friend of my mother's and lived somewhere in the west end. Mother and I went to the bus station to get the bus to Katie's. We were waiting for the bus when I asked if the driver knew where she lived. Well, if the driver did not know where she lived, I was not going to get on the bus and get lost. I was afraid he would just keep on driving, and who knows where I would end up. Taking a bus to Windsor was one thing. After all it was big, and I assumed at the end of the line, so the driver would have to stop there anyway. Taking a bus in the city with a driver who did not know Katie, or where she lived, was far too risky for me. We walked!

Sometime later I complained of being tired. My mother said we could have taken the bus and I would not have to walk. I told her that if she had purchased the pedal car I would not have to walk. Funny the things one remembers. Seemed a long walk down sidewalks and across streets, but tired and worn out we finally got to Katie's. After our visit I agreed to take the bus back to the station, and then on home. Maybe that is why I am not partial to bus travel.

Buddy

Dresden is a town of two thousand, in the middle of farming country, and its claim to fame is that it was the home of the Underground Railway and Uncle Tom's cabin; Uncle Tom being the Reverend Josiah Henson. Slaves walked across the ice on the Detroit River, then made their way for days through the forest to Dresden and freedom. His cabin is still there, but now a museum dedicated to Black History, and he is buried in the small black cemetery there.

As a youngster, I had three aunts in Dresden, and every summer I took turns spending a few days with each one. Well, Buddy lived on the street behind Aunt Mary's. There were lots of kids on the street, but Buddy and I were best friends, the same age, around five or six, and the same size. Now, if you were black, you were not allowed in the restaurants, the barber shop, or the pool room. Fortunately, money prevailed, so they could access the bank and the two grocery stores. No discussion, just an understanding on both sides that this was the unwritten rule. I should mention how fortunate I was as I am sure the word *discrimination* was never in my parent's dictionary. Skin colour, size, shape, nationality, and language just did not matter.

I would get permission from Aunt Mary, and the required nickel, and Buddy would do the same from his mom, and we would walk the short block to the main corner, doing our job of kicking the excess pebbles off the sidewalk, and making dust storms with the sand. The ice cream parlour was right on the corner. There were two or three concrete steps up to the door, and Buddy would sit on one of the steps and wait, while I went inside and got our ice cream.

Buddy was only five, but he was black so certainly not allowed inside. We never questioned it, never talked about it, and I am not sure we even realized we were not the same colour. We were just kids and knew the rules, but never questioned why. So, I came out, gave Buddy his ice cream, and both being colour blind, we wandered back down the street together enjoying our treat, and finishing the sidewalk clearing.

The Depression

The Farmhouse

The Depression meant nothing to me. I was born in the middle of it, so was too young to know, or care anything about economics. If we were poor, then so was everyone else. I don't remember being overly hungry; always had a bed and was looked after. I had pets, brothers, and a sister to play with. I had aunts and uncles who spoiled me. What else could a kid want?

The farmhouse was typical of most I think, built to house a couple of generations. The front door opened into the big kitchen, which was like a whole house in one room. The kitchen also had a door to the backyard, a door to the pantry, and two large sliding doors to the dining room and living room. Four bedrooms were upstairs. No hydro, no inside water or bathroom facilities, and heat in the kitchen only by a wood burning cook stove and a Quebec heater on the other side of the room. It also contained a divan (they were not really a chesterfield) and a large table to accommodate a dozen or so people. Despite all the furniture and stoves, there was still room to run around.

Light was provided by coal oil lamps. If you were rich, you also had a Coleman lantern. Using a mantle and different fuel, they were much brighter. We did not have one. Saturday night was bath night in front of the stove. Water was heated on the stove and poured into a copper wash tub. Little kids could fit nicely into the tub. How an adult managed, I have no idea. It was always nice to be the first one, so you got the clean water.

On really cold nights my mom would heat the flat irons on the stove, wrap them in newspaper and put them in the bottom of the bed under the covers. They kept your feet warm, at least for a while. Though they were not very comfortable to bang into in the morning. Lots of mornings when you woke there was frost covering the inside of the window. No one took their time getting downstairs by the stove to dress.

The railway cut through the back of the farm. Trains started to slow down going by the farm, to stop in Comber. You have seen pictures of many men riding boxcars, looking for work during the Depression. Lights from a farmhouse, even oil lamps, are visible from a train a half mile or so away.

I remember sitting in my highchair while my mother cooked eggs, and probably salt pork, for some poor individual who saw the light, jumped off the train, and followed the path from the tracks to the farmhouse. They would knock on the back door and look for food. They were termed bums. Some were bums I suppose, but probably most were men with families somewhere. They were just trying to find work, had no money or anything else, and were hungry. Mother always gave them something. Perhaps the visitor had helped do chores before coming in for food.

The Provisions

I do not remember my siblings being around at these times, but I am sure they were around somewhere. Farms provided eggs and usually had lots of meat stocked away, along with preserves. There was no in-house refrigeration, just an ice box, and salt pork was a staple. We had a stone milkhouse next to the back of the house. Milk was kept there, along with salt pork. Just as it sounds, bacon and other bits were put into barrels with salt to preserve them. We got lots of salt.

Oranges and non-local fruits that we take for granted were all luxuries then and not available except at certain times of year. We got the Eaton's catalogue and I picked out all the toys for Christmas, the only problem being that I never got them. Christmas seemed to be the only time that I remember knowing that we were not exactly rich. Toys were pretty scarce. Aunt Ollie always sent a box with stuff for us kids. She was dad's sister, lived in Toronto and owned a china shop. Christmas was the only time we got oranges. New clothes were also scarce. I do remember a neat truck that Aunt Ollie sent one year. Wish I had it now. But you know what? Kids can still grow up okay without getting a lot of junk.

We had a large garden and mom canned tomatoes, pears, strawberries, peaches and of course chilli sauce. Passenger trains probably ran four or five times a day. Waste of all types was flushed out as they went. If you have been on a train, you will notice the sign in the bathroom (cramped quarters) that requests that you do not flush the toilet while the train is at the station. There were no holding tanks, just a pipe to the outside. Fresh strawberry shortcake (and other delicacies) was a staple of the dining room, along with china and silverware, in most dining cars. Consequently, wild strawberries grew in large quantities along the tracks.

The Walks

I recall enjoying walking the tracks in the spring with mom. We did not spend a lot of time together outside. I imagine she was busy cooking, washing, and cleaning without the aid of all the equipment we take for granted. Anyway, I was not yet in school, so I thought I was really doing something by carrying a basket as we picked strawberries along the railway line. I probably ate or squashed as many as I put in the basket. It is one of those very fond memories that you dig up from your childhood. A bright sunny day, the red winged black birds flitting around the ditch by the tracks, just the freedom, solitude and company of your mother doing something together. Depression or not, I was a happy and lucky kid.

Muggs

The Arrival of Muggs

Not sure where or how, but I remember a man bringing this tiny ball of fur to the door one day. Muggs arrived for Gordon. He was his dog. I think Gordon named him, but I am not sure where the name came from. I think there was a comic character named Muggs. Over the months Muggs grew. He may have been Gordon's dog, but he loved us all and we loved him. All kids should have a dog like Muggs. Dogs give unconditional love. You can hug them, feed them, kick them, or otherwise abuse them, and they still come back and want to be friends. [Editor's note: Muggs was never abused by anyone in the family].

Gordon went to school and Muggs and I roamed the farm. He looked after me. I took the basket and gathered the eggs. I also took Muggs to keep that monster rooster at bay. The rooster was a Red Rock, I think. I do know that he was taller than I was, and felt I was competition for his hens. What do I know, I just wanted the eggs.

Eggs

I went into the chicken coop, stuck my hand under the sitting hens, stole the eggs and put them gently into my basket. Muggs waited at the door, guarding it from the rooster, who wanted to get in and do away with me. When we left the coop the rooster followed, billowing out his chest and prancing around making dust fly. Angry roosters are not fun friends. Muggs wanted to run ahead to the house, so I called him back and held onto his collar. If the dog got too far ahead the rooster would attack. More than once I was knocked to the ground by that mangy rooster.

I did not want to run with the eggs. I was entrusted with this task and enjoyed doing something worthwhile. I realised the importance of bringing all the eggs back in one piece, rather than looking like an omelette. Holding onto the collar so that Muggs would not run on ahead, the rooster would follow a few feet back, but not attack. It was always a dangerous game. Especially at the gate, things got tense.

Let go of the collar, tell Muggs to get the rooster, put my basket down to unlatch the gate, transfer the basket safely to the other side, call Muggs and get him inside the yard, then hustle to close the gate before the rooster comes charging. I still see him jumping up, spurs extended, attacking the gate as I tried to latch it. Every morning was a new adventure and battle with the rooster. He would have made mincemeat out of me if it were not for the dog. He would even attack my dad in the barnyard. Dad would just give him a lift with his foot, send the rooster flying, only to see that rooster turn and attack again. He lived a long time, but after we moved to Tecumseh, he ended up as chicken soup.

The Haymow

What I really started out to tell you though, is my episode with the haymow. Hope you know what a haymow is. There was a ladder straight up against an inside wall of the barn to the mow. Not in school yet, Muggs and I were out for our morning exploration of the barnyard. The mow was a great space. It ran the full length and width of the barn.

Oftentimes it was full of loose hay to feed the horses and cows. One was not supposed to trample this mound of hay, but kids liked to play in it. It provided a soft landing when one jumped or fell from the beams holding the barn together.

Not sure why, but I thought I should investigate the haymow. I was too young, too little to go up there by myself, but there was no one else around. What was I to do but climb? Up I went, until I got to the floor of the mow, and reached in to grab hold to pull myself up and off the ladder. Loose hay does not provide much of a hold, so I woke up on my back on the barn floor. I have no idea how long after, minutes I suppose, haymows being about twelve to fifteen feet in the air. A fall that far, at four or five years old would knock a bit of air out of you.

Rooster

I woke up and, in a few seconds, realized where I was. My nemeses, the deadly rooster, was standing on my chest staring at my face. Ask me if I remember being scared. Think about the thoughts of a four- or five-year-old being pecked to death by a monster rooster! I covered my face with my arms and hollered for Muggs. He of course was probably outside sniffing around.

In short order, though, my faithful companion and protector came running in, and with a few snarls, barks, and a lunge at the rooster, saved me from death by a chicken. For some reason Muggs was the only thing on the farm that the rooster would back down from. Even the Clydesdales did not faze this rooster. Muggs waited for me to stagger up, hold onto his collar and drag me to the house, to explain to mom my drama with the rooster. Every kid needs a dog like Muggs but could probably survive childhood without a killer rooster.

The Hounds

Muggs was Gordon's dog, and Gordon looked after him. Our neighbours owned hounds, lots of them, and we had Muggs. When he was not fully grown, occasionally, one or two of their dogs would get out of the yard.

They had a fence and gate all around to keep the hounds in. Well, sometimes they would get out, come across the road, and beat up on Muggs. He would end up scared and bruised, and Gordon would patch him up and look after him.

One day he grew up. We heard a terrible commotion out front. Across the road, inside the fenced in yard, there was a large circle of howling, barking, yipping hounds. Inside the circle was Muggs. He was having the time of his life. A dog would rush in, be grabbed by the scruff of the neck, and go flying back out. It was bedlam with the neighbours, and I am not sure who else was running around, yelling, and trying to stop the carnage to the hounds. Gordon and I ran over, but it seemed Gordon was not in a hurry to call off Muggs as the neighbours demanded. Muggs was getting his revenge.

Sometime later Muggs got very sick. It seemed he had eaten some poisoned meat. Gordon was sure it was intentional, but who knows. Anyway, he spent all night in the basement with Muggs, maybe the whole day too, I don't remember. I don't know what he did for him, or to him, except cradle his head and talk to him, but Muggs survived.

The Move

We moved to Tecumseh. Both Muggs and the rooster went with us. We wandered the fields behind our house, just like the farm, but not as large and not all ours. Muggs pulled me in the wagon as fast as Gordon could ride his bike. I think I was eight when we moved. Gordon is five years older. The highway in front of the house in Tecumseh was not very busy. The war was on and not a lot of people had cars nor could get gas to put in them. We would go down the road a way, Gordon on his bike and me in the wagon pulled by Muggs. Muggs would be told to wait while Gord took off on his bike.

When the time was ripe, he would call Muggs and away we would go. Gord delighted in getting the dog to run like a shot, pulling me in the wagon, and at the last minute when we caught up, turning into the driveway. Of course, the dog would follow and so would the wagon for a foot or so, then the sharp turn would tip it on its side and spill me onto the edge of the road. After a few rolls and bruises, he would promise not to do it again. Of course, he did not, at least not until the next time I got into the wagon.

Gordon moved out at a certain age, but Muggs stayed. Eventually we moved to Pillette Road in Windsor. Muggs moved too, but he was getting old. He would be about thirteen or so, not sure, when it did not make sense to have him around in agony. Neither Gordon nor dad had the courage, so one day mom and I took Muggs to the humane society. His face said he knew as well as we.

War, Milkweed, and the Radio

[Modified with permission, based on Alex's story *A Small War Effort* published in the November 2010 issue of *Our Canada*]

The War

The war was on. I doubt that I knew what war was. I certainly did not know where Germany, France, Belgium, or Italy was or any of those places that parents were concerned about. My older brother Edward was somewhere in, or going to, one of those places, and I was not sure why. I was six, went to school a mile down the road, to Comber each Sunday for church a few miles the other way, and to Tilbury some Saturday nights to see Gene Autry or Roy Rogers at the movies. We lived on a hundred acres that I explored with Muggs, and that was a big enough world for me. I loved it.

A creek traversed the farm. There was a wooden bridge of sorts connecting the fields. I lay on my stomach on the bridge and fished with a stick, string and bent pin holding a reluctant worm. Muggs sat beside me lest I fall in. Zeppelins often flew over the farm. They flew low and trailed large banners proclaiming *V for Victory*. It was all very amazing to me.

Most things connected with the war had no effect on me. Sugar was rationed, meat was rationed, as were tires, gasoline, and other stuff.

I remember the little tokens my parents had to buy sugar. We raised animals, so meat was not a concern. Honey was a good sugar substitute for lots of things, and Mr. Allyn down the road raised bees, so honey was not a problem. My dad made ice cream in the little hand cranked ice cream churn. He was also the best homemade bread baker around. What wasn't plentiful were toys and new clothes. I did not care. I was not hungry, I was warm most of the time, with a whole farm to roam and a dog to keep me company, and for a time a goat and a pig. There was not much more I wanted or needed.

We were taught to knit at school, and we learned with scarves. Socks were next if you could get the hang of it. All to send over to some of those strange countries for the soldiers fighting the war. We took a quarter each week to buy Victory Bonds to give the government money to pay for the war. We collected milkweed pods. I liked that. Farmers did not like milkweed, and this seemed like a good way to dispose of it.

All rubber, at least for tires, was natural and came from Brazil and other South American countries that grew rubber trees. It was all shipped north by boat. The Germans subs and other ships of war made it very unsafe, if not impossible, to ship through the North Atlantic. Any rubber around was needed for the war, so vehicle tires just were not available for use at home.

The Milkweed Pods

We were asked to collect milkweed pods. The National Research Centre, or whatever their name was then, was working on a project to make rubber out of milkweed pods. For years I thought they succeeded and were making rubber. I thought that until years later when I met Jeanne Dobson [who received the Governor General's Commemorative Medal for her work with the Girl Guides of Canada]. Not sure how the conversation started, but she also collected milkweed. Her dad oversaw the project in Ottawa, and she assures me that the project was abandoned as it just did not work. No milkweeds were ever successful at becoming rubber.

I have no idea how many areas, schools or kids were involved, but we were. It was a great adventure. Early fall when the weather was still warm, and if you like the outdoors, this was a great excuse to wander all over the farm. The corn was twice as high as me, the weeds at the edge of the fields and ditches were tall goldenrods, purple asters, and lots of other wonderful colours, and milkweeds. It was like an adventure into another world for a six-year-old. You could not see the house from the far reaches. Sometimes the tip of the barn appeared, but to my mind I was in a foreign land.

I had a wagon with sides and used a sickle to cut the weeds. A sickle is not a safe thing for a six-year-old, but we were entrusted with all kinds of implements then. I never ventured into those far reaches without Muggs, so my mother knew I would come to no harm. He kept me company, chased rabbits and bugs and other things, and I cut milkweed and loaded my wagon.

When it was full, I would transfer the sticky cargo to a burlap bag and head out for more. There was a nice bush on one corner of the farm. I explored it too, but milkweeds did not grow under the big trees. I never wasted time there when I had this important job to do. The farm was cut in two by the railroad line. I never went over it into the other fields by myself. Getting run over by a train hurts and I was told the boundaries and stayed within them. Not sure how many bags of milkweeds I collected, nor exactly how they ended up in Ottawa, but I bet my dad was happy to have all those weeds gone from the farm and done away with rather than as just one more chore. The sight of a milkweed always brings back memories.

The Radio

Highway 98 that our farm was on was the testing grounds. Jeeps, small army trucks, large army trucks, Bren Gun Carriers and even half-tracks were driven and tested. All the automotive manufacturers in Windsor were converted to making army vehicles of some sort. Even Hudson had a small final assembly plant in Tilbury, and it was converted to make Jeeps, I think. No one wanted to send vehicles that had any defects overseas. Too many lives were at stake if things did not work properly. All were tested.

They left the factories in Windsor in large convoys and drove down 98 to Tilbury and back to Windsor. I remember one sunny summer day sitting on the front porch with my mother watching this endless parade of brown- and camouflage-coloured vehicles roll by. We waved at the drivers and they waved back. We were all one in winning this conflict. How long they went on, I don't remember, but I do remember my mother having a little portable radio and listening to *Ma Perkins*, one of the current soap operas, as the show rumbled past.

We had no hydro, and I recall my dad bringing home from Windsor this wondrous little box. It would be about a foot square and run by batteries. By today's standards it was a monstrous size for a radio, but it was full of tubes and the batteries took up half of its space. It was only used for war news, other important events, the odd radio comedy or drama, and of course the really important things like *Ma Perkins*, sponsored by Oxydol.

They started out as soap operas, I guess, and never lost their real purpose, to sell soap! Batteries did not last long and were large and expensive. The radio did not blare all day. It was out of my control and in any event, I did not touch it or even think of turning it on. I don't think I really cared. I liked to listen to some of the stories, but was more interested in the outdoors, and roaming and exploring what I thought was the fascinating world around the hundred acres.

Stuart's Crank and the Ram

The Crank

The school was just past Allyn's farm on the same side of the road. We were taught to walk facing the traffic so on the way home we walked past their driveway. Stuart had a tractor. An old Farmall, faded red, with large steel wheels and big steel lugs. It started with a crank. No one else around had a tractor. They all used horses.

One day, late in the spring, so it was hot, I was walking home from school. I was alone as Marlene was probably not well. She missed a lot of school. It was a great sunny, warm day and I was sauntering along as kids do, kicking the dust, looking down to see what treasures I might find. Low and behold, beside the ditch, was the crank for the tractor. I was sure that wherever Stuart and the tractor were, they were going to be there forever. You can't start a tractor without a crank. I was halfway home, but I took the crank and ran all the way back to Allyn's. Stuart was not there but Mrs. Allyn was, and she told me how grateful he would be. I felt very proud of my good deed. They had a daughter, but no boys, and Stuart and I got along just fine.

Sunday mornings Mrs. Allyn would pick mom and us kids up and we would all go to church in Comber. She drove for sixty years and never had a licence. Sometimes Stuart would be with her, but he would stay at our place and drink beer, or whatever, with my dad. They always seemed to be happy and in a good mood when we got back. Anyway, a couple of Sundays later, I was sitting between Mrs. Allyn and mom at church. She put something into my hand and said it was from Stuart for finding his crank. It was a little jackknife, just a six-year-old size. I cherished it and had it for many years, until one day it got lost. I am not sure how or when, but we parted company.

After we left the farm and I had a car, I would go back and pay a short visit. Stuart was retired and aging but there was not a time that he did not mention the crank. It was also many years later, when I was grown, that I learned that he lost lots of cranks. They would fall off their resting place on the back of the tractor. He always had a spare.

The Ram

While I was reminiscing about the crank, I also remembered Stuart's father. He lived with them or probably vice versa. He raised bees and had some sheep. To continue getting more sheep he had an ugly old ram. The ram had the same temperament as Alex Stacey's goat. Their yard was fenced, and the gate closed, as the ram had the run of the barnyard, and it was not fenced off from the house.

Charlie Allyn was apparently well off. He bought a brand-new Ford in 1938 or 1939 and somewhere there is a picture of me, Marlene, and Mr. Allyn, on the front fender of the car. He parked in the garage but often left it in the laneway by the house throughout the day. The ram was not pleased with this arrangement. It was a sunny day and the new car, with its shiny new paint, reflected anything around. The ram was nearby and saw opposition to his status on the farm. He was king of the sheep and no other ram staring at him from a car door was going to take over. As the story goes, the ram backed up and after kicking the proper amount of dust, lunged at his opposition in the car door. The score...one very dazed ram, a sick front fender, and a door to be replaced. Farms are fun places.

My Goat

Harnessing a Goat

He was not a mean monster like the one that held me captive in the piano box. I do not remember who gave him to me, but he was just a little squirt. A real kid. He acted like one, too. Kids on farms had all kinds of pets, so having a goat was not that unusual. For a little while, I fed him from a bottle with a nipple. Guess he lived in the barn, but I am not sure. I was in grade one, so probably six years old. I think he arrived sometime in the spring. Our dog Muggs chummed around with me, but I had time for a goat too, and the dog seemed to accept him.

I had a name for the goat, but I can't remember it. Muggs, the goat and I ran all over the farm. We all grew together but the goat grew by leaps and bounds. He was also great at doing leaps and bounds. Much to my father's dismay, there was hardly a thing he could not jump or climb. I thought he was a neat little guy.

He grew and I felt it was time he was useful, instead of just getting me in trouble by climbing or chewing everything he came upon. I decided that he could pull me in my wagon since he was such a good runner. I found some old belts, rope and all the needed bits to make a harness for him. It was hard to get him to stay still long enough to get it

33

on, but I managed. I hooked him up, climbed into the wagon, and gave the proper instructions to pull me down the lane by the barn.

He jumped, twisted, and finally decided to just chew his way out. My harness was a mess, and my friendly goat was running and jumping across the yard. He did not exactly come on command but was not afraid to come and see me when I called him. I repaired my harness with the help of my mother, who helped put it together in the first place, and got him hooked up one more time. He won, so I threw out the remaining bits of belt and rope and let him go back to his jumping and chewing.

The Doubters

The one-room school was about a mile down the highway, and of course populated by kids like me. We all lived on farms and were poor to varying degrees. There were about twenty-five or so kids when I was there from grades one to eight. They were not sure that I actually had a goat. Daily I would tell of my exploits to very dubious classmates.

I invited the doubting Thomas bunch to come and see. One day after school about fifteen kids took me up on my offer and walked home with me. It never dawned on me to ask or even tell my parents. I probably thought no one would come. I think I was dismayed that they did not believe me, and to prove my honesty, on the spur of the moment I invited them home.

Where my mom was, I am not sure, but she was not home when the pied piper and the troop of kids arrived. Dad was working in the barn. My friend the goat was his usual self running around the barnyard. I took all the doubters out back and they and the goat had a great time chasing one another.

House doors were rarely locked, if they even had locks. It seemed that some of the kids were missing. Father soon heard the commotion and came over to see what was going on. He, for some strange reason, did not like kids running all over the barnyard, scaring the other animals while chasing a silly, little goat.

We went into the house only to find two or three (I am not sure of the actual number) of the missing kids. Father was not amused, as the expression goes, because one kid had his arm in the fishbowl, trying to scoop out the goldfish. They were father's goldfish. I do not remember what the others were doing but I do plainly see the kid with his arm in the goldfish bowl. They left. I had no trouble at school after that convincing them that my goat was real. Unfortunately, some fathers are not partial to the antics of goats that are pets and a short time after my classmates visited, my goat was given a new home. I was not too happy about it but at least I had the company of a real kid for a while.

1930 Chevrolet

For a while, my dad had a 1930 Chevrolet when we were on the farm. I can't remember if it had two or four doors. It doesn't matter because it did not seem to want to run very much. When I remember it, the car would be nine or ten years old. Cars were kept a long time, but they needed a lot of fixing and coaxing. I only recall it being around a year or two. Most of the time it was shoe leather or riding with some neighbour.

We went to the Saturday night show in Tilbury. At least, Gordon, Marlene, mom, and I did. Dad dropped us off and went to The Recess. The Recess was the local draft room. It is still there and seems not much has changed in half a century or more. Dad picked us up after the show and we were heading home.

Somewhere around the Rowsom farm we collided head on with another vehicle. How or who's fault I don't know. No one was hurt. Guess it is hard to get hurt riding at twenty-three miles an hour in a big old car built like a tank. Not sure what the other vehicle was nor do I remember anything about the driver. I recall a man but no passengers. Anyway, we stopped nose down in the ditch with the right front wheel lying almost in the middle of the road. I can only imagine that someone went to the closest farm and called the police, or a car stopped and did that errand. There was not a lot of traffic on the road and not much at ten o'clock on a Saturday night.

Seems we waited a long time. I remember thinking that the wheel was going to get run over in the dark and then it would be no good to put back on the car. My parents and the other driver were engrossed in conversation beside his car on the other side of the road. I heaved and grunted and finally got the wheel upright and rolled to the edge of the highway by the car. Check out one of those and you will see moving a wheel like that is no small feat for a six-year-old.

The police came, measured, asked questions, and took us home. Some months after the accident (I do not recall seeing the car again), Dad came home from Windsor all smiles. He had been to court over the accident. Somehow, he knew all the politicians, top businesspeople, and lawyers. He boasted about hiring the best lawyer in the city. I recall as I got older reading about the expertise of this lawyer.

In any event, dad won the case against the other driver. The only mystery that caused the police and the judge or jury some consternation was how the wheel got to the side of the road. All the evidence apparently, and testimony of the two drivers, would indicate that the wheel should have been somewhere near the middle of the road. In spite of that he had won anyway but seemed that it would have been open and shut had the wheel been where they thought it should be.

I quickly told him that they should have asked me, because I knew where the wheel was, and told him how it got to the side of the road. Just a note of caution, never move wheels after an accident until the police tell you to. Or at least do not tell the father!

The Woodbox

As I got older, I was responsible, along with Gordon, for keeping the woodbox stocked. It was a big wooden box, living in a corner of the back porch, just within reach of the door. The wood pile was in the backyard. Guess dad and Ed cut and split it in the proper size to fit the stove. Gordon and I took turns carrying the wood to its home on the back porch. We took turns weekly. This was my first kick at this chore. The box was filled every night.

One Sunday night dad came in from the barn and ordered the box filled. Gordon said it was not his job, it was a Sunday and so it was my week. I had just started school and it started Monday. As far as I was concerned, my week started Monday. I think they all ganged up on me, as Gordon argued that the week started Sunday, not Monday. He should have been a lawyer. I lost, put on my coat, went out into the dark, and carried wood to fill that blasted woodbox. I remember thinking how unfair it was that the week started on Sunday for wood, when school did not start until Monday. Funny how some lessons stick in your mind forever.

Summer Vacation with Aunts and Uncles

The Family

I had a very extensive family. Today people seem to get scattered, and kids do not know aunts and uncles, much less cousins. I had lots of both, and we knew and saw most of them. Perhaps because in different times people did not move around so much and shared similar backgrounds. Most originated on a farm, even if they did not stay there. Most were not well off, knew what hard work was, and keeping up with the neighbours was not in the forefront of one's existence, so they still seemed to have a lot in common.

Mother had three sisters in Dresden. Dad's sisters had all moved to Toronto. I have no idea why those in Dresden stayed put (all born there) and those born on the farm in Comber headed to Toronto. We did not see the Toronto gang often but did hear from them. Mother's sisters were closer. We visited them and they all seemed to like kids and enjoy us.

For many years, from the age of five or six until I had to spend my summers working, Marlene and I spent a good part of our summers in Dresden and Port Lambton. One would go to Aunt Mary's for a week or so, and the other to see Auntie Rae or Aunt Lola, and then we would switch. Seldom were we together. They always argued about who would have which kid when. We usually went to Uncle Alex's together. Don't

37

know why, but that is the way it was. Uncle Jack and Aunt Lola had a small farm, but he was also an electrician, and he went out most days to do wiring or whatever for local farmers and businesses. They let me climb every tree around and investigate all the farm buildings. They had a cow and a team of horses, along with chickens and an assortment of other interesting animals and stuff. I liked their place.

Aunt Mary

I usually started at Aunt Mary's. She was the oldest sister and lived across the road from the river on a street just over the bridge on the main street. I think she passed away when I was seven or eight. Aunt Mary appeared stern and grouchy and seemed to be. But she was a pushover, at least for me. She lived on a street in town with other houses around, so there were lots of kids my age. We played cowboys and Indians, explored Uncle Tom's Cabin, which was just a rundown shack in the middle of a weed bed, walked to the haunted house, and just had fun.

There is nothing like playing tag or cowboys and Indians on the back streets of a small town in the early evening of a summer's night. It is just getting dark, the fireflies are out, and kids are running through yards and down sidewalks, hiding behind bushes and trees. There is no tomorrow, only the fun and excitement of tonight. That is what I recall of my stays at Aunt Mary's. I remember that and the lilac bush with the bees' nest in it.

I was five and had a sailor suit. Since it was 1940 and the war was on, I guess parents thought kids would look great in a sailor suit. It was just like a real one with bell bottoms, hat, and all. I liked it, perhaps because Edward was in the navy. Anyway, we lived on the farm, but the kids in Dresden thought I lived in Windsor and was a city slicker. Wow! They lived in town and I lived on a farm. I got out of the car at Aunt Mary's.

After the required greeting, I rushed to the back street to find my summer friends, like Buddy. There was a large lilac bush in front of his house right at the sidewalk. He was home and there was a smattering of other kids playing at his house. We had not seen each other since the previous summer. They admired my outfit but cautioned me to stay away from the lilac bush since it had a nest of bees in it.

Could you imagine a kid, supposedly from the big city, and with a brand-new sailor suit on, being afraid of some puny little bees? If those small-town kids were smart, they would know that all you must do is give the tree a good kick and shake, and then run down the sidewalk and the bees would get up and leave. The only trouble is, I must not have been able to outrun bees, and when they got up and left, they seemed to know who did the shaking and kicking.

I had bees in my face, in my eyes and in my hair. My face was so swollen that it overlapped two mirrors. My head was full of bumps, my nose made Groucho's look minuscule, and my lips were so large that I had no hole for a mouth. I could not see out as my eyes were concealed by giant lids. What a mess! Aunt Mary plastered me up with some concoction and surprisingly enough within a few days or, so I was okay. I do not recall the pain or being sick or any of that stuff. I just remember that I was the visiting hero for a while because I had the guts (stupidity) to kick the tree when they all wanted to but knew better.

Aunt Lola (Laura) and Uncle Jack

At Uncle Jack's I had fun with wire. He and his father had helped string the first Bell lines in the territory, so he had a lot of heavy wiring cluttering up the garage. I took some of the stuff he did not want and climbed as high as I could go in the tree just outside the kitchen door. It was the tallest tree in the yard. I tied the wire to a branch and then did the same thing to the other three or four trees close by. It looked like a spider's web of wires from one tree to the next. Were I the uncle and aunt, I do not think I would have put up with it. I was five, six, seven, not sure, but when I recall this escapade, I wonder that I never fell and broke my neck.

The wires were so that I could slide down from one tree to the next. My connections never met expectations. I would climb to the top of the highest tree with another short piece of wire that I could hold onto, looped over the wire going to the next tree. Hang on and push off against the trunk, and I was supposed to slide down the wire to the next tree. My telephone wire would bend, and I would slide a few feet through branches and go flying down to within a few feet of the ground, but nowhere near my destined tree. I tried to tighten the wire but to no avail. All I got were scratches and bruises. Even then I guess I lived with bandages constantly.

I took the wires down and returned them to the garage. The only tree I could not scale was a tall poplar, right by the road at the edge of the driveway. I am not sure I would let a kid do this either, but I managed to commandeer several boards, and hammered them onto the tree like steps on a ladder for about twenty feet so I could reach the bottom branch and make it to the top of the tree. My ladder stayed visible on that tree well into adulthood.

Saturday night was shopping night in Dresden. Uncle Jack would drop Aunt Lola and I off at the grocery store and he would go to the main corner in town and hand out Watchtowers. He had become a Witness some years before. Sundays he would drop Aunt Lola off at church where she would teach Sunday school and he would go on to his meeting. They had many discussions and arguments over their different religious paths.

I do not think he had an enemy in the world, and few agreed with his religion, but when he passed away it was one of the largest funerals that I ever attended, especially considering the size of Dresden. I always looked forward to my stay there, even if Aunt Lola thought a scrub brush was better than a washcloth, and really believed that cleanliness is next to godliness. In all fairness they all thought the same, and although I got lots of dirt on me, I bet it never lived long enough to even think about creating any kind of bacteria or infection. I think these aunts and uncles considered us much like grandparents think of their grandkids and treated us as such. I bet we filled a void for them, and we were both happy with the treatment and were better for that relationship.

Auntie Rae (Rachel) and Uncle Clarence

My next stop was Auntie Rae's. She lived almost across the road from the fairground, and often had cars parked in her yard during fair time and had some borders. They had a small farm, and it went down the lane beside her house to the highway behind and over to the next farm towards Chatham. There was a large barn with cows, chickens, and the usual assortment.

Uncle Clarence's parents were well off and built them a new house when they got married. It is still there on the bend just before her back laneway, on the highway coming from Thamesville. I do not know why they moved. Uncle Clarence was a big, tall, good-natured guy who liked to spend his time at the stockyard, which you could see from the living room window. It was just by the railway tracks a few hundred feet away. I hardly remember him as he died when I was six or seven.

They had a 1928 Whippet that they bought new in London where they were made. It was a little two-door like a model A. Auntie Rae drove it to town and to Aunt Lola's. The yard had some very old large maples and she put a hammock between two of them just outside the kitchen door. Marlene and I spent hours tipping one another out and generally devastating the poor hammock. Auntie Rae and Aunt Lola fought constantly but called each other daily to make sure they were okay, and I guess to see if the sister was still alive to argue with.

Many Sundays Uncle Jack would go to a meeting all afternoon, and Aunt Lola would come to Auntie Rae's after church and stay for supper. Sometimes Uncle Alex would drive down too. He always parked his car under the tree by the kitchen and would go out and sit in it with the door open and listen to the ballgame. Guess that was better than listening to his sisters squabbling.

Often Florence and Clayton would drive down from Chatham, so the house would be full, but the magic fridge always came through. They were all sort of like extra mothers to me, but for some reason Auntie Rae seemed to be the best replacement. I tried to repay her in later years, although I don't think one can begin to really repay the love and understanding given to a child. I enjoyed my visits there and never stopped going back.

Uncle Alex

Port Lambton was different. Uncle Alex never had kids, never got married till in his forties, and never had a messy house or anything out of place. There were five bedrooms and an ensuite bathroom attached to his bedroom downstairs. Almost unheard of then when most still had an outhouse. Even Aunt Mary's house in town had an outhouse. There was a formal dining room, living room, glassed in porch, fireplace that worked and built-in bookcases on each side of the fireplace. Unlike what I was used to, his house also had central heating, so the fireplace was just a luxury. There was of course a bathroom upstairs for the four bedrooms there. It was a neat spot for a kid to run around in and he did not seem to mind our treatment of the furniture or our noise.

I remember Aunt Gert, his second wife, being alive the first couple of summers I visited but I was there after for visits when there was just him and me. The dining room was never used when I was there. Two or three people could eat in the kitchen, and for supper he went to the restaurant. I used to think that was pretty cool since I did not get to eat in restaurants very often. He did that for twenty-five years, every day that he was home. I wonder if he got tired of the menu as I think there was only one restaurant in town. Port Lambton must have had at least two hundred people in it.

If you check the map, you will see it is just past Wallaceburg on St. Clair river. You can see cars driving on the American side of the river, and with a good pair of field glasses almost read license plates. The Snye Channel out of Wallaceburg is not far down the river. It is narrow and many mornings the fog would slow the freighter traffic to a crawl on the river. I used to love waking up early in the morning, five o'clock or so, and hearing the foghorns from the freighters calling back and forth.

I slept upstairs in the first bedroom at the top of the stairs in a brass bed. The other three rooms were equally furnished. I am trying to remember who made the bed after Aunt Gert died and I was still a kid! The megaphone sat on the floor by the fireplace. When a ship was coming down Uncle Alex would get the glasses out to see the name if he could not recognize the shape. If it was one of his buddies, he would take the megaphone to the front steps, or sometimes cross the road, and as the ship got across from the house, call the captain. They would carry on a minute or so of conversation until the freighter passed. Cell phones have ruined all that.

What does a six- or seven-year-old do for a week, visiting with a sixty-year-old uncle who never had kids? I am only guessing at his age. I just know that if I knew him, he was retired, so maybe my sixty is kind. We would take the Hudson on the car ferry to Marine City, Michigan, across the river. His neighbour ran the car ferry. Uncle Alex had a bank account in Marine City so that was an excuse to go somewhere.

No one else I knew, relative or otherwise, had as fancy a car and I liked to ride in it. Also, he never said something was too expensive or we cannot afford it. I never asked for anything but if I thought it was time for ice cream or ogled a particular toy, it seemed to appear. Don't ask why because he made excuses why they were in his garage, and I never did find out, but he had two wagons. One was a large red metal wagon with big wheels, and the other was a neat little silver wagon with sides that covered the wheels. A real modern looking conveyance that would still fit in today. Port Lambton was slightly hilly, and it had sidewalks at least on the main street where he lived.

I spent hours taking turns pumping those wagons up and down the sidewalk for the few blocks that I was allowed to traverse. Many, many, many times they tipped, especially the little one that I was really fond of. My knees were bandaged most of the time I stayed there. I think I incurred more scraped knees on those sidewalks than anyplace I can remember. He must have spent a fortune just in bandages for my knees.

Uncle Alex smoked cigars. His basement was full of them. He was very regimented though. He would sit in his rocker by the fireplace and light one after lunch, smoke part of it and finish it after supper. One a day. Visits to his place were so different for a lot of reasons, I guess.

Aunt Lola's was a farmhouse as was Auntie Rae's, with few luxuries, and had a very lived in atmosphere. No one starved, but I think money was a concern and extras were budgeted for. Uncle Alex's house was a mansion by comparison, both in size and furnishings. Luxuries were not a problem; he did not need anything, had an expensive car, had been retired for years and still had money to survive well.

The summer I attended Cadet Camp we got a weekend off to go home or wherever if we had an adult to look after us. I took the bus to Sarnia, closer than going to Windsor and Uncle Alex picked me up so I spent my weekend in Port Lambton. He had a roll top desk. Saturday night he opened it up and took out an envelope and handed it to me. He said he bought these in my name during the war and forgot about them. They were two Victory bonds for one hundred dollars each. Wow! I was fifteen, and two hundred dollars with interest for ten years was a ton of money. You could get a good used car for that.

I really do not remember what I did with the money, but it was more than I was used to seeing at one time and being given in such a casual manner. I am not sure that I really appreciated nor understood who he really was. He wore a dress shirt and tie every day. I never saw him in scruffy clothes, if he even owned any. His sisters adored him, maybe because they were older and knew much more about him than I. I do know that every night he said his prayers kneeling by his bed. I often think of my summers in Port Lambton.

Mummers and Hounds

You may have read that my dad came home one day with a portable radio. Since we had no electricity, it was battery powered and used sparingly. On Sunday evenings in the winter, we sat around the radio in the kitchen, and listened to two or three programs that were on every week. The one I remember was *The Mummers*. I was five I think and allowed to stay up and listen. Our programs started at seven as I remember, and probably were over at eight.

The Mummers opened with hounds or wolves howling, and always had scary stories of graves opening and bodies coming out and doing all sorts of things that Frankenstein-type monsters would do. The stories always sent shivers down your back, and made you sit closer to your mother or whoever was nearby. They were scary, especially the sound of the hounds, but I liked them anyway. The magic of radio was that you saw the story as your mind imagined it. My hounds were always monster sized with gaping mouths and dripping blood from long sharp teeth. They were too fast for anyone to ever outrun them.

It was dark and was probably the end of March. Dad requested that Gordon and I go out and take the dozen pullets (young chickens) that were nesting under the back porch and put them in the barn. They were supposed to live in the barn, but for some reason decided to bed down under the back porch. I was not afraid of the dark, not until after that evening. If we hurried, we could get the task done before *The Mummers* came on.

We only used the kitchen and bedrooms in the winter; the living room and dining room not being heated. The bedrooms were over those two rooms, so they were not heated either. One got undressed by the kitchen stove, at least the kids did, took a lamp and hurried through the dark living room, and up the stairs to the cold and dark bedroom. You could always see or imagine shadows and things after an episode of *The Mummers*, but they never bothered me. Because of the lack of heat, you snuggled into the bed, your head mostly covered so nothing could get you anyway. Once in bed, you were safe.

You know I am sure that chickens are not too smart. They were all huddled together under the porch. We had a flashlight and just reached under them and grabbed their legs. You took two in each hand if you could hang onto them and ran to the barn and tossed them into the open door. The barn door was one of those double affairs that opened to let a wagon inside. It was also very high. The door was open a couple of feet, so we just went to the edge and threw our quarry inside. No need to use the small door when this one was already ajar.

I was not afraid of the dark at this point but was not going to push things by going right inside this monstrous dark cavern. We made a couple of trips. There was a fence separating the house from the barnyard and we left the gate ajar. There was also a ditch on the barn side of the fence. It was not deep, just sloping to let the water run. It was empty of water that night.

Probably half the brood had been transferred. I was at the barn door and just about to let loose my handful of feathers. Gordon had rid his load and was turned around to head back to the house. Out of the depths of that dark opening into the barn came several loud, blood curdling howls. I froze, my blood turned cold! The hounds from *The Mummers* were in the barn, and obviously on their way out to get me. I turned and my legs finally started to move.

Gordon was a fast runner and already halfway to the house. When it came to hounds and little brothers there was no contest. I was history if the hounds wanted me, but he was not waiting to find out. I hit the ditch and did a couple of somersaults. Remember it was pitch dark. Lamplight from a kitchen window does not do much to light up a farmyard. Gordon had the flashlight.

When I got up and was finally running again, Gordon was already on the porch. I was sure that I was dog food and could almost feel the teeth in my back. I hit the steps and was inside. I really do not remember anything after that. Even after we discovered the cause of the howling hounds, the sound and sight of that dark cavern has never left my mind. Our neighbours lived across the road and had at least ten hounds, of all descriptions. They used them to hunt skunks and raccoons. For some reason, they had decided to try their lungs as I reached the barn door. The inside of a large barn can cause quite an echo on a quiet night. Just ask me.

Hunting

Most farmers were also hunters. A rifle or shotgun usually sat somewhere around the back door for quick access. Farmers hunted, not particularly for sport, although it probably was a form of relaxation, but for food. The gun at the back door was to ward off predators, like hawks, skunks, or foxes, that thought barnyard fowl were easy pickings for lunch. Wolves and coyotes also took a liking to sheep and calves. Deer were also a problem in some areas. Deer could chew up a cornfield or mess up wheat or oats fast. Crows and rabbits were not friendly to farms either. The gun at the back door was mainly to protect the food supply. Some of those mentioned above were also good for the table and were sought out for food. If it was not bothering anything, and you could not eat it, farmers did not shoot it. Animals, domesticated or wild, were part of life. They provided food.

One afternoon Edward went to the bush to shoot some squirrels for supper. He took the twelve-gage pump. Sometime later he returned with a bag full of bits of fur. Not exactly appetizing, and not much meat for supper. May not sound very nice, since people think of squirrels as cute little guys. Maybe they are, but they are also one big pain sometimes, and cooked properly you would be hard pressed to know it was not chicken you were eating. Father was not impressed with Edward's catch. I was six or seven, and was there when Ed came in. Dad said, "let's go Alex and show him how to shoot squirrels," or something to that effect. He grabbed the twenty-two and we went off to the bush. A shotgun can make a mess out of a lot of things, especially something as small as a squirrel.

Knowing where to hit it, a twenty-two will hardly leave a mark. I remember dad explaining where to aim and why, as squirrels scampered around the hickory trees. He even let me shoot one. We returned home in an hour or so with enough food for supper. You probably do not want to know how to skin and clean them, but that was the next job. This is one of the few outings I remember with my dad. I think that is probably not fair though, since he did take me to Comber with him on the wagon to have grain made into chop, and I do remember following the furrow, gathering worms as he guided the furrow plow. Guess I did learn a lot from him in a short period of time, while we were on the farm. If you want to know how to shoot squirrels with a twenty-two, just call.

The Flagpole

Our school, when I was on the farm, was about a mile or so down the highway. We did not walk the "when I was a kid, we had to walk ten miles to school, and it was all uphill both directions," but we did walk, rain or shine, cold or warm. The flagpole was beside one of the front windows and had two pieces of metal on one side to pull the rope up on. This winding gadget was about four feet off the ground and was like a large spike in diameter, but not really pointed on the ends, just rounded off. Each morning one of the older boys hoisted the flag and took it down when school was over. Because the metal spike, as I picture it, was high, several of the boys would climb onto the windowsill to be able to wind up the rope. Otherwise, it was out of reach.

One morning a few of us were in attendance on the front steps as a student performed this task. He slipped and while making a grab for the pole, the top spike grabbed him. It went right through his arm just below the shoulder. I can still picture him hanging by his arm, his feet not touching the ground, with the spike sticking out the other side. What happened next, how the teacher lifted him off, and kept him from bleeding to death, I do not remember. Ambulances did not exist, and I don't remember if she had a car or not. No phone in the school, so I imagine someone ran to the closest farm and got help. I recall fleeting glimpses of classroom life, getting wood for the stove, the outdoor facilities, and the water pump in the yard, falling off the swings and other scrapes, but this one incidence sticks above the rest.

Ink

I recall sitting at the kitchen table one night, working, or probably playing, with an ink pen. The older students used them, and I wanted one. Mother got me one and father did not think I needed it. Just a slip of wood that a nib went into. The nib got dipped into the inkpot, and held enough ink for a few words, until it had to be dipped again. I imagine dad thought it wasteful, since I was just learning to print, and kids were hard on nibs. Press too hard and they break, or at best spill all their ink onto the paper and make a mess. At least it would still work without hydro, which is more than I can say for my computer and printer!

Hay

The Thrashing

Like thrashing time, haying was a big adventure for me and a lot of hot hard work for those involved. We have progressed to square balers, automatic loaders, huge round bales, and now to humungous square bales. All to take the manual labour out of haying. Hay is cut and baled from the seat of an air-conditioned tractor, with the stereo going and the cellular phone at the ready. Not so when I was a kid.

The hay was cut with a hay mower pulled by a team of horses. The mower was just a seat over a set of wheels, holding a long blade out the right side. When the mower moved, the teeth on the blade went back and forth, and mowed down just about anything in its path. I liked the noise it made as it went about its job.

Once the hay was cut, and this could be acres and acres, the same team were hitched to a hay rake. Just another seat on a gadget about ten feet wide, with large oval shaped tines on the back. As it was pulled along, the tines gathered the hay. When they were full, a handle was pulled to lift the tines, and leave the hay in a nice pile. Eventually when the field was done, all these neat piles ended up as rows across the field. It was left like that for a few days to dry; then the real hard work came.

Hay was stored in the mow. A rail ran the length of the mow up in the peak of the roof. A set of trolley wheels was attached to the rail, and they held the hay fork. The fork would be about three feet high, and a foot and a half wide, with sharp tongs on the bottom. It was attached to the trolley by a long rope that extended out the far end of the barn. The team of horses would pull the hay wagon out to the field, and Dad and Edward would load the hay onto the wagon with pitchforks.

Hay was heavy, and the wagon was loaded right to the top of the racks. It was very hard work and usually very hot. The bits of seeds would get down your shirt and stick to the sweat. You were always itchy. There were racks on the front and back of the wagon. I loved to ride on the wagon, especially on the way back to the barn. You could sit on top of the hay and sink down so just your head popped out. If there was lots of hay, and they were available, other farmers would help. Guess they took turns from one farm to the next. There could be three or four wagons working, each with a couple of people, and of course horses to pull the wagons.

The wagon full of hay was parked under the haymow door. If there was no one else with a team to help, the horses were unhitched and driven around to the other end of the barn. One person directed the fork into the load of hay and yelled to the other end of the barn that he was ready. I liked to be the runner to scoot to the other end, and tell them it was okay, because it was a long way to shout.

The team was now hooked up to the rope, and they would pull the fork full of hay up to the haymow. The load of hay would move along the track to the far end, or wherever it was to go. The horses were stopped. Another rope attached to the tines was pulled, and it released the load. If there was help, someone was in the mow to tell the driver when to stop the horses. If not, then whoever was on the wagon scampered up into the mow, after the fork with its load had disappeared through the door into the haymow.

I was only allowed into the mow when this was going on, and if someone was with me. A load of hay that large, should it fall on you, would probably bust you into bits, or at least smother you before anyone could dig through it. Sometimes the load would fall off the fork before it was supposed to, so this job was not without its dangers. As the haymow started to fill up, the hay got higher and did not have as far to fall to the mow floor.

The horses pulling the fork would be taken around the other end again, hooked to the wagon and the process would start over. If there was enough help and an extra team, they would just stay there hooked up to the fork, as another wagon would be waiting, and one team would just be used to pull the fork full of hay into the mow.

The Haymow

The part of the barn under the mow held stalls for horses and cows, but the far end of the barn had an area about thirty feet long, and the whole width of the barn did not have a haymow. It was open right up to the roof, perhaps fifty feet or so. This area was also filled with hay and was the first part to be filled up. It was usually filled only to the floor of the mow, while the mow held hay almost to the roof.

Haymows were great places to play in. Barns are big buildings, and about halfway up to the roof from the mow floor, there were beams crossing the barn. Big beams that a careful kid with good balance could walk on. If the mow was empty, one did not want to make a mistake and slip. It was a long way down and the floor was hard. When the hay was in, however, it was sometimes piled up to these beams and over, so if you fell off it did not hurt. The only problem was to squirm, crawl and dig your way out of a pile of endless hay that surrounded you. Sometimes that was a real challenge.

It is strange that I rarely remember doing things with Gordon and Marlene. Most of my memories are just things I did by myself, or with Muggs or the goat. Gordon was five years older, and liked to tease or otherwise pick on me, so maybe I just blotted him out, and Marlene was not a well kid, and did not run the farm like me.

I do remember that Marlene and I climbed up to the haymow when it was full. We would be five or six, I guess. We ventured to the end of the mow overlooking the far end. It was full of hay, up until a few feet from the mow floor. It looked like a good place to jump into. It was a soft landing, but once there we were trapped. We could not climb back up. Hay is not a good thing to try to climb on. Try as we might, we just kept sinking and getting nowhere. There was no door into the stable, and in any event, hay was piled tight against that wall.

How long we struggled I have no idea, but we were getting panicky. There was a beam of light at the far corner. A small door not quite closed, and if we could get that far we may be able to get out. It did seem an eternity of crawling, digging, getting buried and climbing out, but we finally reached the crack of light. It was a tight, scratchy squeeze, even for a couple of little kids, but I recall the relief of breathing dust free air and seeing light as we emerged into the barnyard through that crack. I don't remember ever going into that part of the barn again.

When I look back it was sure different from watching television, being driven to hockey, baseball, or ballet. I wonder how I would fare now as a kid?

Christmas

Farm Christmases

I can only recall one Christmas on the farm. Dad and Edward brought in a huge tree. It even had a bird's nest in it. The ceiling in the kitchen was either ten or twelve feet high and the tree hit the roof. Part of the decorations were little candle holders that were attached to the branches, and they held real candles, a bit bigger than those on a birthday cake. It sure looked pretty but I wonder if someone stood by with a fire extinguisher. I do not remember any disaster.

We had oranges and pomegranates, which were only in the stores at Christmas. Aunt Ollie sent a box of toys for us kids. I recall a neat semi-truck that the cab unhitched, and the trailer sported dolly wheels, just like a real one. Whatever happened to it I do not know. I also got a wooden Noah's Ark. It was about a foot long and filled with wooden animals. The ark got busted along the way I guess, but years later I remember seeing the odd animal still kicking around in a drawer. Maybe if we had not moved so much, I would still have them.

Christmas in Tecumseh

Tecumseh was different. We had a tree but not a ton of presents. The war was on, so maybe the festivities were not the same. Lots of things were not available and money seemed to be one of them. I just do not remember Christmas as being a big deal, except that we always had a goose or turkey and a big meal. Other than helping with the cooking, I do not recall dad being a big proponent of Christmas celebrations. He was a good cook, though. Gordon was not one for toys, being more interested in sports than I, and of course he was enough years older that we had not much in common when we were growing up. He wanted to play ball and hockey, and I wanted to fiddle with toy cars, trucks, toy farmyard animals and things.

In 1946 or 1947, not sure, but the war had ended, and dad was laid off from the railroad. Being out of work meant not a lot of money for Christmas presents I assume or anything else. I was old enough to be at the end of the toy car stuff but not quite, and perhaps like Sam had devastated the few I owned, so just wanted a couple more. Mom got me two. A little tin four door sedan, about eight inches long, and a smaller truck. I thought the car was great and was not perturbed by the lack of other stuff. Aunt Ollie was gone by now, so no big box from Toronto. Relatives were not in the habit of giving gifts to the whole family, so you did not expect anything from outside the household. Kids had no money, so only gave siblings token presents. Two or three small inexpensive presents were the norm for most of us.

Roger

I went over to see Roger in the afternoon. Roger's parents never seemed to be affected by the economy. His parents and mine were good friends, even if the lifestyle was as far apart as black and white. Roger's uncle was there. He was very nice and was a bachelor who lived down the highway a few miles. I am not sure what he did, but I always thought he was rich. He asked me what I got for Christmas. I remember saying, "everything". Not sure if I was embarrassed because I did not get much, or if I did not want to say that I got toy cars and trucks, when I figured I was too old for such stuff. Roger got an electric train along with a host of other bits and pieces.

In all the Christmases until I got married and held the celebration at home with our own kids, those two are the only ones that stick in my mind. Perhaps that is why Christmas is no big deal to me.

Tornado

It was 1946. We lived in Tecumseh, and the porch from the living room faced Windsor. We were eating supper and Gordon had just arrived home from delivering papers at Little River. Dad was at work in the railway yard, across the road and a few fields away. It had really rained and now the noise of the hailstones, literally the size of golfballs, took us to the front porch to watch them. As quickly as it started the hail stopped and I went into the yard to collect some.

The sky was a weird colour, and we could hear this rumbling noise. Down the road about three miles away, we could see this great black cloud. We had not heard one go over but wondered if a plane had crashed and was burning up, sending big smoke clouds into the air, or perhaps a house was set on fire by lightning.

The hail had stopped but the wind was fierce. Standing in the front yard we saw pieces of wood the size of two-by-fours, along with all kinds of household debris go flying over the house. In the meantime, the large cloud down the road was still there, but seemed to be moving a bit. The rain and hail abated, but the quick downpour had dumped the rain of a dozen storms and water was everywhere.

Vince Morrand lived across the road and a couple of houses towards Tecumseh. He had a reputation as an ambulance chaser. If there was a fire, or a hint of a siren in the air, Vince would jump into his car and start the chase. Vince had noticed the dark cloud also, backed his truck out onto the highway, and headed towards the black cloud. Gordon and I were still in the front yard, awed by the size of hailstones and the various material flying overhead.

Vince stopped and we were eager to jump in and find out what was going on. As we ran to the truck, mother, and Marlene still on the porch, we all noticed dad running through the field, waving his arms, and yelling whatever. We could not hear him as he was too far away, and the cloud down the highway was still making its awful, deep throated rumble. Dad had boots on and obviously had a great deal of difficulty even moving, much less trying to run through the mud created by the downpour.

Gordon and I wondered what the old man had been into, and not wanting to take the time to find out, rushed to Vince's truck, lest he leave without us. Mother hollered something as she watched dad struggle across the field, but we could not hear. Down the highway we roared. A 1936 Ford sedan goes pretty fast when chasing something as exciting as a tornado and it does not know what it is.

We got closer to the big cloud, and it started to move towards the railroad tracks on our right. We were almost up to it, about five hundred feet or so, I think, when the darn thing went through the field and crossed over the tracks, just a short distance from the highway. There was an entrance to the railway yard just before the devastation, which we had not seen because the tornado covered it. Vince, determined to follow this thing to the end, turned onto the cinder roadway leading to the railyard. We crossed the main track and had to stop because the gate was closed.

The railway yard was still big security. It was a marshalling yard during the war for army vehicles that were being shipped out. It was guarded twenty-four hours a day and fenced off. My dad was a guard there and happened to be working when the F4 tornado struck. We all jumped out as soon as Vince stopped the truck as close to the gate as he could get.

The big, dark rumbling cloud was on the far side of the fence. It was getting smaller and smaller, moving away from us. It seemed to wind down and disappear. It evaporated into thin air, but its effects did not. We stood mesmerized at the gate, as wooden boxes containing army trucks were torn from their moorings on flatcars, lifted into the air and dropped, some almost within touching distance. Wood and metal flew in all directions as we watched in wonder, too stupefied to know how close we may have been to oblivion.

Dad knew. He was not hollering against the wind and waving his arms for nothing. He had witnessed tornados on the prairie. They tend to follow a road, or any straight flat surface, and he was afraid it was heading down the highway, and our house would be right in its path. We went back to the highway and viewed the destruction at Little River. It was not a nice sight.

Gordon and the Chair

You know that big brothers can be a real pain. They can be cruel, bullies, and seem to enjoy picking on their smaller and younger siblings. Gordon fit that category sometimes, although when he was not picking on me, he was a pretty good brother, and more so when he got older. As kids we were completely different. Gordon was much more rambunctious and prone to raise hell.

For this incident, I would be eleven or twelve perhaps, and Gordon five years older. He had been a particular pain for a week or so. He was tall and tough, and I was neither, so pounding the crap out of him was not an option, as much as I wanted to do it. Like most households, for meals we all had our set places at the table. The kitchen had the standard wooden chairs with chair pads on them. If you can't beat the crap out of your older brother, one must find some other means of getting even. It would be nice too, to put him on notice that bigger harm will come if he does not cease and desist.

Devious plans take a lot of thinking, and what I came up with would not do much harm, but simply send a warning that I was capable of stealthy retaliation, and he would never know when it would strike. So, I found a thumb tack, a long and sharp one, that looked mighty dangerous if sat on. Just before bed one evening I went into the kitchen and carefully pushed the tack through the chair pad on Gordon's chair, from the bottom of course. It was placed just right, so that as he plunked his butt down, his right cheek would come into contact with that sharp point sticking through the pad. I was sure it would work great, and being very small, it would not be noticeable hiding in the pad. I could hardly wait for breakfast.

I made sure I was up early the next morning because I did not want to miss either the howl or look on Gordon's face. Mom and dad would be there, so there would be no instant retaliation from the guy who sat on the tack. To a kid, revenge is so sweet when a great plan comes together. Mom was in the kitchen and I anxiously awaited the arrival of my dear brother, wherever he was, as he was up before me.

When things go wrong, they do so in a flash, and there is just no time to change direction. It was summer and Gordon was working at the cannery. He rushed in the door, from a visit I assume to our outdoor facility. He announced he was late for work, no time for breakfast, grabbed his lunch that mother had packed, and rushed back out. Feeling betrayed, disappointed, and once more on the losing end, I never noticed father starting to sit down at the table. Why on earth would he pick this morning to sit in Gordon's chair? After all, he had his "Father's Place" at the table. Sometimes a father's rationale is harder to fathom than big brothers!!

No sound would come out of my mouth, and it would have been too late anyway, and probably not loud enough to overcome the cry from my dad as he quickly flew off the chair. Pretty agile for an old guy. My only satisfaction was that my great scheme worked. If only it had been the proper victim. Rats, now I was back to the drawing board.

Church and Sawing Wood

This is an old memory, not in George Street, nor in any church, but about church. It took place about fifty years or so ago in Tecumseh, Ontario. That is where I spent my public school years. Strange place for a United Church kid. Tecumseh had, and still has, a magnificent Catholic edifice, as it was very much a French Catholic town. The United Church congregation met in the school on Lesperance Road, out by Riverside Drive. The church was built on the road parallel to Lesperance, a block or so from Riverside, but still the same distance from town. This was about a three mile walk from where we lived on #39 highway, the other side of town towards Windsor. But I digress...

My father could spout the Bible like it was imprinted in his mind. He never went to church. My mother went to church. Going to church on Sunday for her was as predictable as Sunday dinner.

Many Sundays, in the wind, rain, heat, snow and blistering cold, my mother, sister, and I would walk the mile into town, and take the bus the other two miles to church, or walk all the way, and usually walk all the way home. Bus fare was expensive, but it did go past the church on the way. Sometimes we would get a ride into town and only have to walk the mile or so from Tecumseh the rest of the way home. It was no big deal. Lots of people walked. Gordon was not fussy about Sunday school, church or anything connected, and was old enough to go or not, I think.

I was about eleven or twelve, and it was the middle of January or February, not sure and it does not matter. What matters is that it was cold as .... We heated and cooked with wood, and had a wood cook stove, and a Quebec heater in the front room for heat. My older brother Gordon and I were responsible for cutting and splitting the wood, as well as making sure the woodbox on the porch was full.

This particular Sunday morning was bitterly cold, and it seemed all of us kids were suffering from colds and not able to go to church. Did we really have colds or not feel well? I do not honestly remember, but mother went by herself, walking to town as normal. I imagine she told the minister how sick we were.

Sometime in the middle of the morning, Father found the woodbox empty. Shortly after, Alex and Gordon, colds notwithstanding, nor cold weather either, were outside, each hanging onto the handle of a crosscut saw, pulling feverishly to cut up a railroad tie to fill up the woodbox. I don't think I was old enough, nor perceptive enough, to understand why, but for my mother, if one could not go to church, then you were really sick. You were certainly too sick to cut wood.

I think I mentioned earlier that it was a bitterly cold day. Now, you know that the banana belt of Canada does not experience really low winter temperatures, but the effect from the great lakes that surround Essex County makes minus ten feel like Whitehorse, when everyone is advised to stay inside. This Sunday was one of those days.

With no kids to walk home with her, the two boys especially being ill with severe colds, and such a long walk on such a bitter cold day, the minister offered to drive my mother home. I imagine that she really did put up a fuss, but finally agreed. The car drove into the lane. What the minister perceived I do not know, but my mother's eyes were glued to the two sick boys pulling feverishly on the crosscut saw like they were working out for a marathon. And on a Sunday. Remember this would be 1947 or thereabouts. No stores and nothing open on Sundays. Most kids, including us, spent the rest of the day after attending church, with our good clothes on. Couldn't do much or have a lot of fun with your good clothes on.

Too ill to go to church! Was mother embarrassed? Mother was mortified. She had a disposition that would put an angel to shame, but the rest of that day she was not fit to live with. I never found a way to apologize, to tell her that I really was not feeling well, that I really did have to cut that wood (under orders), and that we really did not intend to embarrass her. I have no idea what she told the minister, but I think she would have preferred the cold walk home.

I suppose the moral is to do your job and get the darn woodbox filled on Saturday so you will not embarrass your mother on Sunday. For some people, *GOING TO CHURCH IS IMPORTANT!*

Chicken Coops and Twenty-Twos

At our house in Tecumseh, we had a back porch that was about three feet off the ground with a railing around it and a roof. Great place to sit in the rain or rest your twenty-two rifle on the railing to get a steady shot.

The single shot twenty-two belonged to dad, or my grandfather. It was made in the original Cooey factory in Cobourg, so long ago that it had no serial number on it. I remember it leaning by the kitchen door on the farm. Standard fare for farms, and needed to get rid of skunks, foxes and wolves that looked on the domestic farmyard animals as lunch or supper.

Everyone knew and respected what it could do. Usually, it was loaded. Kids did not think of it as a toy, but were shown early, and left it alone until old enough, at least eight or so. I think Eaton's catalogue sold them in the twenties, and perhaps earlier, for ten bucks or so.

Of course, the twenty-two went with us to Tecumseh. There was an old chicken coop, probably about the same distance from the house in the backyard as our little barn is now. At one time it actually held chickens. For now, it was vacant with just the screen doors and windows hanging on the wall inside. Gordon and I saw no reason why one could not take a large crayon and draw a big bullseye on it; one big enough to be visible from the back porch, but not so big as to be an easy target.

We crayoned or painted our circles on the chicken coop one Saturday when mom and dad went to Windsor. How old? I am not sure, but I think I was about eleven. We got a box of one hundred Beebe caps. Twenty-two shells came in Extra Longs, Longs, Shorts, and Beebe Caps. Beebe Caps were the babies; short, stubby little shells that did not go too far, and did not do a lot of damage, unless you were a person and got hit by one.

A long rifle shell was dangerous within two miles, so none of those little characters were to play with. Oh, they also came in mushrooms. Mushrooms have a soft nose, so they expand when they hit something, and rip a jagged hole, rather than going right on through with a nice clean round opening. I am sure you wanted to know all that, but you need to understand why we bought Beebe Caps. They were the cheapest and did the least damage.

We took turns. Turns trying to see who could hit the most bullseyes on our circles. I do not remember about Gordon, but I expect he did okay or better than I, but I was a very good shot with a twenty-two. I could ping off bottle caps on a fence post from a respectable distance. In any event, we used up our box of shells with the resulting number of holes in the side of the chicken coop. It looked more like a large, grey, sitting-on-its-side sieve, that had no possible use. Was father a bit upset?

For some reason, we never considered his mood when we started putting holes in an unused chicken coop, and we never even thought about the screens inside. Unless you wanted to keep out giant eagles, those screens were not much good. I know because dad thought he should inspect them after he noticed the holes on the outside of the coop. I remember thinking that it was a bit unfair, since we had forgotten about the screens and felt the coop had no value. He went snooping inside for other damage, and Gordon and I were in trouble because he decided to store screens in a no-good chicken coop.

When you are a kid, you just can't win, but I am sure it was Gordon's idea, and of course I had to endure the consequences also. I wonder if the bullseye has worn off yet?

No Television

We had cold, running water but not hot water, an ice box instead of a fridge, no telephone, a wood cookstove and the same for heat in the living room. Television was a maybe once it was perfected for the masses to use. I did not care, what does a kid know? I had food, the railway yard, asparagus to cut, peas to can, tomatoes to pick, and corn to hoe and harvest.

I was happy and content. We did not have some of the luxuries like a car, phone, and fridge that some of the neighbours had, but who cared? Not me. Oh, sometimes I wondered why we were not up with the Joneses, but mostly I managed to be content in my own little world.

I was in grade seven or eight. Bernie's father was a contractor, and seemed to be doing okay since they were the first people I knew that had a television. A number of us who chummed around together at school were invited to his house after class to see it. I had never seen one before. I recall all of us sitting around in a circle in his living room. The television sat on a table. It was a very large box with a seven-inch screen. We watched *The Lone Ranger*, in black and white of course.

We never got a television while living in Tecumseh, nor the two or three years we lived in Windsor. Dad left for Victoria after that, and we were scattered. Mom and Marlene lived in one place and I stayed with Gordon and Vera until I went to Victoria. Maybe because I did not grow up with it, I think of television as a blight on society and the worst plague of the century. I suspect my view is in the minority but what can I say! The internet and television will merge I am sure, and I guess we will spend our time glued to a monitor, but it will be a bit different since the internet is somewhat interactive.

Chickens

Running around like a chicken with its head cut off!

You have heard of the above? Did you ever see one? Probably not. We often had roast chicken for Sunday dinner. No Loblaws, just send Gordon and Alex out to the barnyard to fetch a chicken. We just caught a likely looking supper suspect and took it over to the chopping block. We took turns. One would hold the chicken by the wings with one hand, using the other hand to hold the feet. Stretch the neck out over the block and the other executioner would wield the hatchet.

With a good, sharp hatchet, one chop would do it. You had to be quick to stick the chicken's neck under the block (a piece of log), because blood would gush out and you could get really splattered. Sometimes you would accidentally lose your grip, or more often if we knew father was not within seeing distance, after it became detached from its head, we would set the chicken back on its feet as fast as possible. The chicken would run around rapidly, no head, shaking its neck and flying blood all over.

We just had to stay out of its way, wait until it dropped after a minute or so, and take the deceased to the house, where a pail of boiling water awaited. The body was immersed in hot water for a minute or two, taken out, put on several newspaper sheets, and removed of all of its feathers. The boiling water made the feather removal much easier.

Sometimes mother, sometimes father, and in later years even the executioners did the above, then removed the insides. Within a few minutes of barnyard freedom, the chicken was in the oven. Guess you do not know when it is your time. I suppose that does not sound very appetizing if you are going to the local supermarket, but given today's traffic, it was probably easier and faster, and I bet a much healthier chicken.

Bike

The Used Bike

I wanted a bike. We were poor. Most of my friends were in the same boat so it was not a problem. Being poor did not mean an unhappy childhood. I remember most of it as being a great time in my life. The mind is a great machine for shutting out the bad bits and highlighting those treasured memories. I was eleven or so when a relative gave me his old bike that he had sitting around for years and no longer used.

Bikes came in standard frame sizes of twenty-four inches for little kids. Twenty-six inches was the next step up and generally the size for all females, and a bike for a real man was twenty-eight inches. This bike had twenty-eight-inch tires and was too much for me. I think this measurement was from the front post where the handlebars were attached to the post for the seat. The wheel sizes also matched that of the frame. Pretty sure that standard measurement still exists today. This old bike was a heavy-duty delivery bike with a double frame, a large steel basket for a carrier on the front, and a hefty steel carrier on the back wheel. Lots of stores delivered by bike and used these large baskets on the handlebars to carry stuff.

After many take apart and learn to fix sessions, I learned to ride it by riding under the bar. If you cannot reach the pedals from the seat, or even resting on the cross bar, then riding under the bar is the only solution (you have to ask someone, someone old, how to do that). Stopping and getting off was easy if the house or some other structure was around when I wanted to stop. It is not easy, but after many scrapes and bandages you get the hang of it. Houses are not always around when you need them, so I fell off a lot. Bandages are still an important part of my life.

I loved that bike. It gave me freedom, but it was a love hate relationship because it was like an old car. If it was not a tube that blew out, it was bearings that were grinding, or a chain that never wanted to stay tight, or at least stay on the sprockets, or handlebars that loosened, or brakes that did not want to brake! Guess I should be thankful and credit that bike with making me mechanically inclined. If I did not learn to fix it, I would never be mobile. It was either repair or walk. I took that large carrier off and stowed it until I needed it to carry papers. Without it on, the bike was like a truck minus the trailer.

The Repairs

I took every bit apart one summer and painted the frame metallic green. It sparkled and looked brand new. Uncle Jack gave me a bit of leftover car paint, and that's how it got to be metallic green, rather than red or blue. Spokes got bent or busted so that the wheels did not always look round anymore. They had a habit of rubbing on the forks and making scraping noises. I think they make the spokes, and a bunch of other stuff, out of far better steel than was put into my bike parts. I bought enough new spokes to redo the whole back wheel, and I proceeded to remove all the old spokes. Look at the spokes in a bike wheel and notice how they go. They don't just shoot straight up from the hub to the rim. There is a definite pattern of criss-crossing. In any event I merrily used dad's fencing pliers and cut out all the spokes.

Did it ever dawn on you that the tension of the spokes holds the rim straight? It didn't on me. When the last few spokes were cut that rim went into convulsions and almost made itself into a figure eight. Did I ever get it back together? Yep. Not sure how many days it took, but I finally figured out the pattern and got that rim back into a circle, with shiny new spokes and no rubbing on the forks. Next time, one spoke at a time! I always had a summer job of some description and that bike seemed to eat up everything I made. The hardware store in town that sold bike parts just loved me.

Gordon

Gordon borrowed my shining green bike, with all new parts, one morning to go to work. His bike was broken, and he did not want to walk or may have been late. He had a summer job at the canning factory. He was a big shot then, probably nineteen or so, and drove the tractor around the yard. He left my bike against the fence. The fence was a standard resting place for bikes. Lots of people rode their bikes to work. Only mine suffered the fate of being backed into by the tractor, driven by my brother. The poor bike was, well, it was a mess and should have been brought home by ambulance. It was weeks before I managed to buy all the new parts the poor bike needed. Not sure whether Gordon helped put it back together or not, but I do know that I paid for all the bits and pieces.

The Ditch

Once it was back together, I had a run in with the ditch at Easter vacation. I really was not a showoff, at least I don't think so. It was nice and warm, and lots of rain. Enough rain that the ditch in front that ran along the road was running over our driveway. When we were out of school for Christmas, Easter, or summer holidays, we had to take all our belongings with us. There were no lockers and so everything was stuffed in our desks. I was in grade six or seven, I think, and we took copious notes in pen; ink pen because ballpoint did not exist at that time. We were supposed to take all these notes home to study for our final exams, not just bum around because it was a holiday.

We normally walked or rode together to and from school. Not everyone had or rode a bike, so those that did would fiddle around back and forth, as kids do. We arrived in front of our house, everyone fascinated by the rushing water, and wondering how deep the ditch was, and how deep it was over the driveway. My sister Marlene did not have a bike. She got up enough nerve to gingerly walk through the water on the driveway. It seemed to be only six inches or so deep. My notes and all that school stuff was in my carrier, held down by textbooks.

I couldn't see being a sissy and walking my bike across that little bit of water, like everyone suggested. Simply go a short distance down the highway to get up speed and the momentum would carry me through. After all, the water was not that deep and only covered about three feet or so of the driveway. With an appreciative audience waiting to see the water fly, I pedalled down the road, turned around and gathered steam.

The waiting gang of half a dozen or so kids, gathered at the edge of the road on the far side of the drive, waited in anticipation.

I hit the driveway like a Tour De France rider. The water flew as the spokes picked it up. I was doing great for two or three seconds, until the front wheel hit the trough that the water had washed out of the driveway. The driveway was covered with cinders and packed down by traffic, but the running water washed a neat little path about six inches deep and a foot or so wide. Of course, it was under the water and you could not see it. A little experience would have suggested that the water would do that, and just maybe you should walk through it first, and check for holes and channels made by the fast-moving water.

What did I know, I was only a kid in grade six or seven. I don't remember ever leaving a bike so fast. I catapulted over the handlebars, landing on the edge of the driveway partly in the ditch. I was battered, bloody, humiliated, and soaking wet. When I came out of my momentary daze and looked around, all I could see were my books, papers, and a year's worth of notes merrily sailing down the ditch carried by the current. Were there cheers from the crowd? I don't remember. I do remember trying to fish my notes out of the water. I don't know why I bothered. Water seems to do strange things to ink. It runs and you can't read it. I know there is a lesson in here somewhere and perhaps you will pick it out.

Five on a Bike

The hand-me-down bike and other monsters like it that were used to deliver groceries and as such must have been the forerunners of *in thirty minutes or your order is free*. It was very heavy and had to be manhandled to steer, especially at slow speeds, or with a load in the basket. Only really, really large and heavy items were delivered with the luxury of a truck.

A couple of years after I got the bike, I could actually ride it, start, and stop, without the aid of the house. Freedom at last. A handful of us kids were just messing around at the edge of town; Tecumseh, that is. Why we decided to try this or whose idea it was, I can't recall exactly, but I was the only one with a bike, and decided to give everyone a ride.

I think I just saw it as a challenge and decided to try. Our experiment was going just fine until the Ontario Provincial Police (OPP) happened by. Even then there must have been crooks to chase instead of harassing innocent fourteen-year-olds, don't ya think!

Like I said earlier, this was a big bike with lots of spare room because I was not very big and took up little space. You know, I can't remember the name of more than two of those kids involved in the stunt, but that does not matter. The five of us were of slightly different sizes, so we were situated on the bike accordingly. I was on the bike and one of the smaller kids scampered up the back carrier with help and perched himself on my shoulders. Another climbed onto the handlebars, which was not an uncommon way to give another kid a ride, and one straddled the back carrier and helped steady our act, while the last passenger hopped onto the crossbar between the seat and the handlebars.

I could pedal standing up, so we had lots of room, and after a couple of aborted tries we were merrily cycling down Tecumseh road at a reasonable pace. A bicycle built for two, indeed... five was much better. Riding double was forbidden, even then against the law, I think, although lots of people did so. Riding five seems like a tough feat and I was not very big, but I was nothing but muscle from hoeing, chopping, cutting, running, and doing the normal chores some of us kids did regularly, so physically it was no big deal to me.

The police car went by and then pulled over. I, of course, stopped immediately, and when the officer got out, I had dislodged all my passengers except the kid on my shoulders. I imagine, unlike riding double, there was no law against riding five on a bike. The OPP guy was aghast, but I bet when he got back to the station and then home, he talked about our escapade to everyone in hearing distance. We got a pretty good lecture and I promised not to do such a thing again, and why would I? We just proved it could be done, and that was enough.

Cinders*

When I was about twelve, we lived in Tecumseh and some friends lived on a side road a short way from our house. There were lots of houses and schools, and large factories heated with coal. Coal does not completely burn, and some types leave what are called cinders. Cinders were bits of unburnt coal and were very black and dirty with some sharp edges. When the stoves or furnaces were cleaned out, the ashes and cinders were used to put on roads, just like they use gravel today. They would eventually pack down and the rain would wash out the black stuff. So, this road that my friend lived on had just received a fresh load of cinders. Riding a bike on that stuff was very difficult until it packed, because the wheels would sink in, go sideways and be like riding in sand, except it was black and very dirty. Cars would make a black dust storm after a fresh load was spread on the road.

It was Sunday night, and no one was around, until I saw my friend's family car with the whole family going home. I wanted to ride my bike to catch the car and see if he could play with me. My mother did not want me to go. You know about mothers! She said I would fall and get hurt on the cinders. I assured her that I could ride just fine and off I went. The car was not going fast but raising a cloud of black dust. I peddled like a demon through the black fog, hoping my friend saw how I could ride and even catch up to the car.

Moments later I was sliding along in the cinders, black dust flying, and my bike a few feet away lying in an ungraceful heap, with the back wheel spinning and making its own little cloud of dust. I limped home pushing the dirty two-wheeled contraption that caused my demise. My left arm was a bloody black and red mess. Skin was hanging from below my elbow, and red blood washed the black off as it dripped down my arm. The rest of me, face, hands, and knees, were black, bruised, cut and a bit bloody, but the arm was the real prize. Mother was not happy. She was normally very sympathetic to my almost daily encounters with cuts, scrapes, and bruises. This night she turned into a Dr. Jekyll and said if I had listened to her and stayed home, I would not be such a mess. I could look after myself.

We did have running water, but no hot stuff unless you put the kettle on. The cleanup operation was not fun or a pretty sight. I came out fairly well, except for the arm. Marlene, feeling sorry for me, helped in the operation. The large cuts in the arm were all black inside with coal dust. We washed and washed, but some of it just would not leave. We bandaged over it. It healed, and today the scar still has a small black streak under the skin. For years it was very visible, but has been getting fainter, and maybe someday when I have used up all that coal dust, it will not even be noticeable.

School and Elephants

You know that I attended the Catholic school in Tecumseh. It had over six hundred kids, and outside of three lay teachers, we were taught by nuns, or sisters. At most, there were three protestant kids at any one time, and for some months there was just me. My fights and battles are probably chronicled in other stories, but this one is about the circus. The circus was being held at the Windsor Arena. It was a big event.

I had never been to a circus. In fact, I had only been to Windsor a couple of times. I was in grade eight, making me thirteen, I guess. For many reasons that you may find elsewhere, come spring in grade seven or eight, I started to leave school early. I mean early in late morning, or not return after lunch, and finally without recrimination from the nuns, but not with their actual blessing.

Charlie and I decided that we should go see the circus. He was one of the few kids who was smart enough to pay attention and get good marks. We hung around together, although he lived on the other side of town by Riverside Drive. The circus was on during school hours, and some schools in Windsor actually took their classes to see it. Not our school.

We were the only two students to witness it that year. We left at the first recess, taking the bus to Windsor and after asking for directions, finally found the arena. It was still morning, and the circus did not open until two or three in the afternoon. Some details are a bit foggy after fifty years.

Being closed, we naturally migrated to the back door of the arena, where all the action was taking place anyway. Animals and all sorts of circus contraptions had to be unloaded, taken inside, and set up, as this was the first day. We sort of hoped that we could slip inside unnoticed, as we did not have any money to buy a ticket.

Most circus guys seem to be big, tattooed, and tough, and really big if you are a short, skinny thirteen-year-old. We got corralled at the big back door where the elephants were being taken in. We told our story honestly. I do not remember what my buddy did, but I was given a shovel, a large wheelbarrow, and instructions to follow this elephant with its handler.

One elephant could choke up any decent septic system in one sitting. Having spent some time on farm chores, this was not a big deal as far as work was concerned, only a big deal as far as the size of the wheelbarrow loads were concerned. I did this during the preparation time only, and true to the big, hairy, tattooed guy's word, got to sit in the stands during the entire circus. Notwithstanding the phoney notes, and explanations to the "mothers" the next day at school, circuses bring back a special memory for me for some reason. Go figure!

The Outhouse

The School

As you know, I attended the separate school in Tecumseh. The public school was down by Riverside drive and too far to go. All the teachers except two were nuns. We addressed them as "mother or sister." The Mother Superior was not a happy principal. I do not recall ever hearing her laugh or seeing her smile. Perhaps if I had her job and dealt with six hundred or so ruffians, I would not be too congenial either.

The high school was across the road and just down a few doors. The dinky one-man police station was close to the high school, and still had its outhouse intact sitting out the back, although it had not been used nor needed for some years. The policeman was Santa Claus without a beard. He was not very tall, and I am sure if he wanted to, could have laid down and rolled rather than walk.

Everyone, young and old, called him Gerry. I have no idea what his last name was. The high school was much smaller than the grade school, as it had less than a hundred students. Obviously going to high school was not a big priority for kids in Tecumseh, although some went to Assumption in Windsor.

Our school had the typical double doors going to the playground. Once inside, you could go down the corridor to the classrooms on the ground level, or just about across from the doors and ten feet or so away, was a large stairway leading to the second floor. Classrooms were there, and to the right and down the hallway you would find the principal's office. The dreaded Mother Superior spent her days there.

The Prank

It was Halloween, and as we entered the school you had to hear and notice all the commotion from the top of the stairs. "You have to see it, go upstairs." Kids were lining the steps and laughing quietly while trying not to. I fought my way through the crowd and turned the corner. As I said, I do not remember Mother Superior being overly joyous at the best of times, and this morning she was livid. An angry red face peering out of a nun's habit is not a nice sight, unless you are a kid, and know that the anger is not directed to you, but to the old outhouse from behind the jail.

The outhouse sat in all its glory in the hallway, just in front of the door to Mother Superior's office. All us kids thought it looked magnificent there and could not understand her utter dismay. Some nuns are grouchier than others I guess, as it was easy to detect the grins and sly smiles that the other nuns tried to conceal. When facing Mother Superior or the kids, they all did their best to put on a "what a dreadful deed" look, when we all could tell that they were enjoying the joke as much as we.

There was too much commotion, too many curious kids and not enough nuns to keep the stairs and hallways clear. We were asked, told, commanded to leave the hall and stairs. As soon as one group obeyed another would fill the void. Six hundred kids are hard to herd, and this was a spectacle that no one wanted to miss. Someone had been sent to fetch Gerry. After all this was serious and needed the attention of the police.

Seems some high school students had broken the lock on the door and carried the offending outhouse up the stairs sometime during the night. I have no idea who did it, and I doubt that Gerry spent much time on the case trying to find out.

The Police

I was fortunate enough to be clinging to the rail at the top of the stairs when Gerry arrived. Not heeding the command to leave, the kids on the stairs had to suck in their chests to make room for the law to get through, as he laboured up trying to catch his breath on each step. It was pretty quiet now that the police force was on the scene. We all called him Gerry, but that did not mean that we did not respect what he stood for.

He got to the top and rounded the corner past my vantage point. Mother Superior met him with a grimace and a tirade, about how could he have let such a dreadful act happen, and how bad the perpetrators were, and he better get the outhouse out of her school and get busy finding and punishing the criminals responsible. Most of her words were lost on the crowd, and obviously on Gerry.

I guess the messenger who was sent to summon him had not told him why he was so desperately needed by Mother Superior. He saw the outhouse. He saw Mother Superior. He burst out laughing, so that his stomach bounced up and down. The solemn group of onlookers no longer had to contain themselves, when the local law enforcer felt as they did. The noise from Gerry's guffaws was drowned out by the laughing, cheering kids. Mother Superior, who for the last while was completely incensed, was now beside herself and retreated to her office, completely disgusted with kids, the local law and probably the world. If only camcorders were around then.

Things settled down after laughter caused tears, and Gerry's stomach quit bouncing. The other nuns got us sorted out and sent in the right direction for class. Mother Superior emerged from her exile, and some of the older boys were recruited to remove the offending object from the hall. I can close my eyes, think for a moment, and the scene is there. The colours are fuzzy, the noise is not as loud, but Mother Superior's face is there, just a few feet away from Gerry's bouncing stomach.

Paper Route and Bowling Alley

The Paper Route

Gordon had the paper route. He grew out of it and I took over when I was twelve. The paper route has its own stories, but I want to talk about the bowling alley. After a year or so, I also saw greener pastures and quit the paper route. For a time, I did both, but just could not handle them.

If you needed something, or wanted something completely unnecessary, you better have some kind of job so you could pay for it yourself. Some kids did not share this dilemma, but the great majority did. We delivered and collected as I think kids do now. Some guy from the paper came to the house every week to collect their portion. My recollection is that I was always short. Not everyone paid on time, but maybe I was just a lousy collector, or spent more than my portion.

I think we got paid three cents a paper. I had fifty-two customers, spread over about four miles along the highway and the tracks, of course. That would work to about nine dollars and change per week. It took me a little over an hour and a half each night to do the route, and probably twice what I earned for parts to keep my old bike going. It was not a winning proposition.

Hardly ever did I ride into town after eating supper and delivering papers, but one spring evening I wound up inside the bowling alley. Some of my school chums set up pins at Tecumseh Lanes. It was on the highway, inside the town limits and at the corner of, I don't remember the road, but it was gravel and in town. I lived out of town and did not hang around there in the evenings like they did. I had little knowledge of the alley, except a friend lived close by.

The gang waited for it to open, and most of the kids just hung out or fiddled around on bikes. I had never been inside, and I was twelve or thirteen. The doors opened and the kids swarmed in. This was a serious alley, boasting eight lanes, with leagues going from seven to nine, and nine to eleven almost every night except Saturday and Sunday. It was a nice night.

Some of the kids who were supposed to work decided it was more fun to fool around on their bikes. Guess they were not used to the word *responsible*, and being poor and broke was the norm, so why change it by working. Even then, when money was scarce for most families, it was difficult to get kids to deliver papers and set up pins. Pin boys came and went. Some were good at it, needed the money and worked regularly. Others just played and worked occasionally. The serious ones set up two alleys at once. A few could take two alleys of ten pins.

The kids swarmed in to see if they could work, to buy a pop or just annoy the owner and be booted out. I went in out of curiosity. I was a quiet, shy kid, so I just went into the entrance and peeked around. Bowlers got pretty upset if there was no kid to set up the pins, the owners more so. One of the owners (a father and son) asked me if I would work. I had no idea how but agreed to check it out. I was shown the back. I observed for a few minutes but had to go home since it was almost dark, and I was not supposed to be that far away. I agreed, if my parents were willing, to come back and work Sunday night.

The Bowling Alley

No McDonald's or fast-food places for kids to work at. The bowling alley was the only place for ambitious kids who wanted to work and make money. They paid I think, five cents a lane for setting up five pin, and six cents for ten pin. If you made five dollars a week, you got to bowl free on Saturday night. Kids would set up one lane for the first shift, or two lanes, and others would take over for the late games, taking one or two alleys, depending on your experience and ability. Some could set up two lanes for both shifts, but most could not, or did not want to.

For a league with five bowlers on each team, taking two alleys meant you could make a dollar and fifty cents in two hours for a five-pin league, and two dollars and ten cents for two alleys of ten pins. It was hard work. If you worked say five nights and took two alleys both nights from seven to eleven, with a mixture of five and ten pins, you would average eighteen or nineteen dollars, plus tips. Compared to papers, when I added the tips, this was big money.

You must imagine if you have not been there, what it is or was like, at the end of a bowling lane. The alley stops an inch or so from where the last pin sits. The pit starts after that. It is the same width as the alley, but about six inches or so lower. The balls and pins all end up in the pit. The pit is about three feet longer than the alley, with a wall about the same height at the end. There is a walkway, only a foot and a half or so wide at the top of the pit and running the full length of the alley. The ball return curves up to this walkway, and there is one beside each alley.

Pinsetter

The working end of a bowling alley is not a spot to take lightly, and no place for a novice setting up pins for a serious ten pin league. I found that out with the very first ball that came down my lane. I am not sure, but I think I had four or five minutes of instruction, and do not recall ever seeing a ball thrown until the game started. The pinsetter would sit on the walkway beside the ball return, legs hanging down into the pit. Experience, and knowing the bowler, would tell you how fast the ball is coming, where it would hit the pins, which ones would fly, and in which direction. It was a learned art. The back wall of the building was made of concrete blocks and formed the backdrop to the little walkway behind the pits. I know, the picture is as clear as mud.

While we hung our legs into the pit, we did not do so when anyone was throwing a ball. Too distracting for the bowler. You simply lifted them up and held them out straight or rested them on the ball return. Good exercise, I guess. When the ball finally hit the pins, you also learned where to put your legs, to protect the rest of your body from flying pins. Five pins do not take off to the same extent as ten pins and are not near as dangerous. Most five pin bowlers at that time were kids or old geysers. Rarely dangerous.

Ten pin bowlers and the pins they hit were a different kettle of fish. Taking care of two alleys called for a lot of caution. I found that out on the very first night. It was not unusual for a ten pin to fly out of the pit, hit the concrete wall behind, and slide along the walkway for two or three alleys. Experienced pin boys let the others know in advance, and all were prepared and out of the way. I wonder if we were covered by Workers Compensation Board?

Head Pin

Sunday night came and I was sitting on the walkway, right in the middle of the alley, legs held high, when the first ten pin ball rocketed down the alley. I had practiced with a couple of veteran pinsetters, so I was ready. I watched the ball hit the pins, saw an errant pin in the air, and woke up with an awful headache and one large bump on my forehead. What an awesome start...one ball, and I was gone. I remember several people standing over me. The goose egg on my forehead was ginormous. It probably did not feel too good either.

I sat around for a while, wet cloth on my forehead, and then rode my bike home. I am sure, although I do not remember, my mother not wanting me to do this dangerous job again. I did it for four more years and paid my way through high school. A bruise like that is a sign of honour at school when you are twelve. I was a hero for a couple of days. I never got clobbered again.

Paper Route and Dogs

This particular customer was near the end of my route. It was an unkempt farm, much like most were in the late forties. The laneway was reasonably long, with a large hedgerow on the left side. The driveway ended past the house in a large circle in front of the barn. The house had a side door with a big porch.

My routine was to ride my bike down the lane, throw the paper onto the porch, do a u-turn, and get out as fast as possible. The speed, in my mind, was necessitated by the large dog chained to the clothesline. The line ran from the back of the porch to a pole, or some building in the yard leading to the barn. The dog's chain was attached to the line, and he could run along the line as far as his chain allowed. He could get within a few feet of the steps to the porch, but not quite.

I never purposely annoyed the dog. I only rode as close to the porch as necessary to throw the paper to make sure it landed by the door. I think I was just a bit afraid of him. He always lunged at the end of the chain and never sounded very friendly, although liking dogs, I always talked to him. I tried to reassure him that I was just a humble paper delivery kid, and would never cause him, or his charges, any harm.

Every night save Sunday, the growling and lunging dog and I had our conversation. I rode in, very gingerly, always wondering what would happen to me if that chain or clothesline should break. I had that picture in my mind of the *Hounds of the Baskerville*, ripping me to pieces, tearing off arms and drinking in the blood dripping from my limbs.

I pictured that dog breaking his chain as I turned on my bike. He lunged and landed on my back. I went down with teeth sinking into my shoulders. I was entangled in my bike, as the razor-sharp teeth tore into my flesh. *At last, I am getting even with that annoying kid on the bike, who keeps throwing that thing onto the porch.*

I did not like to deliver the paper to that house, even if the wife was very nice on collection day, when I actually had to climb the steps and knock on the door.

Winters were the worst time. It was hard to ride in the snow, and it was dark. I could not tell how close I was to the end of the dog's chain. Some nights I was sure I could feel his breath through my pant leg as I turned around. Being the chicken that I was, I often got off the bike at the steps, threw the paper, and turned the bike around on safe ground, a few feet from the end of the dog's reach, got back on and rode out the driveway, always listening for galloping paws behind me.

You know what kid's minds are like! This was one of my customers that preyed on my mind until I got there and left. I never had peace of mind until I was out of that driveway, out onto the highway, and could no longer hear the snarl, growl, and groaning, creaking chain. Only then was I safe.

It was winter. For Windsor it was really cold, and a fair bit of snow on the ground. I still used my bike because the large grocery store carrier held the papers. Sometimes I rode, and mostly walked because of the snow. On days when it got too bad, I pulled a sleigh with the paper bag sliding off most of the time. Walking with the bike was easier.

I reached my dreaded laneway. It was dark. The hedges along the lane made it seem even darker, the porch further away, and the barking, snarling dog even closer. His voice bounced off the barn and echoed in my ears as I rode the snow ruts up to the porch. The dog hollered. The chain he was on creaked and groaned. I prayed that the space beside the porch was cleared of snow, and that I could hurl the paper onto the porch, do my u-turn and get back out to safety on the highway.

The kitchen light shone its glow onto the porch. As I quickly tossed the paper, my nemesis' shadow lunged at the end of his chain. I turned the bike, jumped back on, and started to spin through the snow-covered lane.

I was almost at the highway. The ruts were not that deep, and the carrier was just about empty. My friend attached to the clothesline had become very silent, except for a rattling chain. I turned my head to see what was going on. One large dog pulling a length of chain was flying up the driveway, and quickly closing the gap between him and one terrified kid on a bike. Well, that sure did not take long, as within seconds I was lying in a heap in the hedge with part of the bike on top of me, and the dog standing on me and the bike. I guess if you don't look where you are going, you may just run into a hedge.

It was winter and I imagine that I had lots of clothes on and mittens. I put my arm over my face and wondered what part of me would be severed first. Did he try to bite me? I really do not remember, as the lady came out to get the paper when she heard it hit the porch, and she witnessed the escaping dog. She ran up the driveway yelling at the dog, and that probably took his attention away from chewing me up, although he did not move off me until she grabbed his chain and hauled him off.

I got untangled from the bike and the hedge, sort of shook up, but no worse for wear. It was probably a good thing that I ran into the hedge, since he may well have jumped on my back, or taken a bite out of a leg. It is also a good thing that the lady was there to rescue me or who knows, I may still be lying there waiting for that dog to move. The next night and many after we carried on where we left off, him lunging and yapping, and me getting out as fast as I could. The chain never broke again.

Papers and the Railroad

Friends

We were just normal kids, for our generation anyway. We had lots of space. Our parents never worried that we would be abducted or otherwise harmed. We lived on what was then highway #39, about a mile or so from Tecumseh, and about ten miles from Windsor. My parents had a bungalow on about three acres of land. The house to the east of us would be about a thousand feet away on higher land and separated by a field. To the other side lived the Renauds. Their house was a little closer, but not much. Eventually another family without kids would build on the space between us and the Renauds. The Renauds had thirteen children, all at home most of the time we lived there.

Clarence was a little older than I, much larger, not good at school, and he was my protector when fights got too rough. There were three houses across the road. Roger's family lived in the new house, and on the other side of the driveway the grandparents lived. It had been a large farm at one time. Their property went back to the railway tracks, about a couple of thousand feet.

Vince Morrand lived in the third house on the far side towards Tecumseh. Roger, Clarence, and I, along with Louis Souliere, who lived a few stone's throw down the road past the Renaud's, all hung around together. Farther towards town there was another family with two boys who also were part of the gang at times. I cannot remember their names. Next to Clarence's house was a short, private road that went a mile or so, and dead ended in the front yard of a house. A couple of wild little characters lived there, and they also kept us company on many of our exploits.

Clarence's parents had about ten acres, running back along the private road. His father worked in town, but they also had a horse, and used it to pull implements to work the garden. They had a few rows of grapes as well. That was a pretty good vineyard. Louis' dad farmed. We spent a lot of time just messing around in the barn and hay loft. Unless you are a boy brought up in this environment, it will be hard to understand the intrigue of a large barn and fields to run in.

The Railroad

As I said, the property of Roger's family ended at the railroad tracks. Originally it was just a single track, but because of the war, seventeen more tracks had been added as a siding behind the main line. These tracks started at Little River and went all the way into Tecumseh, close to five miles I believe. These tracks were used to store freight cars of all types that held army trucks, jeeps, and tanks.

Ford, Chrysler, and General Motors all had factories in Windsor which were converted to turn out vehicles of all kinds used by the armed forces. These vehicles were put on or into rail cars, taken to the marshalling siding in Tecumseh across the road and through the field from our house. They were shunted around to make up trains to be sent to Montreal or Halifax, or maybe Toronto, to be shipped by boat to Europe.

The yard was fenced, heavily guarded and no one was allowed nearby. Our gang never ventured near the yard until after the war. Around the end of 1945 and into 1946, activity slowed greatly, and although it was still guarded, there did not seem as many, and we could sneak in and inspect the goings on. For kids twelve-years-old or so, and with adventurous spirits, the railyard was a great treasure. I did get to experience it though, long before we took it over as our special playground.

The Paper Delivery

When I was twelve, I inherited Gordon's paper route. Beside my last house towards Tecumseh, there was a path that wandered the edge of the field and brambles that followed a little creek to the railroad tracks. There was an old gentleman, and we referred to him as the hermit. He lived in a little dinky shack on the far side of the road that ran on the far edge of the railway siding. Guess he was not a threat to national security, or they would not have let him stay there when the siding was built. He would be about a mile from town, and he subscribed to the paper. The kids in town did not want to go that far to deliver so I did.

So, I ambled along the little path by the creek, jumped across the ditch, climbed the fence protecting the main line, and then scrambled up the gravel and stone bank to the tracks. Many a time in the spring that ditch caused me grief. Trains are big and loud, but not always loud if the wind is strong and blowing in the face. I always stopped and looked and was very cautious. Trains ran very often then, and the passenger trains went very fast. The main line was really a piece of cake, though, compared to the siding.

The Trains

The seventeen tracks on the siding presented the real challenge. Each one had to be crossed very carefully, and they all, almost always, had cars on them. If a track was full and an engine was coupling three miles away, it took a few moments for the movement to hit the cars where I was. The tracks were very close, and you could not see the end, nor tell if they were going to move.

You listened as hard as you could, then very carefully climbed the ladder to the coupling if it seemed safe. You hung on as tight as possible and gingerly stepped over the coupling, grabbing the ladder on the far side, lest the cars start to move. Getting thrown off was not a big problem. Getting thrown onto the coupling between the two cars would have been a big problem. It seemed to me to be sure death, and I wanted no part of that.

Trains do not start off nice and easy. There is a bit of play at each coupling, so as they all tighten up, they do so with a jerky movement. You hang on tight to the ladder, step on the edge of the coupling, and reach for the ladder on the other side. You will appreciate that my arms were not long enough to stretch from one side of a boxcar ladder to the other, and even rail workers were told not to cross cars in this manner. You could hold onto the rod that comes down for the brake, but it was not a great thing to get a good hold on. Once started, you did not stop to ponder, but got over, down the ladder, and did the same maneuver until all seventeen tracks were behind you.

I am sure the railroad police would have taken a very dim view of my shortcut had they only known. Sometimes I would get the nerve to climb to the top of a boxcar, to see if I could see far enough to detect any engines. I was a bit leery of this because I was always afraid that I would be spotted by some worker, or worse still, the dreaded guard. I am sure my hermit really appreciated the risk I took daily just to deliver his cruddy paper that I got three- and one-half cents a week for. In nice weather, I actually enjoyed this little adventure each evening. It was like a lottery each night to see if I could get over and back without incident. Winter was an entirely different matter.

The Darkness

I do not like dark particularly, and not much at all when I was twelve or thirteen. The space between rail cars is very dark with lots of shadows if there is a moon. If it is windy the doors will often rattle. It can be dead quiet one moment and then this strange squeak or low rattle will burst upon your ears. One thing about dark nights though was that you could usually tell if an engine was on your track, because you could see the glare of the light poking around the side of the first car.

I always looked under the cars, and as far as I could in both directions. I always had to be wary of the guard, and a pair of legs on the far side of a car always brought me to a halt, and the hope that my heartbeat could not really be heard that far away. When it was dark the telltale beam of a roving flashlight always signaled a guard doing the rounds. Just be patient and quiet and when he was far enough away I could always sneak past.

Winter clothing was not the greatest, and steel boxcars tend to feel umpteen degrees colder than it is. I was always frozen when I got to the little shack, and always invited in, offered tea or coffee, and cookies, and sat by the woodstove to warm up. Regardless of the warming hospitality, I still would be frozen again when I got back home.

Out of the danger of trains, I still had the path to traverse. It bothered me as much or more than the shadows and noises in the railyard. It was usually pitch black on the path because it was covered by bushes and other growth. I could always imagine someone, not sure who or why, lying in wait for me somewhere along its twisty way. Luckily, it never happened. I wonder if current papers carry that much excitement.

When things slowed at the railyard there were fewer guards and less train shuffling. We explored the yard on many a sunny afternoon. I am sure my paper delivering experiences came in handy to navigate our wonderland.

More Bowling Alley

Money

The knock on the head was soon forgotten when I realized that I had made a lot more money than was ever possible delivering papers. If I worked both shifts, taking two lanes for five nights, I could make more than twice as much money as I did on my paper route. Factor in the tips, and then work Saturday and maybe Sunday afternoon, why the income was more than I could imagine.

I tried again the next weekend and found out that I could do okay. After some time, I became very fast and could set two alleys of ten pins for both shifts. Because I needed the money for school, as we had to buy all our own books, pens, and pencils, I usually worked five nights a week and sometimes Saturday and Sunday afternoons. When I started high school, for a while my routine was something like this:

Get off the bus at Tecumseh, ride my bike home, do my chores (we were not on a farm then, only having three and a half acres, but we had chickens, ducks and rabbits, and wood to cut and chop), deliver papers, eat supper and be at the bowling alley for seven, set up lanes for both leagues, and ride my bike back home. I would be home around eleven-thirty.

Mother was always waiting up for me. She was usually dozing on a chair by the stove in the living room. If tips were good, I would take home a chocolate bar for her. She did not like my routine and was always worried about me getting home in the dark. Winter is the bowling season, and it was dark coming and going. I was not always fussy about it either, because as you know riding a bike in winter is not fun.

Long Days

The bus left Tecumseh at seven-thirty in the morning, and it took me twenty minutes or longer to get there, depending on if I rode or walked. The days were long, but I do not remember feeling any hardships, or 'why me?' sort of stuff. I liked the bowling alley; the owners and the bowlers were good to me, and I got paid. I could buy my school stuff, the odd clothes, and I had enough money to keep my bike in repair. It always seemed to need something.

Most of the winter I could not ride because of the cold and the snow. Guess I was in shape because I would jog there and back...especially back. Clothes were not like now, so winter clothes were heavy, and the standard footwear was not conducive to running or keeping you warm. Cheap shoes and running were one way to keep the feeling in toes and fingers.

The sidewalk and streetlights ended a few blocks after the bowling alley, and then it got dark. When I was going home there were not many house lights on because it was out of town and the houses were scattered. Not a lot of cars either so I usually ran on the road. There was a dirt path beside the fields, but it was narrow, and occasionally there was someone else either going or coming. I may have been in shape, but I was a chicken after the barn and Mummers episode.

I really did not like the dark, so the trip home was never fun. If there was someone in front of me, I wanted to be as far away as possible because you could not see any features or tell who they were. I never wanted to find out, so I would cross the road and run on the other side until I was past them. Moonlit nights were great, though, just because they lit up the countryside, and in the winter with snow on the ground it looked so beautiful. If only it had not created those darn shadows.

One Last Bowling Story

Respect

Many of the kids were rambunctious, mouthy, and knew every bad word ever thought of. I did not swear or use profane language. I always felt it unnecessary to swear and did not like profane language. Unlike most of the kids, I was polite and treated the owners with respect. I was always taught to treat adults like that. They were good to me, especially the father. He was Mr. Kurrie and his son, who was probably forty or so, was just Bill. Mr. Kurrie remarked one day that I was the only kid in the place that did not swear.

The alley was closed for July and August. During that time, the lanes were sanded down, oiled and everything was gone over and refurbished. All the ten pins were turned on a lathe and repainted. One summer Mr. Kurrie asked if I would like to help. I do not know if he really needed me or not, but I worked with him all summer doing the alleys and pins, and he paid me more than I would get at some of the other more arduous jobs I usually had.

Leagues

The Thursday night league was one of my favourites, although a real pain in the butt. It was the only five pin league that I set up. It was a group of doctors and their wives. They started at nine, always late, and never finished until about eleven-thirty. Doctors' offices were often open in the evenings, and so they could not always be at the alley on time. When they did arrive, they spent a lot of time yapping, and not paying attention to when it was time to bowl. They were also lousy bowlers.

Most of the kids, much to the consternation of Bill or his dad, would holler down the alley for someone to get up and bowl, and cause the bowlers to complain. No one was happy with the doctors' league, and they were not happy with the insolent pin boys. Reluctantly, I agreed to set up for them. Remember, we did not make as much money setting up five pins, and these characters keep you there usually a half hour longer.

When the bowlers were finished, the pin boy walked up to the score table and initialled the back of the score sheet, verifying the number of bowlers and games, and ensuring that you got paid as your name was on the sheet. It was usual in most games that one or two bowlers would give you a tip, very unusual for everyone on the team to do that. Five or ten cents was normal, twenty-five cents or more was wow!

Most of the doctors were not normally in the habit of tipping, since the pinsetters were such a bunch of insolent ingrates. I sat and waited patiently, although I would have liked to scream at them also and did not enjoy getting home so late. It did not take more than a couple of weeks though before they expected their regular pinsetter. We got to know one another, and I would chat with those who arrived on time while we waited for the rest. It was the only league that every player tipped the pin boy, and not with a nickel or dime. I made more in tips from the doctors every Thursday night than I was paid for setting pins for all four hours.

The men's commercial league took their bowling seriously, very seriously. I sat pins for them for more than a year or two and knew their quirks. Who hollered over a pin slightly off the peg, who threw curves, hooks, straight balls, made the pins fly, who were the real bowlers, and who were the whiners.

Judging

Attached to the concrete wall above the walkway to the back of the alley and about ten feet off the floor was a little box. A neat wooden box big enough to hold one person. It had a ladder flush to the wall to gain access. The box was open on three sides and was exactly situated so the person sitting in the box could see all eight foul lines. The part against the wall contained a wooden seat, and in front was a panel with eight switches, one for each lane.

Of course, they were not numbered, and were in two rows of four. For serious leagues and tournaments, the foul line judge sat in the box and pressed the appropriate button if called for. It was not that unusual for the wrong button to get pushed in error. Bowlers would glare and the judge would holler his apology and then press the proper button. When the button was pressed, a bell would ring, a light would glitter on the board over the end of the alley, and a light would flash for the pin boy to know to reset the pins. Bowlers did not appreciate the foul line judge, and often heated exchanges would take place. The judge was infallible and while words were exchanged, everyone knew and accepted that once the button was pushed there was no turning back.

The foul line judge was hired and paid for by the bowling alley. He was usually some guy with lots of bowling experience, and someone who was very alert. You had to watch carefully as you could have three or four bowlers delivering at once, and then seconds after them, another onslaught. No time to turn away and wipe your nose or check out who just came in. One had to watch very carefully, and if just a fraction of a toe went over, not on, but over the foul line, then push the button immediately, not a few seconds after they backed away from the approach.

Playoffs

It was playoff time. May, June, I do not remember, except that it was warm and spring moisture made the floor, including the approaches, damp, and sticky. Where was the regular guy, I have no idea, but Bill asked me if I would sit in the box. I had done it a couple of times before during the season and was not pleased with the adverse comments to my eyesight. The only compensation for two hours of sweat, fear, and tense fingers that could not find the right button, was the pay. Twice what one got for fighting off pins in the pit. I reluctantly sat in the box.

Things were going pretty well. These guys lived bowling and had the same fright and respect for the foul line as I did when I pushed the buzzer. Last game, tenth frame. What's his name (I can almost remember but not quite), who was the worst offender, whiner and yeller at the kid in the box, stuck his toe out too far. The buzzer brought the silence to a roar. The offender ran right over and stood under the box. The kid is too young! He pushed the button in panic! I may have been close but not over!

The opposing team of course backed my judgment and praised my eyesight and quick skill in pushing the button. The uproar brought Bill to mediate. Words flew in all directions and cooler heads questioned if I was really sure. I do not remember names, but I can conjure up the scene today. I was steadfast. I professed to simply doing my job. I do not remember if that buzzer affected the outcome of the match or not, but it is a lesson I guess in sticking to your guns if you know you are right. I do not ever remember being asked to be the foul line judge again.

Chicken

Discrimination

I don't know, but I was a pretty quiet, shy kind of kid, perhaps even timid would be a good word. I went to public school in Tecumseh after we left the farm. The school had six hundred or so kids. All French and Catholic, except me and Marlene when she went. For a while there was also Fred. He was a short kid like me, but round and freckled faced with red hair. He could and would take on any Catholic kid or otherwise, big or small, either singly or by the dozen, for any reason. He would get up, wipe off the blood and charge again.

He saved me from many scrapes. Alas, he was only around for a few months and moved on. I often wonder what happened to him. He was the product of a broken home, I think, and learned early in life to stand up for himself or perish. Marlene was sick often and missed a lot of school. In any event, I soon discovered discrimination, although I did not know the word then. Kids were kids, so I thought. I never knew there were Catholics or Protestants, or black or white. We were just kids. Not in a Catholic school in that era, apparently. According to the priests and nuns, and the kids too, since they got the message from the former, I being a non-Catholic was going to hell, and there was just no saving me unless I smartened up and became Catholic. I had no idea what the heck their problem was.

I have made the statement many times that I did not grow up, I fought my way up. Being the nature I was, and still am to a great extent, I found that very difficult. It did not take more than a millisecond for all the kids to know that the new kid was Protestant. Most really did not care. I think their philosophy was like mine. So what, is there really a difference?

Over time, a couple of years, two gangs emerged at school. The kids I got along with and chummed with and those who really took the priests at their word. One such kid lived on Tecumseh Road, just at the edge of town. There was no way I could get to or from school without passing his door. There was a sidewalk there, and only on his side of the road. Crossing the street did not help because there was not enough shoulder to walk on, and anyway I did not want to openly display my fear of him by crossing the road.

Chicken

His nickname was Chicken. I do not remember his real name. I think his nickname came because he was tall and skinny, and perhaps to some resembled a chicken with a long neck. Not sure. He was much taller than me and decided to be my special, personal tormentor. I did not need a special one. I had lots. He delighted in waiting in his doorway for me to pass in the mornings, and then hound me the rest of the way to school. Now, to be fair, that only happened when Clarence was not walking with me, but that's another story.

The same thing on the way home. I was afraid to tell my father or Gordon about this terror in my life because they would just say "stand up for yourself and pound the crap out of him." I think I may have, but I did not enjoy being bloodied and bruised. Some of my friends, and others on the other team, seemed to enjoy a good scrap, and a bloody nose or bruise here or there did not seem to deter them.

When I was twelve, I started to work at the bowling alley. One spring evening we were waiting for the owner to come and open. He lived in Windsor. There was always a gang of kids, those of us who worked at the alley, and just a bunch of hangers around types who frequented the front. Perhaps twenty kids.

I was short for my age and Chicken was the other direction. He did not work at the alley but lived a stone's throw away and always inhabited the sidewalk in front. I do not think he had a lot of friends. He had been a plague on my life for more than a year now, and I was getting a little weary. His haranguing did not stop at going and coming to school where there was no audience, it carried on in front of the bowling alley. Other kids there were echoing the sentiments of dad and Gord... just beat the crap out of him. Don't take that!

The Fight

I had enough. One can run and convince yourself to feel good about it if there is no one around. When you are surrounded by peers, being a coward is not an alternative. The road beside the bowling alley was gravel, crowned in the middle with lots of loose gravel on top and at the edges. I do not remember exactly what triggered the final retaliation, but we ended up in the middle of the road surrounded by the whole gang of onlookers. Lots of shouts and cheers, none for Chicken, all for me to stand up and teach him a lesson.

Gravel flying like most scuffles of this kind, as two kids pair off, throwing punches but not really inflicting any kind of damage, except to egos. I was finally angry enough to lose my fear. I got one good punch to his gut, making him bend over enough that I could land another on his nose, sending blood squirting. That was the end. The owner drove around the corner. The crowd of workers cheered and headed for the door. Chicken walked his bike home with one hand and the other holding his nose.

I was a hero with the bowling alley gang. Word spread through the school with the same speed as when I started, and they discovered that I was not Catholic. I would not say we ever became close friends, but never again did I have to consider crossing the road to go by Chicken's house.

The Moral

Got room for a footnote: there is a good lesson in the above. The world is full of bullies, and I think more so in this generation with the *Me Society*. I lived in daily fear for a few years as a kid, not thinking about it as a career, but it was there at school, and going into town on weekends. Not a nice environment. Most kids survive, and some get scarred for life.

I think I was lucky. My home environment, especially my mother, helped immensely. I learned that you can be compassionate and caring, but sometimes you still have to look out for and take care of yourself. I had lots of confrontations after Chicken, but once you know you are right, have done nothing wrong, and you really won't break from a bruise or two, well, living with the world becomes a lot easier. Confrontation is for the weak and cowards of the world but can be halted by the strong. (Or in my case, a kid who has just had enough).

Borrowed Jigger

Many exciting days were experienced at the railyard. A jigger may not be a name you recognize, but you may be familiar with the term *handcar*, or not. This was a little platform mounted on four miniature railway car wheels. Work crews and all kinds of railway people used them to scoot along the railroad tracks. If you have not seen one in real life, I am sure you have seen them in old movies.

They were just large enough for a person to stand at either end and pump the large handles that were in the middle of the platform. When you pumped the handles, it ran a mechanism that turned the wheels. Not really unlike a bicycle sprocket set up, but you used your arms and not your legs. One person could get this little gadget purring pretty fast once you got it under way. Two people really pumping could turn it into a rocket on rails.

These little guys were stored at various spots along the right of way. Usually there was a set of rails running ten feet or so, ninety degrees to the main track. Two people could easily lift one end, turn it, and set it on its storage site. You pushed it to the end away from the main rails, applied the brake and there it stayed until the next crew or workers needed it. Our private rail entertainment centre had a jigger stored off the main line. Louis and I often eyed it enviously.

One fine summer day there was not a guard or worker to be seen. We had never tried to move it, so we were surprised that two fourteen- or fifteen-year-olds, with a bit of huffing and puffing, could get it onto the main line. We were not sure of the times but had a good idea of when the trains came through, and like the workers there was not a train to be seen.

Trains, both passenger and freight, ran often and if this little jigger was caught too far from its home, it could end up just being numerous steel and wood splinters, not to mention what the two people pumping the handle would look like, if they did not see the train and stayed on the jigger.

The beautiful day, the absence of railroad busybodies, and no trains in sight meant the temptation was too much. We got the bright yellow jigger onto the main track. All jiggers were painted bright yellow. Two kids pushing on the handles, like sitting on a teeter-totter, could really make that little machine go. We sailed up and down the tracks like the wind, being careful to not get too far from its resting place, lest a train came upon us and we had nowhere to put our machine.

One person faces each way so both ends of the track are covered to watch for approaching trains. We rode until our arms wore out and we became fearful that some do-gooder would spot us and report this little dinky train running back and forth on the main line. We returned our borrowed jigger to its home a few minutes before the passenger train flew by.

I think such an act is a criminal offence, and the railroad and justice system do not take kindly to people stealing jiggers. I guess they are concerned that someone may just get killed by a train. We did not think that would apply to us since we spent so much time there and felt very knowledgeable about what went on in the railway business. Anyway, we did not steal it or anything like that. We were just borrowing it for a while and would not do any damage to it.

Most jiggers are motorized now. They are also enclosed like little dinky cars. What a bunch of wimps these railroad guys have become. When we moved to Peterborough and I worked for Smith Corona Marchant, one of my customers was in the Sylvester Steel factory in Lindsay. The building is still there. Mr. Sylvester was an old gentleman then, no employees, just he, a secretary, and a large empty plant.

For years he had made jiggers. Jiggers like the one we borrowed, called handcars, because you made them go by hand. Motorized ones were now what was popular, and the call for Mr. Sylvester's handcars was down to so few a year, that he could put them together himself and still only work one day a week. I felt sorry for him, his empty factory, and the fact that kids would not experience the exhilaration of borrowing a jigger on a beautiful summer day and feel the wind as they pumped full speed along the tracks. To me, it is unfortunate that times have changed.

Bikes and the Railroad Yard

Busted

We got caught. We had been spotted before. Hollered at and escaped over the fence and through the field. Let's face it, some of those guards are like some of today's finest, but they had no donut shops to frequent. We were pretty agile kids and at least could run. We had lots of occasions where a speedy exit was necessitated, so got lots of running practice.

Things at the yard were winding down. Just one guard. He rarely walked but drove his car slowly down the road. The gate at the roadway was even left open. We rode our bikes to the road behind the last track. Dad no longer worked there, so that threat was gone, or so I thought.

Hiding behind the last boxcar we spotted the guard's car, way down at the far end. We scooted across the road and hid our bikes in the long grass beside the road and headed for the row of boxcars. We needed some nails or whatever so started our search. It was about the middle track and if we were quiet, we could hear the guard's car and make sure we stayed hidden.

Not too long after we heard the car drive up and a while later drove back past. We had walked quite a distance from our starting point and did not realize how far we had gone. It was getting dark so we knew we should get home or suffer the consequences. We heard the guard's car coming and going a few times. He seemed to be driving awfully slowly.

How are we going to cross the road, get our bikes and ride out before he sees us, if he keeps that up? We stayed between the second last row of cars and walked to what we thought would be the spot opposite to where we had hidden our bikes. There were three of us. When the sound of the car got near, we crouched down beside a wheel until the sound passed. A wheel on a rail car is plenty big enough to shield a kid. Finally, the pesky guard's car disappeared to the far end and we bolted over to our bikes. Not there.

Bikes Stolen

Yikes, someone has stolen our bikes, all three of them. The indentation is still in the grass, so we know this is where we left them, but they are gone. Our parents will line us up, execution style and shoot all three of us. Bikes are expensive and we are poor. We also lost them in a forbidden part of town. I don't want to go home. It is almost dark. No such thing as a cell phone, so I can't call home to explain that I am at Roger's and may be a few more minutes.

Guess what? We did not have a phone at home to call anyway. We hatched a plan that thirteen- or fourteen-year-old kids actually thought would sound real. We would walk up the road as bold as brass, the road that we were not supposed to trespass on, and when the guard came along, we would enlist his help to find the thief that stole our bikes.

You see we were not really messing around the railyard. We were wandering the field behind and left our bikes there. We only used their road to get to the field. I know! But we really were not the type to lie or do really bad things, and this did not seem like a lie, just a slight distortion of the truth. After all, our bikes were really in the field, and the consequences of our real whereabouts that evening could be disastrous if we told the guard where we really were. We assumed that he did not know.

It was not long before a set of headlights got closer and stopped as we stood at the side of the road. We approached the driver's door as he got out. No one missed the open trunk with three bikes hanging haphazardly, but secured by rope, to the bumper.

We presented an awesome case, all innocence. Why would he have our bikes secured to his car, when we were just in the field looking for birds? Wouldn't you know it? This old geezer guard was better with words and mind games than we were. He gave us back our bikes, was going to tell my dad, but we really would not go to jail if we just stayed away, so we did not get run over by a train, or otherwise have our lives shortened. We learned a good lesson and did not go back for weeks, or months, I really do not remember!

I do sometimes though, when I see a siding full of cars, still picture that guard and our bikes. Just in case you are wondering, Father was not too pleased, either.

The Railyard

The Guards

You already know about the railroad yard. Well, the war was over for a couple of years, the army vehicles no longer rolled out of Windsor, the siding was down to a couple of guards, and trains were not shuffling cars around all day, every day. Curious kids could sneak around and investigate all the marvels. The guards had little guard houses every mile, or a bit closer, I think. The little houses had wood stoves and a chair or two. The guards walked back and forth the length of the yard, stopping at their little shacks for a rest to warm up or grab a cup of tea or coffee. The yard was fenced in front of the main line. There were roads at either end and a roadway running the full length after the last set of tracks.

We walked the road to the gate and simply climbed over or went through the field behind Roger's place and climbed the fence. After very carefully going over the first few rows, one of us would be elected to climb to the top of a car, see if we were close enough to see the road, and determine where the guards were. If they were walking at the far end or just out of sight, we knew we were safe for at least a few minutes.

It was always exciting. A game of don't get caught, all the time checking for the sound of an engine or boxcars starting to move. Getting caught by the guard was one thing, getting run over by a train was something else. By this time most of the cars were empty, and the railroad used it as a storage yard for all kinds of rail cars. There were boxcars, refers, flat cars, gongs and even the odd stock car. We avoided the stock cars. The flats and the boxcars were a variable horde of treasure. They had all kinds of good nails.

If you are a kid that likes to make things, you need good nails. Nails were probably cheap, but if you are poor, you did not have money for even cheap nails. Bolts, lots of nuts and bolts, and bits of steel fasteners. We carted home as much as our pockets could carry. Our mothers wondered why we always had holes and rips in our pockets. Bib overalls were great for those excursions. They had lots of pockets and were tough. We scrounged all kinds of treasures and revelled in the dangerous game of hide and seek with the guards. I think they knew the game too. We just had not met to set up the rules.

Riding and Jumping

Most of the tracks were full of cars all the time. Often an engine would hook onto a mile or two of cars to sort them out and get the ones they needed out of the middle of the bunch. If you could escape the sight of the brakeman, the guards and those other meddlesome adults working there, you could grab a ladder, stand on the bottom step, and hitch a ride until you felt it was time to ditch, because the increasing speed was going to cause major problems when you tried to get off.

A ride on a ladder of a fast-moving flat car is exhilarating to a fourteen-year-old. Boxcars are high and difficult to climb into unless you have help. We had help. We would boost one of us inside and then he could help pull the next one inside. They were great fun to ride in. Lots of room. You could try to run around inside while it is moving and shaking or sit with your back against the wall and pretend you were a hobo.

Letting go of a moving car and jumping off the step takes a bit of practice. But you soon learn to point yourself in the right direction and land running, otherwise you are in for an awful tumble. Getting out the door of a moving boxcar takes a completely different strategy. Safer to stay there until it stops and take your chances with those pesky railway guys. Boxcar doors are pretty high off the ground. They are not fun to get out of even when stopped. Getting out backwards with your legs hanging down is asking for trouble, especially if the car is moving. If your legs land a bit too close to the tracks, the wheels may just remove them. Landing on your back in cinders and doing rollovers is no fun either.

Hard to explain to your mother where all the scratches came from and why your clothes are such a mess and a bit torn. Don't ever admit to your problem of exiting from a boxcar, when everyone for miles knew the yard was out of bounds, and certainly no place for kids to be playing. Guess adults just did not understand. Never will know what their problem was! For a time, my dad was a guard there. I suppose he would not have approved either, but that just added to the excitement and intrigue. All that made the adrenaline flow faster...watch out for trains, train workers, guards, father, and hope you do not have to answer to your mother about your whereabouts for the last two hours.

Who needed Disneyland when you had a playground like the railyard at your doorstep? If you were not old enough to be part of the war like Edward was, did not really understand what the war was all about, then growing up during that time and living where we did was one great adventure.

BB Gun

The BB Gun

I just thought about how God protects kids and the stupid. We saw no harm in our little game, but it seems dumb now. Cowboys were the movie heroes of the day when I was little and as a young teenager. Gene Autry, Roy Rogers, Tom Mix, and a host of others spent their time chasing and catching the bad guys. Part of their stock in trade was a Winchester 30/30. It was a lever action rifle, and they could work without ever removing the gun from their shoulder (I did own a real one when I lived in Victoria). A Red Ryder BB gun was a kid's copy, and every boy with blood in his veins wanted one.

Not all had them. Some parents are fussy. I had one when we were in Tecumseh. Actually, I think it was the one Gordon had on the farm, and I just inherited it because he was too old for it then. Unlike the real 30/30s, this little copycat was spring loaded, and no kid I knew was strong enough to hold it against their shoulder and crank the lever. You had to rest it on the ground and work the lever.

BB guns are dangerous little guys at very close range. Within forty feet or so they sting, and I am sure could put an eye out of commission. You did not shoot a BB gun at people. It got the same respect as a real rifle, except for our game of tag. It could also kill a bird at forty or fifty feet. We did not shoot birds. It was great fun, though, for pinging bottle caps and tin cans off fence posts, or putting holes through paper targets, and for playing tag.

The Game

Not sure who thought of this, but we all enjoyed it. Our little gang of Roger, Louis, Clarence and whoever else was around, would head for our favourite playground - the railyard. I had the only BB gun in the bunch. Things had slowed down greatly, so we just had to check for the guard, and make sure no engines were working.

We drew straws and one of us got the gun, counted to ten and everyone else scattered. We would run under and around the top of the boxcars. At the count of ten, the kid with the gun would try to find a victim and shoot them with the gun. If you got hit, you were it, got the gun, counted to ten and things started all over.

The most fun was being like the real cowboys, running along the tops of the boxcars, and jumping from one to the next with your make believe 30/30, trying to shoot the fleeing bandit running ahead of you. Boxcars are pretty high, but they have a steel walkway on top from one end to the other. It is skinny but big enough to easily walk on or, in our case, run on. I think the distance from one car to another is somewhere around three feet or so. A good jump but seemed to pose no problem for a thirteen- or fourteen-year-old.

If you get the chance, climb up and try it sometime (without the BB gun). Why no one slipped and fell in between or rolled off the edge I do not know. We had the odd scrape and banged shins on ladders, but thankfully no major catastrophes. Like I said, God looks after kids and the stupid. Lest you think we were really as dumb as this sounds, we did have rules. No shooting above the shoulders, and no shooting at close range. We wore overalls and they were tough, very loose fit and were great at taking most of the sting from a BB gun.

It was summer and warm, but we also took jackets as protection, and tried not to hit anyone in the hand or any exposed areas. Let's face it, a BB gun is not that accurate, and trying to hit a running target when you are running, especially on the top of a boxcar, is no easy feat. You had to keep a close watch for the end of the car, lest you just keep running instead of jumping, and end up a pile of broken pieces on top of the coupling.

We may have been stupid, but not stupid enough to have the guard see us, and certainly not dumb enough to dare give the slightest hint of our game of tag to our parents, or even siblings. I doubt to this day anyone ever knew.

The Golden House, Car Aerials and Cops

The Golden House

It was springtime I think because it got dark about 8 o'clock. I went to work at the bowling alley and they did not need me. Another guy, I can't remember who, and me were just riding around on our bikes since we did not have to work. Tecumseh had about two thousand people and about one hotel for every hundred residents. I think there were seven.

The Golden House was at the far end of town. It was not like the others, which were mostly just draft rooms. They had a good dining room, a lounge, and a Chinese cook. I guess he could speak English, but he only hollered at us kids in Chinese. Perhaps that is because we annoyed the heck out of him. Most kids seemed to delight in tormenting him without realizing what they were doing or without any thought that maybe this was not nice.

The Cook

He was not picked on because he was Chinese, but because he spoke a strange language and seemed to be easily provoked. The parking lot was full of cars. The alleyway beside it also ran behind the police station, a half a block or so down the road. Kids delighted in sneaking up to the back door, which went into the kitchen, ringing the bell, and hiding behind cars in the lot. The poor Chinese cook would open the door and of course there was no one there. After a couple of times, he would stand in the doorway, a large meat cleaver in hand, and shout in Chinese. Guess no one who indulged in this pastime gave any thought to the fact that this poor guy may just have a room full of diners who were waiting for him to cook their food.

My friend suggested that we could remove our boredom this particular evening by ringing the doorbell and watching the antics of the poor Chinese cook. I had heard about this pastime but had not taken part. We left our bikes at the far end of the lot beside the alley. It was dark, so it was easy to sneak up beside the cars to the back door.

After leaning on the bell, it was just as easy to run and hide behind a car, peeking out to watch the antics of the poor cook.

After a couple of times he appeared, determined to find the culprits. He came out, hollering and running towards the parked cars. The meat cleaver sure did look big, sharp, and menacing. By this time, we were at the back of the lot and on our bikes. As we pedalled furiously down the alley, we saw him return to the door. Safe at last, almost to the far end of the alley.

The Police Car

A car was coming slowly down the alley. What kind of a car, or who, one could not tell, because all you could see was a set of headlights. My friend crossed in front of the car and rode through someone's driveway out to Lesperance road. This was not his first episode and I think he knew more than I. The car was close and being the nice polite kid that I was, I stopped and waited for it to pass. The only trouble was that it did not go past me. The police car stopped. I did not have the guts to run. Besides, I did not think I was in any kind of real trouble.

I walked my bike back the short distance to the back door of the police station. The building was small. One little cell, I think, and an office with a small desk. I sat on a wooden chair on one side of the desk with my interrogator on the other. Not a nice experience for a thirteen-year-old. I was scared. Scared because I would have to tell my dad.

The Questions

In any event, I don't really think the cop was much concerned about the Chinese cook, but he was checking the alley and the lot because kids had been breaking aerials off the parked cars. We appeared likely subjects. Perhaps my friend was part of this problem and knew enough to get away.

I guess I whined and cried sufficiently to convince the cop that I was innocent of breaking aerials. I told him what we were doing, which in my mind, was bad enough. He at first threatened to lock me up and go get my father. He relented when I think he knew I was not the guilty party he was after and let me go with the promise that he would be out to visit my father the next day.

It was not a happy bike ride home. It was after ten. I had to not only explain why I had not returned earlier since I did not work, but what I was doing until this time of night. Dad was in bed. Mom always stayed up till I got home. I explained my predicament to her and asked her to explain to dad, to soften the blow. The police officer never showed up. Father was not pleased in any event, since he knew the Chinese cook. So, I hope you get the lesson...do not ring doorbells on the back door of restaurants with Chinese cooks.

Chores and Tomatoes

Chores

Asparagus, peas, tomatoes, corn, it did not matter, there were still jobs at home. The wood had to be sawed, split, and taken in. The ducks, chickens and rabbits had to be fed. We had three and a half acres that were planted with tomatoes for the canning factory, corn, and the normal garden of all kinds of vegetables. Three and a half acres does not seem like much, until you are the kid that must cultivate it and hoe out all the weeds. It was not easy, and always hot and sweaty. I did not mind too much as I liked working in the dirt and helping things grow. When the peas were over, there was always work at home, and of course when there was time, the railyard was still there.

Tomatoes

Later in the summer the tomatoes ripened and had to be picked. Not that there was no work for little tomato plants as they were growing. I hoed weeds out of the fields of tomatoes that were so long you could not see the end. Thistles and pig weed get big, so you need a large and sharp hoe. These plant-wrecking hunks of metal on a stick sure made for good arm and shoulder muscles and a tired kid at the end of the day. One could see for a long way down a row. Leave one weed standing a quarter of a mile into the field, and someone told you about it. Sometimes it was a long walk to correct a mistake over one lone weed.

A neighbour had a field that went from one concession to the next. They are a mile apart. We could not see the end. The field was not as wide as long, but too far to walk to the shade of a tree for lunch. We carried a bread bag with a few slices, salt, and pepper, wrapped in paper, and a jackknife in our pocket. When it was time for lunch you just sat in the dirt, picked a good-looking tomato, and made a sandwich. Like asparagus, there were several kids, each taking a row. When lunch was over, the residue from the tomatoes along with any rotten ones started to fly. We all went home dirty and splattered.

The tomatoes were put into, what else, a tomato basket. I have not seen one for a long time, but they were about two and a half feet tall, small at the bottom, and getting progressively larger at the top. They held a lot of tomatoes and got heavier as we went along. When the basket was full you just left it there and got another one. Sometimes there would be a drought for twenty feet or so, with very few ripe tomatoes. If the basket was near the top, you had to drag it along until you found enough to fill it up. One did not leave partially filled baskets.

At the end of the day, five or six, whenever the field was picked clean of ripe tomatoes, we quit. The tractor would come along pulling a wagon, and we would have to heave the full baskets onto it. They were heavy, and a farm wagon is not exactly low to the ground. The baskets had their peculiar shape so they could be stacked, the small bottom fitting in between two tops. We got paid so much for each basket, nothing for loading the wagon, but were expected to stay and help do it. No one really complained. I guess we were just glad to have a summer job and earn some money. I don't know if McDonald's looks good or not, but this was just the way it was.

The Canning Factory

The Factory

Tecumseh Fine Foods was the only game in town that I recall, besides retail stores and many taverns, of course. Go through town on highway #39, cross the tracks just at the far edge of town towards Belle River, and the factory was on the bend just over the tracks. It was a local endeavour, and sometime after I left town it was purchased by Green Giant. I contributed many hours to the success of Tecumseh Fine Foods. They provided jobs for a lot of kids.

I am not sure whether the peas came first or the asparagus. They were both early in the spring. Ask any decent farmer and they can tell you. I think of peas because if you were in grade eight or high school in Tecumseh, and your marks were sufficient, you could get out of school early in the spring to work for the canning factory. They actually canned all the peas, owned the asparagus fields, but shipped it out to another factory. I worked both for the asparagus harvest and peas, then tomatoes and corn.

Lest you think I wasted my childhood getting into trouble at the railyard and just messing around, let me explain the routine for asparagus. You had to be thirteen I think, but I am not sure. In any event, when I think about it, thirteen or fourteen years old is young for the slave labour we provided. A gang of kids, thirty to forty, all teenagers, arrived at the gate to the factory at six or six-thirty in the morning.

The Ride

The time is a bit foggy, but I know it was early, cold, and sometimes very wet. A truck would arrive. A five-ton stake, if you know what that is. It is a vehicle with a large wooden box, and in our case, no top. It is called a stake, because the sides are made up of racks, each about three feet long and held to the truck with stakes. The stakes are sort of two-by-fours that fit into slots in the side of the truck bed. They lock together at the top with a pin affair. The stakes are about three feet or so high. If you stood up, these sides would come up to just below your shoulders, if you were a small kid like me. We did not stand up.

The stake truck was the bus to take the workers to the asparagus fields in Harrow, about thirty or forty miles away. The field boss would open the back gate and climb up into the truck. That way he could look down and see all of us wet, shivering urchins, willing to work like slave labour. The ones that had been before and he recognized as good and obedient slaves, he would holler for them to climb on.

They usually needed about thirty kids. Through a series of very abrupt and short yelled out questions, he would pick the required number. "Are you sure you can do this all day?" "Ever worked in the fields before?" or, "you don't look very strong to me." For whatever reason, I got on the truck the first morning I went, and every time after that. It was not a fun ride.

We sat, leaning against the racks, and bounced with every crack or bump in the road. Trucks are very bouncy when they are empty. Thirty or so kids are not much weight for truck springs. We sat in groups, trying to keep warm, holding lunches in paper bags, and trying to keep our bums from getting too bruised.

Generally, they were a tough bunch, with language to match. The regulars sat together just behind the cab. That is the best place for wind and less bruises on your rear end. Sometimes it rained, and the driver would kindly put the tarp over most of the box. We usually arrived wet and very cold anyway.

The Boss

If it rained, we just sat around under the shelter of the barn overhang and waited until it stopped. No pay for this, nor the ride. You only got paid when you were actually cutting asparagus. Does anyone wonder why we have unions? Asparagus fields are large. They could be a half a mile or so long, and as wide or wider. We were all issued a knife. It had a handle, was about a foot long, and had a V shaped cutting edge on the bottom. You can buy them today for cutting dandelions. We also got an eleven-quart basket. Each kid got a row. We were lined up behind our rows and given instructions by the field boss.

He also worked in the factory during pea canning. You may hear about him later if I remember. This guy could have taught drill sergeants, or maybe he just did not like kids. "Cut each shoot off at the ground. Do not put the knife in too deep and hit the roots. Do not leave any. Put them in the basket with the tips facing the same way. If you find any taller ones that were left from a day or two ago, cut it off and leave it in the row. Do not walk on the plants. If you see weeds in the rows, cut them down. Keep up, no stopping until we get to the end. Do not break the shoots." Ya, ya, ya, we know.

Sometimes we would wait out the rain and a kid would not feel well, or maybe realize this was not to be a fun day, whether it was raining or not, and decide that he, or she, was not really cut out for this. Your choice, sit around the barn until five o'clock when the truck goes back with everyone else, or if you really are not well, if someone goes back to town earlier, they will take you. Nice bunch.

The Work

There is only one proper way to cut asparagus. You bend over, knife in your right hand. grab the shoot with your left, jab the knife, put the tip in the basket hung over your left arm and keep going. Pretty soon you are almost warm, except for your frozen hands. It is still only eight fifteen or so, if you started on time, and the shoots and knife are wet and cold.

By nine your back is complaining, but the sun is out, and it is starting to warm up. When the basket is full you leave it in the row, and someone, maybe the field boss, or his eighteen-year-old 2IC brings you another one. By nine thirty the coat has been removed. By ten o'clock, the first sweater comes off, and now you have extra stuff to carry along with the basket.

The abominable asparagus boss never ceases to holler or curse at some kid for asparagus infractions. A few with permanent bent over backs are already done their rows and are sitting in the dirt at the end.

Most are scattered throughout the field parallel to one another, and some are lagging far behind. The laggards are incurring the wrath of the field boss. Some may just leave their basket and head back to the barn. He notes the name and time to satisfy the payroll department. They will just sit it out until the truck takes us back at five.

We get a five minute or so break at the end of the row. Kids just lay back in the dirt or grass, to ease the ache in the shoulders and back. Only too soon we hear the familiar bark, and stumble to our feet and find another row. Lunch time, I think, was a whole hour. It is spent eating for ten minutes out of our paper bags, and the rest sleeping in the shade of the barn. From feast to famine, it is now time for no shirt and whatever you could dispense with. Unlike the freezing morning, it is boiling hot for the rest of the day.

The bumpy, bouncy, bum bruising ride home is usually quiet. We are too achy and tired to grumble or discuss the day's events. The stake truck deposits the load of kids at the factory gate. I walk the mile home, have supper, and make sure the alarm is set at five-thirty for tomorrow.

Peas

The Vinery

I think asparagus was first and the peas were next. Too bad Colleen was not of age then. What a ball she would have had with tons of peas. [Colleen dislikes peas]. Factory peas were grown like hay, no rows, just a field of peas. They were cut the same way, with a how mower, raked into rows and loaded onto wagons, and taken to the pea vinery.

That's where I started. No plush jobs inside the factory. You started out in the boondocks. Pea vineries were located on some obscure concession road eight thousand miles from anything, except fields of peas. We were taken there in the inevitable stake truck, or pickup, and left until five o'clock or so when we received our bumpy ride back to the factory, dumped at the gate, and left to ride, walk, or get home, however, just be sure to show up at the gate the next morning at the crack of dawn. I actually liked it, I think!

The Factory

Picture a very large upside-down U structure. The inside was large enough for a truck to drive through. The two sides contained large steel drums on the top and a wooden structure to hold the drums up. Wagon loads of peas would back up to the drums, and the peas, vines, and all, would be pitched into the open end of the drum. A diesel engine would spin the drums and pound the pea vines until the peas came out. The drums had little holes in them, so the peas fell through and were deposited into the two side structures, which were full of shelves.

We put pea boxes on the top shelves on both sides, and they caught the peas that fell through the holes in the drum. When the boxes got full, they were removed to lower shelves and replaced with an empty one. The boxes were about twelve by eighteen inches and were very heavy when full. The top shelf was too high to reach, so there were a couple of steps running the length of the building so we could reach the top shelf. If you were looking after moving boxes you really had to keep watch and run from one end to the other to find and move full boxes.

The Crew

The crew consisted of a foreman, and I think four kids. The foreman was sometimes an old grouchy guy, but more likely he was an older teenager that had worked for the factory for four or five years and knew the routine. We took a lunch, snacks, and drinks. There were no facilities of any kind there. If there were no loads of peas coming, after making sure everything was shipshape, we just sat around. Some days the wagon loads of peas did not stop and we went home feeling like we had worked in asparagus all day.

The foreman looked after the diesels or tractors that ran the drums, kept the paperwork for the loads coming in, and mediated squabbles among the crew. Two kids worked inside moving boxes of peas and two worked on the stack, one for each drum.

The Stack

Pea vines are wet, and very heavy. The spinning drums pounded the heck out of the vines and pounded the peas out of their pods. The peas ended up in the boxes and the vines, pods, weeds and whatever else were thrown out the far end of the drum as a wet, heavy soggy mass. That soggy mass was pitchforked into the stack. There was a prize for the best stack, and all hell to pay for a messy one. I am not sure why, but nice, square stacks were important in the pea industry. The real pea vinery boss, not the grouch from asparagus, but must have been related, came by at least once on most days. He checked our site, but most importantly he checked the stack. When we started of course, there was just a bare area behind the vinery.

As the first load came in you were to fork the vines into a nice, neat square of soggy, smelly green stuff. We put out stakes for the perimeter to start our stack. They knew from previous years about how big it had to be. I would say about thirty square feet. It grew very fast. I should tell you that the new kids, like me, were started on the stack. There was no need to buy weights or go to the gym if you worked the stack. We tried to start with a nice, neat square, but soon the pea residue reached the top of the drum, about fifteen feet or so.

If it was a busy day, you stood there, up to your boot tops in pea residue, and by the afternoon it always seemed at least 90°, and probably was some days, with the drum throwing pea stuff out faster than you could move it. This stuff is not solid, so you sank up to your waist when you moved around. Once the loads were gone and the box movers had done their job, the kids on the stack had to fix it up nice and neat, or else. No one cared if you spent an extra hour while they sat. I wonder what we smelled like after getting pelted by wet pea stuff all day. The sides were to be nice and straight, the stack square and the top even. Give me a break, these guys did not know the behaviour of wet pea goop. I do not remember getting a prize.

Like working in the asparagus field...get off the truck at the gate, get home, eat supper, do chores, wash the green stuff off and go to bed. No shower as there was no hot water in the house. And hope you hear the alarm for five the next morning.

Inside the Factory

Inside Work

Was this after my stint in the hospital or before? I am not sure, but I got to skip the vinery stint and work inside. I did not work days, of course. This was a twenty-four-hour operation when the peas were running, and without seniority you worked midnights. The midnight shift was just that, twelve to eight.

I worked in the warehouse. For a while I had the neat job of pushing kettles of canned peas uphill, from the canal into the warehouse. You unloaded the cans onto a conveyor gadget that put labels on the cans, then put the cans into boxes when they exited the labeller. I do not want to mislead you, but I think that was how it worked. There was not a lot of automation. The boxes were also sealed by hand, loaded onto skids, and piled up for delivery.

There were three cookers. The cookers were tall pressure cookers that held three or four kettles full of cans. The kettles were large steel things, sort of a barrel stave affair with lots of holes, but spaces too small for a can to go through. They were round and held, I don't know, but they held a lot of cans. The kettles were perhaps three feet around and would hold cans piled up about ten high. The kettles had a big steel handle, so a crane could pick them up and deposit them into the cookers and lift them out.

When the cans came off the line someone put them into the kettle. When it was full, someone else pushed it down to the crane site by the cookers. It was downhill from the line to make it easier to push, but it was uphill to the warehouse. The steel kettles rode on little dollies with large casters on them. The crane sat over top of a canal that ran to the cookers. The canal was a cement affair about three feet deep, and I guess about that wide, just wide enough to hold a kettle.

The Crane

I graduated from pushing kettles into the warehouse and labelling them, to running the crane. I thought it was a neat job. The crane house was no more than a metal cage, about ten feet in the air over the end of the canal. It had a steel ladder against the wall so you could climb up. It was surrounded by a metal cage and had a seat, and some switches and levers.

The operator, that was me, moved the crane over the canal, lowered the chain and hook to snag a handle on one of the kettles that had been pushed down, and left in the appropriate spot by the edge of the canal. You got the hook onto the handle (that was the most difficult part for me to get the hang of), lifted the kettle up and sent it down to the cooker. The person (kid) in charge of the cooker, would motion you how to manoeuvre it, so it could be lowered into the cooker.

He would be about twenty-five feet away at the end of the canal. We lowered the kettles into the cooker until it was full. He would lock down the lid and do whatever was needed to start the cooker up. It took twenty minutes or so to do a batch. When the peas were cooking, I could sit in my little box or wander around into the warehouse and annoy other people, or actually help them finish their job.

When the cooking process was over, I was notified and got my crane into action again. The hook was lowered into the cooker, and I fished around until it hooked onto a handle. The kettle was lifted out and lowered into the canal, which was constantly changed with cold water. I would slowly, those were the orders if the boss was around, slowly bring the kettle through the water, back under the crane house, and then lift it out and drop it on a dolly. Some poor kid would then push it uphill, as I did, into the warehouse. The slow movement through the canal was to cool off the cans after the cooking process.

At the vinery we could have a handful of fresh peas whenever we felt like it or had time. At my crane job I could bring the kettle right up under my feet, reach down and pick out a hot can, whack it on a convenient piece of sharp metal to open it, and just dump fresh warm peas down my throat. Now you know why I would not eat peas for years.

The Boss

After emptying all three cookers, the canal water got pretty warm. Remember, this is Essex county, and nights do not cool off much. Our asparagus grouch was also now the boss of the warehouse. I think his name was Rudy. He had a pronounced accent and no last name that I recall. His demeanour in the warehouse was the same as in the field. I really had no problem with him, perhaps because my dad was a foreman in the factory on the day shift. I actually worked and did my job, and he and dad were friends.

Not all the employees (mostly kids) thought much of Rudy. My crane job was a snap but pushing kettles into the warehouse and packing boxes was hard work. I was not big, but some of the kids who worked the warehouse could have made a fortune as professional wrestlers.

The canal was empty, and I was sitting in my box waiting for more kettles to play with. I could hear a commotion in the warehouse just around the corner, lots of shouting and scuffling. Rudy's voice was part of the din. It only took a few minutes for the warehouse crew to emerge with Rudy in the middle. They hollered at me to get off my crane and help. Rudy was not one of my admirers, but he was the boss, about the same age as my dad, and an adult. I wanted no part in their endeavour. They succeeded without my help. After a lot of yelling, kicking and flailing arms, Rudy ended up in the canal.

He splashed and hauled himself out. I had real mixed emotions. Rudy probably got what he deserved. But he was the boss and that had to be some kind of humiliation, not counting working the rest of the night soaking wet and explaining to his peers why and how he got dunked into the canal. We had a new warehouse crew the next night. After a time, I worked the cookers for a while, but it was not nearly as much fun as running the crane.

Corn

Asparagus, peas, tomatoes, and peppers were all history when the corn was ripe. Fine Foods canned corn. I worked in the factory during corn canning season but did my stint in the field first. Louis' uncle had a contract with the factory and had acres of sweet corn. No machines to pick the corn, just kids. Five of us, including the uncle to drive the tractor, made up the team. The tractor and wagon would bend down two rows, and a kid on either side would pick two rows. You broke the ears off and tossed them into the wagon.

If you were unlucky, you got the two rows behind the wagon. They were bent over and so it made it hard to get at the ears, and you were always behind. We took turns. Eventually the load became uneven, and someone climbed up and threw the corn around to spread it out. Those on the ground did not stop, and it was a dangerous job, with kids throwing ears of corn at you while trying to straighten out the load.

When the wagon was full it was taken to the factory, about two miles into town. The uncle was a different sort than our friend who controlled the asparagus fields and the warehouse. We were always paid extra, got to go into town with the load and have ice cream or some such treat. He was not married so had no kids but knew how to treat them and look after them. We should have introduced our canal friend to him! Like the asparagus, peas, and tomatoes, it was just part of summer. I don't think I would trade those summers for anything!

I Don't Feel Well

Onset

It was four o'clock or so. I was on the bus from Windsor to Tecumseh, on my way home from school. I am not even sure of the time of year, but I believe it was late fall, because I had not ridden my bike to town because of the cold weather. I was fifteen. My stomach started to send signals that it was unhappy, and the rest of me did not feel so great either. I just wished the bus would hurry up so I could get home. I was a pretty healthy kid without any medical problems, so I did not like the feeling.

I got off the bus and found that walking was a real effort. The legs just did not want to do their job. Bernie lived at the far edge of town toward our place. He and I were friends in public school, but he went to the Catholic High School in town, and I took the bus into Windsor to attend Patterson High School. I managed the few blocks, banged on his door, and asked him if I could borrow his bike to ride home. Riding was not easy, but far easier than trying to walk. I had diarrhea big time and was relieved to stumble off the bike at our back porch. I have to tell you though, that diarrhea is not fun when you have an outhouse and have to make numerous visits throughout the night.

Leukaemia

Guess me and mother thought it was just a severe case of the flu. I dislike bloody details and talking about diarrhea, but the blood in the outhouse was a sign that perhaps this was more than the flu. By morning I could hardly walk, and my arms and legs wore a bluish, purple tinge. My stomach felt like a raging monster lived inside. We went to our doctor in town. I do not remember getting there, but I know that I could not walk without a lot of help. The doctor thought that it was some sort of skin disorder and sent us to a skin specialist in Windsor. I have no idea how we got there. I can picture his office and almost remember his name, but not quite.

After very few minutes, I recall him saying that he had only seen three cases of this in his time in practice, and two died. I am not sure if he said this to mom, thinking I was out of hearing range or not, but his comment was not reassuring to a fifteen-year-old. I really did not care. My stomach hurt so bad that sudden death would have been a relief. He immediately put me in Grace Hospital. I wonder if I had clean underwear on? That would be important to a mother.

Apparently, I had a rare case of leukaemia that ate up white blood cells and the red guys, well, I don't know what they did, except they came to the surface and turned my arms and legs a purple colour. It may have been the other way around with the blood characters, but I looked pretty sad, could not walk, could barely move my arms, and nothing would stay in my stomach. The stomach lining was full of holes and even water ran out immediately. This was only day two.

Pain

I remember a couple of things above all the rest: the constant pain, the needles, and my mother's visits, twice a day. Hospitals had strict visiting hours, and nurses came around and asked people to leave if you were there even five minutes over. The norm was one to three in the afternoon, and seven to nine in the evening. Unless a patient was dying, there was just no way you were allowed in at other hours. We lived on the far side of Windsor from the hospital. Mother took a bus to the terminal and another one to the hospital. The return trip was the same. I think it took over an hour each way. She came twice a day, without fail, all the seven weeks I was there.

How my mother managed the bus fare I do not know; it was not cheap, even then. How she managed the time, I don't know that, either. I guess I do know that I am still on the minus side of the ledger as far as any repayment goes. I often think that I could have done more for her in later years, but that is not part of this story.

Doctors had no answer as to what the cause was, nor the cure. I ate nothing and could not even drink water. I would hold my knees under my chin to try to ease the pain in my stomach. I took no pills because I could not drink anything. Apparently, I had no stomach lining to hold stuff in. I was constantly hooked up to bottles of whatever, and every four hours got a shot of morphine, or some such drug to ease the pain. I received umpteen needles for the morphine, and I have no idea what else, every day. The poor nurses were at a loss to find a spot to stick the needle into. My thighs and shoulders were like leather from the constant injections.

One day, a nurse having tried a few times, took a spirited shot at my shoulder, and managed to embed the needle. The needle broke off leaving a bit sticking out of my shoulder, and the rest in the plunger in her hand. The needles were my worst nightmare, outside of the constant pain. The stomach did not seem to care about morphine or anything else. It just wanted to hurt, and the monster would not leave, no matter what kind of drugs the doctor tried.

At first the drugs relieved the pain for a while, but after a week or so nothing would do the trick. A shot would let me sleep for about fifteen minutes, and then the pain would return. I do not want to sound dramatic, nor play up the pain, but I spent weeks with tears in my eyes, and pleaded with the nurses to give me more shots or whatever, to get rid of the torment in my gut. I was always thirsty but could not drink because water and anything else just went through like a sieve, and only added to the agony in the stomach. I guess when stomachs get ticked off, they can be nasty. The nurses could not increase the dosage and the doctors were afraid to, less the drugs killed me.

My home was a ward with ten beds. Almost all old geysers. Two died while I was there. I remember not caring about that, I just wanted my stomach to quit hurting. It was like the Tasmanian Devil, constantly doing his whirling act in my stomach, and tearing at anything in his path. I am sure I was also a pain for the nursing staff, but I just wanted the pain to stop. I never got out of that bed for five weeks. Never being very heavy, I lost a ton of weight and must have looked like a purplish, blue skeleton. Not a pretty sight, I bet. I do not remember ever thinking or realizing how ill I was. I just knew that I was always thirsty, and my stomach was trying to get even with me for something.

One night it finally dawned on me that this was serious. It had been a very bad day. The doctor had been in a few times, along with a couple of his buddies to see if anyone had any ideas. He had even called a specialist who taught at Victoria Hospital in London. He drove up that afternoon to check me out and came up empty for causes or solutions.

The End

They were apparently at the end of their resources, and I was in and out of consciousness, waking only to ask for something to relieve the pain. The doctor said to the nurse, "he has had enough morphine (if that is what it was) to kill a healthy adult, so go ahead and give him another injection, if it will ease the pain for a while." It was around suppertime. I am sure they were very unhappy that no one could put a handle on this thing, and felt the end was close, because the next time I woke up it was around eleven at night.

Uncle Alex filled the doorway, and the bed was surrounded by relatives and doctors. Auntie Rae, Aunt Lola, Uncle Jack and just about everyone that I was related to seemed to be there. It finally sunk in that maybe the end of pain was in sight. They did not drive up from Port Lambton and Dresden at night, and in the winter, and pop into the hospital long after visiting hours, just because I had the flu. I just remember it as a blur of doctors, nurses, family, and relatives.

Guess if I had been Catholic the priest would be there for the last rites. I have no idea if the minister was there or not. The doctor had called another blood specialist, and amidst all the visitors and commotion, although I remember it as being very quiet, with lots of whispering going on, decided that a blood transfusion would do no harm, and may keep me kicking for a few more hours. One of my bottles was exchanged for a bottle of plasma. I faded out and do not remember anyone saying anything to me or knowing how long they stayed or anything like that. I only remember waking up around five in the morning with a nurse by my bed. I don't think I felt any better nor worse, but I was still there.

The Recovery

The doctors must have detected improvement because they thought a direct transfusion may help. I have no idea what type of blood I have, but the word went out, and a guy that worked with Edward was willing to part with a pint, or whatever amount they needed. A couple of days later he lay on one bed and I in mine, with a plastic tube running between us. When I think of it, I am always reminded of jumpstarting a car, with cables running from one battery to the other.

I don't even know the man's name now, but he sure must have had good blood. The pains got less intense, and a week or so after receiving the blood I was able to stand and lean on my bed after five weeks of not being able to put a foot on the floor. My purple skin slowly started to get white, or pink, again. Two weeks later I went home, wobbly, but able to walk and eat. I missed over half a year of school but returned in January after the holidays. For many years after, my stomach would hiccup and not feel too hot if I got tired or whatever, but thankfully that is the only reminder.

Pillette

Let me set the picture if I can. Some of the details fill my memory, and some are very distant. I went to the hospital from a home in Tecumseh that was far from palatial, but I liked it and had many friends close by. My mother liked it. We had hydro, wood heat, even for cooking, no telephone, and no indoor bathroom. A step up from the farmhouse at Comber, but not in keeping with the local standards.

I did not care. It provided everything that I needed but posed some problems, as things do today when you do not have what the Jones' have. I was in grade nine at high school, 1949 or thereabouts. After I was released from the hospital, we had moved to Pillette Road in Windsor.

This is what I want to explain. I have never talked about it to anyone. Your mother does not even know. Like some dark secret. It is not really a dark secret. Some of the best years of my youth were spent there. But some of the things that kids are most conscious of at the age of sixteen were part of that existence and have not been revealed. Just so you know, here goes.

For some strange reason, the kids that I hung around with and were my closest friends, always seemed to have the nicest houses, and all the latest technology for the times. If there was any technology. Like complete indoor plumbing, central heating, and a refrigerator. I did not care if I did not have such luxuries. But I guess I did care that my friends thought less of me for not having them. Guess what? When I think about all those memories, they did not care either. What they cared about at that time was me. If only kids would realize that. I did not, and they won't. Society more and more emphasizes the things and not the people; so, it will be harder than it was for me.

So, I came home to Pillette Road in Windsor, rather than the little house in Tecumseh. My dad, for what reason I will never find out, arranged with a friend or acquaintance, from Aylmer, Ontario, to operate his feed store on Pillette Road, a smidgen south of Tecumseh Road, just inside the Windsor city limits. I can only imagine that he wanted to keep his connection to the farm community, and his independence of being his own boss. There was still a farming community in the area, and the store supplied the feed and other items that they required. Something you guys will have a hard time to fathom.

At least he got the business, not the building. The building was divided into two with a restaurant housed in the other half. You have to know what this type of building was like inside to get a picture of the premises. Imagine a store front, say twenty feet wide by forty feet long. A door was at the far end which led into the back of the building. The ceiling was much higher there to accommodate the equipment to mill wheat, clean grain, and bag feed. The high ceiling left space next to the showroom wall for an office, accessed by a stairway just inside the door.

It had a crummy little space upstairs, about twelve by twenty, and that was the office. It had windows overlooking the equipment in the plant area, and one end window which looked out over the lower roof to the restaurant. This office became our home for a year or so. Not a lot of room so dad slept on a couch next to a Quebec heater, by the door to the plant. There was no central heating, so wood or coal fired stoves were still in demand. The washroom was in the restaurant next door that was part of the same building. Not a nice environment. And not a home that a fifteen-year-old bragged about to his friends who lived in normal houses.

No company asked over for dinner or to play computer games, not there was such a thing. I think this may be one of the reasons I always thought of my mother as a saint. She endured it without obvious complaint, and while I am sure she felt different inside, she never let it show. I wish you had the opportunity to really know her, and I had the words to describe her. She was not always healthy, but always showed a happy face. Were I asked to name a modern hero, I would have to say, my MOTHER. Despite the living conditions, I did have lots of friends though, and like mom, seemed to live through this housing embarrassment.

Cadets

Training

It was a federal edict. I am not sure but all schools, at least all the time I spent there, had cadets. For boys only, of course. Each spring we had to do cadet training for six weeks or so. I am not sure of the timing, but I think only the prospect of sudden death could get one excused. Remember, I started high school in 1949. Canada and most of the world were still carrying recent memories of WWII. The cadets were army cadets. Soldiers in training, sort of.

Every school carried enough uniforms of various sizes to fit all the males. They were regulation army issue. Course, heavy fabric that made me itch from one end to the other, especially the legs. Hot as they were, and the weather, I wore pajamas bottoms under the pants to isolate me from the picky stuff, and at least allow a drop of comfort.

Come May or thereabouts, we all picked up our uniforms and took them home. We were responsible for ironing, shining buttons, and generally getting them in shape. My hat is still in one of my drawers. How I ended up with it I do not remember, but it is here and whenever I come across it, I think I should turf it. Memories will not allow it, though. One day a week, I believe, we wore our uniforms to school, left class early, and went outside to practice marching. It was great discipline, and probably not a bad thing for kids today, if we cannot rid the world of the idea of war.

Morse Code

We carried Lee Enfield rifles. They were the stock in trade for soldiers in WWII. Ours would not fire, but were just as heavy and awkward, as if they worked. We learned to march with them and to "present arms." I did not particularly like it, but I didn't hate it, either. One option was also to learn signaling. Seems funny, but there were no computers, no cell phones, none of that stuff, so the army relied on Morse Code for communication.

In 1997, Morse Code was stricken from the list, and not used by the merchant navy as a means of communication. I think they were the last group to still use it. If you are not sure how it works, then do some research. I am sure there is still tons of information on Morse Code. You had a little switch called a key. Push the key down and it made a noise, and sent an audible signal heard at the other end. It was sent in dots, a short push, or dashes...just hold down a bit longer.

Every letter had its own series of dots and dashes. The most notable being SOS, three dots, a dash and three dots. The operator knew the code for each letter, and could also listen to the message, and write down the letter as he heard the dots and dashes. Not only the military but also the railroad, even when I worked for the CPR in Windsor, used this code to communicate the arrival of trains and all other important information. Telegrams were also sent using Morse Code.

I was fifteen and had missed over half a year of school because of the blood disease I mysteriously contracted and miraculously escaped from. The teachers felt sorry for me. Mr. Bass, our Latin and math teacher (and an ex-Marine and pro wrestler), asked if I would like to take communications. Why not? It involved sitting in the classroom and learning Morse Code. Like that was fun. Try to learn the alphabet over again in dots and dashes.

I liked it and after a month or so I got pretty good at it. I could send and receive at forty words a minute. Dig through all my saved junk and you may even find my certificate. That was not a bad number for a novice, and even respectable for someone making a living sending and receiving dots and dashes.

Camp

"Would you like to go to Cadet Camp at Ipperwash?" Kids who showed some initiative, or I guess who were good at Morse Code, were encouraged to go to Cadet Camp. Each school got to recommend a small number. My summers were slugging at a pea vinery, picking tomatoes, hoeing corn, and then either detasselling or breaking down corn, or such similar backbreaking endeavors. Camp, cadet or otherwise, did not sound that bad. I had never been to camp before.

Because of my recent bout with death, my mother was not too enthusiastic, but she also knew I was probably not up to my usual summer job, either. One day in July, I boarded one of the buses, along with a hundred or so other kids from the area. We headed for Camp Ipperwash, near Grand Bend on Georgian Bay. If you check your map, Windsor and Grand Bend are not exactly neighbours. With today's transportation, that distance is no big deal, but back then it was a long way away. It did seem a long way from home and for a long time - six weeks. I was still not quite up to par healthwise, but fifteen-year-olds are quite resilient, and I was sure I'd be okay.

There was one other kid from Patterson that I knew, and the rest were strangers. They came from all parts of Ontario and Quebec. I was assigned to the signal core, and he was in the mechanical division. His job was to learn how to drive and do minor maintenance to army trucks. He did not learn well, as one evening he drove a truck into the main gate and partially demolished it. He was not popular.

There were so many exciting events that I am not sure which to include. Maybe I will just leave this and do them separately. You will remember my stay in jail on the last day, perhaps my trip to the base hospital, the week at Uncle Alex's [mentioned briefly in another story], the riot in the bunkhouse, and Saturday nights in Grand Bend. When I get the time and desire, I will fill in some of those [unfortunately he never did].

The other memorable time was the exercise on the last few days. I was the signal man for the Captain on the winning side. I never left his side for the two or three days of our own, small war. Of course, I got into a bit of trouble just as the battle was ending, but that is another story. The Brigadier was also someone to remember since he drove around, or rather was driven around, in a very shiny jeep with white walls and red leather upholstery. Never saw a jeep like it before, or since.

Boblo Island

It sits in the Detroit river, owned by Canada, but leased to the United States for ninety-nine years. I think the lease is up, or renewed, but for my purpose that is irrelevant. When I was a teenager in Windsor, Boblo was THE Amusement centre. It was our local Disneyworld long before Disneyworld existed. The Americans owned it, but all the amusement rides and carnival stuff was owned by a man in Windsor. Tour boats daily took hordes of people from Detroit all summer long. One day a year the boat left from Windsor. On weekends there was a Boblo Island midnight cruise which stopped for passengers in Windsor. The boat had a band on the dance deck. It never stopped at the Island, but just floated up and down the river for a few hours. It was great fun.

The Island had lots of parks, hamburger joints, and tons of rides, like any midway. It was a very popular spot and always busy. There was a barge that went every half hour from Amherstburg, as Boblo was only fifteen minutes offshore from there. I believe it still has remnants of forts from 1812. They were built to keep the Yankees from invading Canada, since it is so close. Anyway, the barge would carry six vehicles and several walk-on passengers. The only vehicles allowed were delivery types taking stuff to the island.

Canada Packers supplied the beef to the concession stands. Lyons Transport had the contract with Canada Packers to ship the meat to the island. It went on Saturday. I worked part-time at Lyons, and working Saturdays was part of my part-time job. I worked there from age sixteen to nineteen, until I left for Victoria. I delivered the meat to the Island on Saturdays all summer.

For a kid of sixteen or seventeen it was a great Saturday and I got paid. The pickup truck was brand spanking new, so it was fun to drive.

I would go to work for eight, do bookwork for an hour or so (that's what I was originally hired to do), then drive over to Canada Packers a few blocks away, and they loaded the meat into my pickup. The guys at the Packers were not pleased about that, but I was not big enough or strong enough to carry them. They were sides of beef. A whole half a cow, covered with cheesecloth. I would then drive to Amherstburg. It was a nice scenic drive and took about forty-five minutes or so.

You must paint the picture in your mind. A butchered cow is about as long as the box on the pickup. The tailgate closed, but just barely. The number of sides usually filled the box of the truck right to the top. The box was literally filled with fresh meat covered in cheesecloth, and it could be 80° outside. I guess the health inspectors were on vacation, or probably did not exist.

I got to the ferry dock after forty-five minutes or so, and sometimes had to wait if the timing was off and the barge was not back yet. Most times I was the only vehicle, since only commercial vehicles were allowed, and if no one else was doing deliveries, the rest of the barge was walk-on passengers. Once the truck stopped, the flies started. You could barely see the meat for the flies feasting through the cheesecloth. It was not an appetizing sight. Once we landed and the truck started to move, the wind dissipated the flies.

It was pretty awesome power for a kid. There were roads on the Island, but they were very narrow and only used for delivery vehicles. People walked on the roads, not expecting any vehicles. I delivered to a half a dozen or more stands scattered from one end of the Island to the other. You just puttered along with the odd honk of the horn and the box full of flies, pulled up to the back door of the concession stand, and suggested someone come out and carry in their side of beef. The exercise took up the afternoon, and the few minutes on the ferry back to Amherstburg was always relaxing, especially without a pickup filled with flies. Just so you know, I never had the nerve to eat a hamburger on the island.

Heading West

Dad's Travels

Dad had travelled to the west coast in the twenties in a model T. Literally no roads as we know them, and if you know anything at all about a Model T, you know they ran about twenty miles an hour, and had a flat at about the same ratio. The flats were not the car's problem, though. For the year, and technology, it was a great gadget. If you get an opportunity, take a ride in one, and imagine going three thousand miles over dirty, muddy roads, carrying a screwdriver, pliers, and fence wire to keep it going! Must have been one trip. Oh, and this was a pickup with a canvas top! Anyway, I can only surmise what it was like, and just relay my adventure, many years, and light years in technology later.

The Move

The above is not the point of my story though. I just think it may add to your understanding of my younger days. I missed over half of grade ten, but rebounded physically, very fast. Thanks to giving teachers, I squeaked through. The next year was not so easy. A household joke as long as I can recall, was that dad was moving to Victoria, BC. He had been there with his Model T, and I guess fell in love with the place. Every time he got upset, or whatever, he was going.

We laughed until one December when I was sixteen. His birthday was New Year's Day, and he said that he was finally going on January 1. The feed store was a losing proposition for many reasons, and he wanted out. January 1, 1953, he boarded the train in Windsor with a couple of battered old suitcases and was gone. He was sixty years old.

Mom lived with a wealthy doctor's family and looked after their two small kids. I think she liked it and they loved her and were very upset when she left a year later. Marlene became a nanny for another family, and I lived with Gordon and Vera and stayed in school. How it was all arranged, I have no recollection, but it did not seem to be that strange at that time. The following year, spring I think but not sure, mom and Marlene left for Victoria, and I stayed behind.

Left Behind

I was actually a pretty smart kid, but on Pillette Road and at Gordon's house, trying to do homework was somewhat of a chore. There was also no encouragement to stay in school and do well. I got a good job after school and on Saturdays at Lions Transport. I worked in the office and helped out driving when needed. I liked it.

I had decided to stick it out in school and applied to the Detroit Institute of Technology for the engineering course. I like to fiddle with things as you know and thought I could be an engineer. That got squashed one day when I ended up in the hospital with an acute appendix attack. I was out of commission for another six weeks. The downshot was that I missed the start of the course and had no money to go, as medical coverage was not what it is today, and I had to pay for the operation and the hospital of course. That took a few months and so the Detroit Institute of Technology was out.

I missed my mother I am sure, had been no farther than Toronto, and the west coast seemed very exciting. School work was suffering, and it would be at least two more years before I could go to the Detroit Institute of Technology if I shaped up and my marks were okay. I think it looked like too big a hill, and the desire was not strong enough. School and I parted in the middle of grade thirteen. I had actually thought of the ministry for a few years but did not have the resources to go through the required years of university.

Goodbyes

It was January or February 1952, I think, and I was seventeen. I paid for my ticket, and had enough for meals on the way, and a few bucks extra. Probably had a hundred dollars or so. Gordon and Edward had driven me to the bus terminal in Windsor. A very unhappy young lady was also with us. Restless feet, adventure, the lure of the unknown, or wanting to see my mother, all combined to encourage me to get on a bus to Seattle, and then a ferry to Victoria. It was very cold, about seven thirty at night, and I recall watching those left behind standing shivering on the platform as the bus pulled out. The bus went through the tunnel to Detroit, and then to Chicago for a change of buses.

I guess I thought I would exercise my wandering feet and return to Windsor and she would be waiting. She was or is not your mother and was not waiting when I returned. All my belongings were on my back and in a little cheap cardboard suitcase (still in a closet here I think, full of stuffed toys). Everything I owned fit into that suitcase. I had been to Chatham, Dresden, and even Detroit, but not Chicago. The well-to-do travelled long distances by train, a few by car, and most average people went by buses. Bus stations were the proper size to accommodate the number of travellers. Chicago was a transfer point, and the bus station was accommodating. I was lost. It seemed as big as all downtown Windsor, but with a roof over the whole place.

Money Exchange

It was late morning when we entered Chicago. I remember being in awe of the waterfront and the buildings. The bus station was huge. You've got to remember that bus was the favourite mode of travel then for the average person. We had some time between buses, and I wanted to get something out of a vending machine but had no American money. Naive or what? I went to the counter and asked them to change a twenty-dollar bill. The young lady had no idea what a Canadian twenty was and had to go ask her supervisor if it was legitimate and could she accept it.

The line-up behind me was typically Yankee impatient. I was a typical seventeen-year-old and embarrassed by the wait. I was used to Detroit. People there were familiar with Canadians and Canadian currency. This situation was new to both the clerk and me. Finally, I got my twenty changed and had a pocket full of American money. They were big on silver dollars and they sure pulled down pockets. That is my recollection of Chicago until many years later, when I was there for a Data Terminal Systems (DTS) convention when I had the business.

The Backseat

A couple of other guys, my age or a bit older, got on the bus in Chicago. They were going to various places in the west. After a few other stops we picked up a couple more. Being a kid and knowing what was cool, I went to the back seat. The adult population on the bus knew better. Backs seats are bumpy, hard, don't recline and have no armrests. The five of us were unaware of such stuff. We were all heading for adventure, and comfort was not important. The destination did not matter. Getting there was the adventure. What a lesson that we forget. Live each day! We ended up with five or six of us and took up the whole rear seat. The bus ran night and day, with stops for a break every couple of hours, and a bit longer for lunch.

Travelling

The bus stopped at major centres only, but because of the highways then, we went through every town and hamlet in the west. It was an express bus. Imagine an express bus that probably topped forty-five miles an hour (no four lane highways then, no seventy miles an hour Greyhound coaches, and no onboard bathroom). We stopped for coffee breaks and lunch. I think it still took four days, as this thing did not go that fast.

Drinking laws in most states were much more lenient than in Canada. Being the age we were, at most stops when everyone went in for coffee or tea, we searched the area close by for a hotel. Riding on a bumpy bus (they were not the nice, soft cushy types of today) after a couple of draft beers sometimes became an endurance test. No washrooms on board then. Kids will be kids.

The driver was impatient and took a head count after each stop. I think coffee breaks were fifteen to twenty minutes, depending on the speed of the restaurant staff. Lunch was only slightly longer. I was last on many times. Lots of things to check out when you are a kid from the farm, and the badlands and mountains were only images from radio programs and comic books. When was I ever going to get the opportunity to see these things again? When we hit town, I had to wander and check out the sights.

This sightseeing stopped when the gang at the back decided that coffee was not really good for you, and if there was a hotel with a draft room close by, we would be better taking our break there. Perhaps it would not have been such an unwise decision today with a bathroom onboard the bus. Oh, well!

Western Winter

Bus heaters were much like the washrooms, almost nonexistent. My coat was not designed for minus thirty, which it was when we got off at the next stop in North Dakota. I think I had coffee and not cold beer. Winter in the northern states is just like Alberta or Saskatchewan. Cold and lots of snow. During the day, the bus windows were so frosted over that to let a small ray of sunlight peep through to see a bit of landscape, my lap ended up looking like it had endured a real snowstorm. with the frost scraped from the window. The cold notwithstanding, we were not very hot on coffee during our stops.

I was a big fan of Western movies, and when we hit Fargo, I was elated to be in this legendary place. Wow! Fargo was a hot spot for any kid who was a fan of the old west. To think that it existed, and I was here! Western nostalgia was one thing and reality was another. It was night, minus 32, or some such thing, but I was happy to be in Fargo. My clothes did not cut that kind of temperature. Memory has a lot of holes, but the temperature I remember. Windsor never heard of such a thing and it really stuck in my mind. Unfortunately, in the dark one cannot see much of a small western town, and it was very cold to wander far.

Being teenagers, if there was a pub within running distance, we would head there and gulp down a draft beer while the geezers had tea or coffee. You can imagine how hard this practice was on kidneys, bouncing around on the back seat, of a very cold bus without a bathroom.

Sometimes it seemed a long way, a very long way between stops. Looking out a cleared spot through the frosted window, at the badlands in North Dakota on a bright moonlight night, still sticks in my memory.

The Bar

We tumbled off the bus, last of course, and went into the warmth of the station. As much as touring Fargo was intriguing, one of the gang with better eyesight than the rest saw a sign across the street. I would love to say it was the *Last Chance Saloon*, but I think not. It was just a typical draft room that no longer exists. We all ran against the cold and picked a round table close to the bar. The place was pretty empty. The bartender came over and informed us that he did not serve black people. If the black kid with us left, he would serve the rest of us. He did not seem to have any concern about age, just colour. He made his pronouncement and retreated to his bar, leaving us wondering if we were in Memphis, or some other spot in Georgia.

This was the highlight of my trip. I do not often make a noise about being a champion for any kind of cause, but this was a victory that I can relish. I suggested to my seatmates that we could survive this stop without a beer. I suggested that our black friend leave, and we would each order two drafts. Two at a time was common. When they arrived, we would tell our bartender friend that we were not thirsty, and all leave. Our black friend got up and walked out the door, whereupon the bartender returned to take our order. We all ordered two drafts. Ten drafts are a real tray or table full. The nice bartender returned and distributed ten beers. He set them all around and waited for his money.

On cue, we looked at one another, "I don't really think I am thirsty, are you? "No, I'm fine. Let's go." Getting up, we said something like, "thanks for serving our friend," and we went out into the freezing cold, leaving a very angry bartender with ten beers to pay for and throw out. Our friend was waiting outside the door. We laughed all the way back to the bus station and had coffee. I wonder if he remembers that incident. I wish I could remember his name, but I can't.

Hotel

We got into Seattle late at night. The ferry did not go till morning. I went to a restaurant across from the bus station, got something to eat, and inquired where I might stay. I was directed to a hotel on the waterfront close by. It was cheap, real cheap. It should have been closed. I only had twenty dollars left so could not afford a decent place. I was on the second or third floor, with the one bathroom down the hall, if one dared to venture to it. The noise from the fighting in the bar down below, and general riffraff staying there, was a bit unnerving. The door would not lock so I jammed the only chair, an old wooden thing, under the knob, and reluctantly slept on top of the bed with my clothes on. The sheets did not look too appetizing.

I was up early, really early the next morning, and walked to the ferry terminal which was not far away. I bought my ticket and had one twenty-dollar bill left. I had never been on a ship that large, nor out into the ocean, especially far enough that you could not see the shore. I think it took five or six hours to get to Victoria. I was impressed with the ship, the ocean, full of excitement about my destination, but had no idea what I was going to do when I got there, nor where I would stay, as mom and dad lived in a small suite in the Westholme Hotel.

The Arrival

Anyway, in my mind, Victoria was just a stopping off point. I was going to get on a ship and see the world. That strikes me as funny now. The only boat of any size I had ever been on was the ferry to Boblo Island, and you could almost touch shore from where it sailed in the Detroit river. I actually really liked planes and wanted to fly.

There was a vacant room right across the hall from my parents. That was my bedroom. I checked out the town but wanted to travel the world. I went to the seafarers joint to see about getting on a freighter. I did not care where in the world it went, or what I had to work at. I just wanted to go. "Do you have a union card?" They had to be kidding, even then! No card, no connections, get lost.

I next found out about the weather ship. I imagine that satellites have replaced it, but maybe not. This ship went to a spot hundreds of miles out into the Pacific. It stayed out for forty-nine days, doing a big circle in the ocean. It was loaded with whatever equipment one uses to track weather and sent the information back to shore. So, I talked to them. Not a chance. They had lots of people with experience and union cards who would go for one trip to earn enough money to bum around shore until they were broke again. I talked to and checked out every kind of ocean-going gadget I could find. Guess a short, skinny, farm kid did not have the right background.

I think the above exercise only took a week or so. I needed a job and money. Obviously, the ship guys did not want me. My twenty bucks was long gone. I got a job at Standard Furniture. It was five floors, privately owned, and the largest store in Victoria. Sort of like Cherney's [a furniture store in Peterborough, Ontario] but bigger. I sold floor coverings. What I did not know but learned about carpet, tile, and linoleum was just amazing. I actually liked it. We got a salary and commission, and they were sorry to see me leave, only to return to Ontario. So much for travelling the world!

Yardmaster

New Job

A true historian would have an assistant check all the dates and pertinent details, or at least have taken months to do that himself. Well, I am not a historian, and this is not meant to be a detailed newspaper, or on the spot reporting of history. It is history nevertheless, and as accurate as my mind recalls. It was 1955 or 1956, I don't think it really matters. I returned from Victoria and within a few days, just by a quirk of fate, ended up with a job at the Canadian Pacific Railroad (CPR) in Windsor. No idea of what I wanted to do or be, but had to eat, and this job paid more than I could ever imagine. I wrote the tests, passed the muster for credit reports, and the references checked okay.

Railyard

The yard runs from the top of Tecumseh Road, where the road takes a ninety-degree bend to the north and continues for a mile or so, and then the road takes another ninety-degree bend and heads west to Huron Line. The entrance to the CPR yard is right on this second bend. The yard runs all the way from Tecumseh Road right to the Detroit river. The main line comes into the yard just feet before or after, the top ninety-degree bend, depending on your direction of travel on Tecumseh Road.

The yard from the Tecumseh Road crossing to the River is approximately three miles long, by my calculations. The road entrance into the yard would be about a mile from the crossing, where the main line crosses Tecumseh road and enters the yard. I have a very clear picture in my mind, but somehow, I think my explanation leaves a pretty blurry picture for you.

As you drive on the short dusty road into the yard, there are two or three houses that are on private lands at the entrance. There is a parking lot, and then the yard house to the right, which is a large wooden building housing several offices and a washroom, an entrance to the yard, and of course it is the command center where the yardmaster reigns supreme. He is god, no matter which shift: day, afternoon, or midnight.

Yard Checker

My job was to be a yard checker. Next to an oiler, a checker was the very bottom of the food chain in the yard, especially the midnight shift, which I was hired for. Come on duty at midnight, not ten after but preferably ten to the hour. I was given a little book, kind of long and skinny, with columns spaced specifically for what we were to enter. A couple of pencils and a flashlight completed my equipment.

My job was to go out into the yard and walk down each track and write down the pertinent information in my book. The information required was the car identification (e.g., CN, CP, GN, PN, OH) followed by the number (about six to ten digits) then the tare (weight of the car), usually six digits as they are pretty heavy, and then gross, I think.

The checker that just left for home had done the whole thing just before he left. His book was turned in to the yardmaster and I was not privy to its contents, but fair to say if the boss took the time to check, and were there any discrepancies, you know who would be sent back out, winter, summer, hail, rain, blizzard, thirty-five degrees above or below. If the car was at the bottom of the yard (meaning miles away down by the river), so what.

When it happened, rarely, I prayed that my numbers were right. No matter whose fault it is, the yardmaster was never happy about it. Some were more considerate than others, but all needed a course in "This is how you treat employees, how you deal with people, how to handle stress 101." It was a great experience, and exposure to life as it really existed, and could be a prerequisite for any kid at a certain age.

I imagine the operation in the yard office has changed considerably, as electronic eyes have taken over from car checkers, and I think automatic switchers pull the pins and move the arms on the switches, so maybe the modern yardmaster just sits in his office and watches a computer screen, instead of having a fit and screaming at people. If so, and it is probably so, what a shame.

Midnight

Windsor, as you may know, is a warm spot in summer, so working midnights was not that bad. The temperature was great, the night sky beautiful deep in the yard, but not impressive at the top end, as the lights around the yard office and switching hut made it almost like daylight. But the sunrise was always magical. Depending on the time of year, the stars started to fade around four o'clock, and the first rays from the sun took over, and from then on it was a light show. The one side fading and turning into shadows, the other sending more and more slivers of yellow, orange, and deep red until the sun itself lit up the yard, and started to send shadows of boxcars, hoppers, tankers, and reefers onto the neighbours on the next track. I started at midnight by doing a full audit and had to end the shift by doing the same. The morning one was always, winter or summer, much more enjoyable, for lots of reasons.

134

Tracks were never loaded with cars for the full length of the yard, but you could probably walk close to a mile on any one track, writing down numbers. The tracks were spaced so there was room to walk between them, with boxcars on either side, but you could stretch out your arms and touch both cars. Cold, windy, winter nights were the worst. No matter the temperature in the winter, because of the proximity of the river, it always seemed cold, really cold. So, you either froze your fingers, or learned to write with gloves on, all the time holding the book steady, and aiming the flashlight at the right spot on the car.

Of course, when the wind gusted, and a boxcar door was ajar, the creaking and groaning sent enough cold shivers up my spine to freeze any part of my body that was not already convulsing with the cold. And occasionally there was a bum climbing in or out of the car. In that case we had few words, I assured them that I was not the railroad cop, and we both went on about our business. Some nights were fine, some so-so and some, well, scared should be replaced with terrified.

I never let my feelings show when I finally emerged into the heat and light of the office. After all, men are not afraid of the dark, right? Throughout the yard there was always this movement of shadows, of flashlights flickering and train cars, some almost silently coasting down a sidetrack. On a bright moonlit night, beyond the lights around the yard office or the switching shack, those moving behemoths would cast menacing shadows as they passed, and then sometimes with a loud crash, announce their mating with the other cars on the siding that they were destined for. It was all very magical, or threatening and scary, depending on the weather, my mood, and the atmosphere of the yardmaster and the men working in the yard.

Ma Bell

The Start

In my day as an employee of Bell Canada, the company was referred to as Mother Bell, or more affectionately as Ma Bell. The company lived up to the name. Changes brought about by deregulation in the last few years have changed all that. You may have trouble believing how Ma Bell operated years ago.

I worked at the CPR in Windsor. It was a fun job and paid well, really well, for a kid. But I felt that it had no future for me. In retrospect it probably had a great future, as they were just getting computerized, and I took to that stuff like the proverbial duck to water. A fellow who was older and there longer than I was transferred to their computer department in Toronto. I could have been next. Anyway, on to the Bell.

For some weird reason I always wanted to be in sales. I had already sold the S&H (Sperry and Hutchinson) Green Stamp program, *The Book of Knowledge,* and encyclopaedias. Bell had an advertisement in the Windsor paper for representatives for various cities. A job with the Bell was prestigious and for life. The railroad was just, well, it was just thought of as any other job. The Bell hired three people out of the hundreds of applicants. My education was not the greatest, but I fared well on their test. One guy stayed in Windsor and two of us headed for London.

The Company

Without the proper research, let me tell you how Bell started. When good ol' Alexander got his listening device going, his company was given the right to provide phone service to all Ontario and Quebec, provided that every household was given access to a telephone. That meant that they had to provide service to rural areas that were unprofitable. They had to run lines to every town and side road in Ontario and Quebec. That was pricey.

The Canadian Radio-Television and Telecommunications Commission (CRTC) controlled the pricing of everything Bell charged for and had to approve of every increase and decrease. Other provinces set up their own phone systems, but Bell eventually also owned Maritime Telegraph and Telephone Company, and over the years a very large real estate company, Transcanada Pipelines, and many other holdings including Northern Telephone, which was the manufacturing arm of almost all the equipment they used.

Over the years they grew to be the most profitable company in Canada, even larger than General Motors. People like to talk I guess, and it costs, or in the case of Bell, makes money. Lots of money. I am not sure how many small private telephone companies got started, but there are still a few in the province, all hooked up to Bell for long distance.

The first phones that I recall were crank jobs with a mouthpiece attached to a fancy wooden box. I am sure you have seen one. We had one on the farm. They had a small crank on the side. The microphone or mouthpiece stuck out from the front of the box. A separate earpiece hung on a hook attached to the side. Hanging up the earpiece hung up the phone or cut it off. Numbers of people used the same line, hence the party line. You would have an identifiable ring. One long and two short, or two longs, or two shorts.

When you called someone local you used the crank and turned it to make the required rings. If it was long distance or out of your area, you toggled the cradle that the earpiece sat on, and the operator came on the line. You simply told her who you wanted to call, and she connected you. I really do not recall any kind of phone book then, although there may have been one. Everyone knew the rings. Some city folks had individual lines, and eventually separate lines came everywhere. Well, almost everywhere.

Batteries

The ringing current (24V) was supplied by batteries that lived in a large box, somewhere beneath where the phone was mounted. There were two batteries about ten inches high and two and a half inches around. Batteries were very primitive then and were changed often. I do know that the busy signal, at least during my term at the Bell, was supplied by a very large generator gadget at their switching station. In any event, some technological advancement was made, so that these batteries were obsolete and no longer needed to make the telephone work. Crews went to every house that had a phone, removed the batteries, and rewired the phones. The batteries were given to anyone that wanted them.

Batteries, yum! I wanted them. I was always fiddling with something, and batteries then were nowhere near what they are now. They were costly, especially if you had no money. They did not last very long. No re-chargeable types then. This free supply of electricity was like Christmas morning, and receiving everything you had prayed for. I had stacks of long, round, crappy batteries, and we did not even have a phone. We had a phone on the farm in Comber, but no phone in Tecumseh when this battery demolition took place. My buddies were not battery nerds, so were happy to collect them and give them to me. What did they know about electricity!

About that same time the province decided to convert hydro from 60V to 110V. Houses only had 60-amp power, and only four fuses to control everything. The Comstock Company was given the contract to convert the whole province to 110V. They went from house to house exchanging motors in fridges, and I am trying hard to think of other appliances, because most homes did not have many other kitchen gadgets with motors that we take for granted. Anything that had a motor in it was replaced, courtesy of the province. We did not have the population of today but try to get a handle on the magnitude of Bell's battery removal program, or Comstock changing every electric motor in the province.

London

The late forties and early fifties were heady times, at least in Tecumseh for a kid with tons of battery power, lots of rotten tomatoes, a Bee-Bee gun and forests and fields to explore. Bell was a large presence in every major city. At one time they had over forty thousand employees, a fleet of green cars, repair vehicles, construction equipment and who knows what all. They put in their own poles, lines to carry telephone wire, installed telephones, and fixed all that stuff. No one could own a phone and all telephone equipment was rented from Bell. Their service and treatment of customers was second to none. They also did a large business overseas installing phone systems. They made no money on local service to residential customers, but the business customers were a different story. The largest profit maker for Bell was the Yellow Pages, followed closely by long distance, and then pay telephones. I have no idea how those profit centres line up now.

I arrived in London and worked in the sales office on Queen Street. The sales departments were divided into three groups called small, medium, and large. These terms meant the size of the business. The large group only had two or three sales staff to call on places like Labatt's Brewing Company and large government offices. The medium group called on medium sized businesses with small switchboards. The small group where we all started called on every other business, from the local garage with one telephone on up. Out of London we went right up to Goderich and Port Stanley in the other direction. We used green cars and rented one from Hertz or Tilden when no company cars were available. The starting pay was not great, less than I made at the CPR, but there seemed to be no shortage of money for travel, meal expenses, and training.

Pay phones and mobile had their own department. Even then in the early sixties, there were phones in cars. Not many, but they were available. The equipment to run it almost filled the trunk. The phone was a radio phone that connected you to the Bell through a special operator. The phone was a push to talk, meaning that when you spoke you held down a button, and when you let it up you could hear the other person. It worked, sort of, and was very expensive.

Sales

We had one green car equipped with a mobile unit, and one sales guy who drove around and tried to sell the stuff. Not often, but once a year or so a storm or some disaster would cut off the phone service in some small community in our area. When that happened, someone, usually a member of the large sales staff, would take the green car with the mobile in it and head for the disaster site. They would drive around town and be available for anyone who needed to make an emergency call.

I never had that opportunity, but Gus was in Seaforth late one night as an ice storm had put them out of commission. If you were out of the car and a call came in, then the horn would blow to alert you. About midnight Gus went into the local Chinese restaurant for a coffee. Every town had a Chinese restaurant. He had just gotten his coffee, no one else in the restaurant, and the horn started to blow on the car.

Our sales manager was just checking to see how Gus was doing. The horn noise was noticed by both Gus and the owner. Gus left, telling the owner that he had to go to the car to answer his telephone, but would be right back to finish his coffee. When he went to go back into the restaurant the door was locked. He got this message through the glass, "You're crazy, I've closed for the night."

Training

The Bell was great on training. I trailed along with Gus my first week in London and then spent two or three weeks in Toronto. Training was serious business. Start at eight and go till four-thirty. You had better be there on time and if you did not measure up, well, no more job. We stayed at just about every hotel in town, from the Royal York to the King Edward and Park Plaza.

These were all fancy hotels, and still are. For a kid that spent life in an unheated farm bedroom, these places were pretty amazing to me. They paid all the meals, up to a certain amount each day, and subway fare.

They had very good courses. Lots were directed to their specific equipment and method of selling, but lots were generic. Their best sales courses could apply to anything, and they gave short, one- or two-day flings on effective letter writing, writing business letters and other very useful topics. Every employee that used a Bell vehicle, or rented one on their behalf, took a one day driving course every year. They also paid for us to go to first aid training.

The telephones that have push buttons on them were the sole domain of the medium and large sales group. They were far too complicated for us beginners to fathom. The system was called 1-A- Key and was probably their most popular system. It also obviously worked well, as they were around forty years ago and were in use until about twenty years ago, when electronic systems came into being. It is laughable when I think of the worksheet that was used to set up one of those systems. Most of us could plan it in our heads now.

The Revenues

You can see how they made money, as the customer was charged for the lines, at least two or more, a separate cost for each set, and a cost for each button on each set. If they had an intercom, it had a separate cost, as well as a fee for each set connected. The hold feature was charged the same way, as well as the lights on each button. All these bits and pieces were options and charged accordingly. And if you wanted numbers to ring consecutively, there was an extra charge each month. All charges were monthly as you could only rent and not buy anything, except for long cords and coloured phones some years later.

Consecutive numbers had to be that and not two different numbers. At some point the switches were upgraded and each exchange could provide a small number of consecutively ringing numbers that were different, and not actually consecutive. Hope that makes sense.

Every town had at least one Bell switching office. These buildings held all the switches to make the phone connections. The switches were called Step and Repeat. These buildings were filled with aisles of these switches that went from floor to ceiling, with just enough room to walk in between the banks of switches and get at them to make repairs. These switches were mechanical solenoid types of characters that made constant noise. The racket was really something. The new electronic switches are quiet, take up no room and are much faster. I often wonder what they are doing with all the old Step and Repeat stuff, and the massive buildings that held them.

We had nothing to do with the switching offices or the equipment, except that we could request them to do a busy study. They would hook a gadget up to a customer's line and run it for a week or two. We would then get a printout that showed how many calls were made in and out, and how many times someone could not get through because the line was busy. This was great information to show a business that they needed more lines, as they were missing calls due to busy signals.

Canvassing

Two special fun jobs that I did in London come to mind. A new subdivision was being built, and although most of the houses were occupied, the roads were not finished, and the Bell lines not yet installed. I took a green car, two girls from the business office, and we canvassed every house in the subdivision. It took a couple of weeks. Of course, we took coffee breaks and ate lunch at a restaurant, all courtesy of Ma Bell. I cannot remember who the girls were, but most of them in the business office were my age and all good looking. I think that was the first requirement when the manager hired the girls in the business office. Were they cute and could they pass the shape test?

We were to find out what kind of equipment they wanted, like coloured phones or extensions. Most homes had one set, and it was usually black. Jacks were new then, but you could rent them with a phone to plug in, as long as you had one set wired permanently in place. The portable set was an ordinary telephone with a jack wired to the end of the cord. Sounds pretty weird, eh!

St. Thomas was the only place in our domain that did not yet have dial phones. They still had a main switchboard. All phones, business and otherwise, came without a dial. When you wanted to make a call, you picked up the receiver and an operator came on the line and said, "number please." She would make the connection.

The local manager had been there forever. He thought his system worked just fine. Several of the businesspeople we spoke to had different stories. A new dial office was being built and the old system being turfed out. That was progress. Four of us went to St. Thomas to contact every business owner. We went Monday, stayed at what I recall as the only hotel in town, and came back to London on Friday afternoon and filed our reports. Since there were four guys, we stayed two to a room, and met for supper and probably a beer afterwards. It was fun in the summertime and took us over a month.

The Heist

The hotel had a draft room on the main floor. This was an old hotel with rooms on the upper floors. The draft room had the bar at the back on the right side of the room. On the left was a hallway to the back door and over this hall and the bar was an open storage space with a ladder leading up to it. This space contained multiple cases of beer, stored there until the fridge got empty.

I have never stolen anything in my life, save for being an accomplice in this episode. I don't know who hatched the idea, but I guess we all agreed. Two of us stayed at the table near the front. One went out the front door. The other guy headed to the bathroom off the hallway beside the bar. We called the bartender over and ordered more beer. While we kept him engaged in conversation, our supposed bathroom pal scurried up the short ladder, and dropped a case of twenty-four into the waiting arms of the one who had gone out the front, ran around and quietly slipped in the back door. He left the beer hidden in the alley by the back door, then walked around and re-entered via the front. The culprit on the ladder sauntered back to the table as the bartender turned to go back to his bar. Obviously, save for us, the place was empty, being a weeknight and about ten-thirty.

Time to leave. We went to the alley to retrieve our beer, and some thieving skunk had stolen it. We were mortified to think that someone would stoop that low. Two of us went back inside through the front. We told the bartender that we decided that we would have one more. The other two more daring souls snuck in the back door and pilfered another case. This time it was not set down but taken directly to the room.

I guess being young and stupid go together. Had we been caught, I am sure we all would have been charged, and Ma Bell, not taking kindly to this kind of antic, I am sure would have canned us all. As they say, only by the grace of God... We did not want our beer to get hot, no fridges in those rooms, so we filled the bathtub up with cold water, and put all the beer into the tub.

Why the tub in my room I will never know, but the next day about four o'clock, there was a knock on the door. We did do our job, but this hot summer day we had quit early, and we were all sitting in my room savouring our stolen treasure. Bell had no problem with drinking. Just do not do it while working. This was a Tuesday or Wednesday, I think. I opened the door. Our boss from London had driven up to see how things were going. He was aware of the heat, so was not too shocked at seeing all of us sitting in one room drinking beer. The first thing he had to do though, was go to the bathroom. We had not counted on a surprise visit, and although I do not recall, I am sure we mumbled some good story as to why our tub was full of beer.

More Training

The business office was a block or so away from our sales office. It was on the second floor of another Bell building and was the contact with the public on accounts, complaints, and residential orders. It had a manager and his assistant, the only two males, and about thirty-five females, mostly young and easy on the eyes. They were the service reps, and most times handled a very stressful job. Because of Bell's monopoly they were extremely customer conscious and had rules and regulations that were adhered to or else. Most salesman types did not have much use nor contact with the business office other than to try to hit on the girls. I was freshly married so while the office was filled with a ton of cute girls, I already had one and so did not care. It was two of those kids that canvassed the subdivision with me.

Every year or two a sales rep spent a year in the business office. Everyone said they did not want to go, but in reality, they all wanted to be selected. It meant you were on your way. The higher ups saw you as someone who was management material, and this was part of the training. There was lots of room for advancement in the sales field, but if you were really going to make it big in the Bell, then you had to go through the business office for a year. I was blown away when after a short stint with the company, I was informed that I was being transferred to the business office. These moves all came at the same time of year, and there was always speculation about who was being shipped where. They moved people all over Ontario with much frequency.

My life as a service rep started with five weeks of training. The training was held in a small room down the street on the second floor of another Bell building. This little room was set up just like the business office, except it only had three desks, or positions as they were called, and a separate desk for the trainer, who sat facing the three desks but about five feet away. You can see the money they spent on training. One supervisor or trainer for three people for five weeks. There were two girls of course, who had just been hired, me, and the female trainer. She was a pitbull, and one of the girls lasted less than half the course, so the two of us struggled along with Miss Personality. The trainer and I did not get along well. She had a reputation in the business office, so I guess it was not just me.

The service reps worked hard and were mainly the face, or at least the voice, of the Bell to the public, but they got no recognition, while the salespeople were the darlings of the company. We learned the business office routine a bit at a time. It was drilled into us until we knew it in our sleep. We had the same phone set up as the business office, except it only went from grumps' desk to ours. She was the customer each time we mastered a bit of the proper telephone language. When we had one bit down pat, we went to the business office and observed while listening to the real thing.

We marched down the street like school kids with their teacher, from our little classroom to the business office. I always dreaded walking past the sales office. I don't like catcalls. The method of training for that job was effective then if you could withstand it. I doubt that it would fly today given the rigidity of the routine, and the demeanour of our instructor.

I hated the course but just could not fail. It would have been too demeaning to the sales department, my boss's faith in me, and to me. Our five weeks dragged on during the July and August heat. I was used to being outside, going where and when I wanted. Being cooped up in a little room with the dragon lady was not fun. But I endured.

The Office

Picture a large room with windows on three sides. You come in the door, and on the left is a private office. Just outside this private office sits another desk. Straight down the wall from that, another small closed off room. The rest of the space has desks all around the perimeter facing the windows. The desks are close to one another in groups of four, with a few feet separating each group. The middle of the room is completely bare. The private office is for the manager. The desk just outside his door is for his assistant. The other room is the monitoring room. This was the business office. In every city they looked the same.

A service rep occupied each desk around the perimeter. The desks were called positions. There would have been about thirty or more positions. There were five or six supervisors, each watching over eight positions or service reps. When I finally graduated from business office training and entered the real world, my supervisor was Margaret. The only older woman in the place. She could have been the trainer from hell's mother. We did get to be on civil terms, finally. Each position held the records for a number of telephone subscribers, about two hundred and fifty, I think. They were of course arranged by phone number. The records showed all the information, such as name, address, and what equipment they had. On the top of each desk and in the middle was a green metal file affair. It was like a three-tiered basket, with three lights mounted on its top.

There was a green light, a red light, and a yellow one. Green meant that you were free to take calls. Yellow said you were at your desk but on the phone, and red said that there was no one at that desk. These lights were duplicated downstairs at the switchboard. When customers called, the switchboard operator would ask for the telephone number, then put the call through to the position that had the records for that number. If the light was red or yellow, she would send the call to the next closest position with a green light on. Make sense? Business customers were looked after by a few senior service reps, except for the one line very small businesses.

Let me back up a bit. As our training progressed, we would march over to the office and actually occupy one of the positions. The first few times, all we were allowed to do was answer the phone, and no matter what the customer asked, our response was, "I am sorry, but I am not trained on that, please hold for a moment and I will get someone to look after you."

The real rep would be patiently waiting, with her headset on listening to the call. She then would look after it. We would go through this routine for an hour perhaps, and then march back to our cell, where we would be told how lousy we said what we said or did not say. As things progressed, we were actually allowed to handle simple requests, with someone else listening in and making facial gestures and hand waving, to alert us to our sloppy ways. For the most part though, we still resorted to our "I'm sorry routine."

Even after graduation the training continued until we were fully competent. Even then we could make no real decisions. Anything slightly out of the ordinary had to be directed to your supervisor. I was not allowed to relate lots of questions that I knew from my time in sales. That was Margaret's territory as I was not supposed to know the answer. As time went on, my calls for Margaret grew less and less. I don't know if she ever caught on or not.

I really felt hemmed in. I was not used to this kind of environment and did not accept it easily, although the job was not that bad once I got the hang of it. The girls were all great and since I am pretty obliging and easy to get along with, they got me out of more than one hotspot.

The phone rang and your light glowed. Pick up the phone on the first ring. Two was permissible, but you better have a good reason. The pattern was always the same. We all had special note pads. You wrote down everything the customer and you said. It was all done in Bell shorthand. They had the best abbreviation system that I have ever seen. I still use some of it today. If you had to get out records, then you turned over the hourglass that was a mainstay of every desk. It ran for thirty seconds. That is how long you had to get back on the phone, or else.

Some days it was bedlam as people turned over the glass, unplugged the headset, dashed across the room, got out a record card, and roared back to their desk. When you took out a record, you put one of your special cards in its place, so people would know where it went. Heaven help you if you forgot or a record went missing. It really was a good system, and very well controlled.

All those little notes you made about every call were kept, and at the end of the day Margaret picked them all up and checked them. They better be accurate and agree with what she thought she heard, or saw if she was nearby, when a particular call was made. These little slips were somehow recorded and each month an assessment was made of our efficiency. Every office did the same and they had a performance index. We were told if it fell below the average, but also told when we were the best. Like I cared.

Let me tell you how they accomplished this little feat to make sure it was accurate, and the local manager was not fudging the figures. The monitoring room held another good-looking young lady. Her job was to randomly listen in to calls. We never knew when, nor who, was being spied on. She took notes like we did. She came around at the end of the day and picked up the calls from each position that she had monitored. Your notes best agree with what she wrote down. Sometimes there was a hot discussion about who heard what. No matter, she was god according to Margaret and the manager, so don't argue. She and I became good friends.

The Benefits

I joined the Jaycees, and the Bell paid the shot. Once the business office and I got our act together, I could get time off during the day to attend special functions. They were very community minded and encouraged the employees to be involved. I got special treatment during my stint in the business office. It became fun and probably some of the best training I have ever received.

Working with a group of the opposite sex does pose some problems. Often, I was the only male in the office. My co-workers looked after me, but they were also not above playing tricks. One morning I went to the washroom and the zipper on my pants broke. I spent the rest of the day with my topcoat on and buttoned up. Luckily, it was a London Fog and quite light.

It sure would be a hoot to spend a few hours with that gang of kids again.

The Prank

Well, things were pretty quiet one afternoon. Unannounced, the VP from Toronto waltzed in on the manager. Some of us saw him. It became obvious that not everyone did. The girl who lived her solitary life in the monitoring room was sitting at one of the desks, just outside her door. It was very quiet and not much to monitor, so she had wandered out. With her back to the monitoring room, she did not see the VP take over her spot. The manager went in with him.

My monitoring buddy turned to face the desk and made a phone call. With a lousy disguised voice, she became a farmer who wanted to order a phone installed in his outhouse. Of course, she just asked the switchboard to ring my station. She thought that I did not know who it was, but I played along because the VP could have been listening in. I turned around to get her attention, but of course the way the room was laid out, all the desks facing out, all I could see was her back. She was not prepared to turn and look at me.

If I put the phone on hold and ran across the room and he was listening, I would be in trouble because the customer gave me no reason to put him on hold. If we got caught, she would be in big trouble. I knew that I was on safe ground because I did not initiate the call. I was trying to keep from laughing, but treating this as a legitimate call, just in case he was listening. I was afraid she would be hung. The monitor is a very serious position, and you just do not do things like that.

While it was a very slow day, calls were still coming in and she should have been in her little cubicle doing her spying job, not out trying to play a prank on me. I did my best to pacify this stupid farmer for quite a few minutes. Suddenly the door to the monitoring room opened and out stepped the VP and the manager. My shocked farmer hung up very abruptly, without even placing an order or so much as a goodbye. The two men walked the few feet to the desk where she sat.

She sat immobilized, probably too scared to get up. The manager introduced her as the real monitor, said what a good job she did, and away they went. Did they actually hear our conversation? Probably not. I imagine the luck of the draw took over and they picked a couple of real calls. But we will never know. After that call we discussed who could shovel the most, so she bought me a little yellow scoop shovel on wheels. Sure would like to talk to her again; and you know, for years I have been trying to remember, and for the life of me I cannot think of her name, or I would try to find her.

The Phone Bills

We, the service reps, got a copy of the monthly phone bills for all those numbers we looked after. They were graded A, B, C, and D. When the bills hit, it was the busiest time. We took our regular calls, at least I did when I was there, and sorted our bills when the phone was not ringing. The As were filed. The Bs were put in another file for checking later, and the Ds were given special attention. They were called within a few days of the bill being received.

When each bill was paid, you could only pay at the Bell Business office then, and we were given a list the next day. We marked them off so we knew who had paid and who did not. Bs were scheduled to be called within a week or so, but those poor D guys were hounded immediately. Pay up or your phone will be cut off by........I am not sure how many days but cut off they were.

The term we used for calling the service department and noting on the bill was 101C. I have no idea what it stands for, except your phone is cut off because you did not pay your bill. If you called a number that was thus disconnected the operator said, "this service is temporarily disconnected." I always knew years after what the problem was when I heard that message.

If a D, usually a small business, wanted an extension, and some of those I was familiar with from my days in the sales department, I had to ask Margaret whether to grant them extra time or not. The back of the bill was noted with the terms, and initialled by the supervisor. Rarely did I agree with her judgement. As I melted into my position and really knew what was going on, I got pretty good at forging her initials. People on welfare, single mothers and small business owners that were Ds every month, but somehow paid their phone bill, although not on Margaret's schedule, got special treatment if they spoke to me. It just seemed logical that she was not available or too busy, so I took it upon myself and made the decisions. Signing her initials may have been stretching it, but I just could not live with her decisions.

You gotta wonder if she wondered why the number of requests for her assistance dropped shortly after I became part of her troop, and why the Ds did not cause as much a problem as normal. She also checked the bills and could see the notations and initials. Maybe my rendition of her initials was better than I thought, or not. As a career, the business office and I would never have survived. But for a year it was great training, and sometimes a lot of fun.

The Party

A Christmas party for the whole office was standard. I looked after it the year I was there. Like my subdivision episode, I was allowed to pick a couple of helpers to make the arrangements.

We rented a hall, hired a DJ, bought the booze to make punch, and ordered the food to be catered. I am not sure if Bell picked up the whole tab or we all chipped in. The party was a Friday night. My two cohorts and I took the Friday afternoon off to do the last-minute running around. We went to the liquor store and headed to the hall with our supplies. I used my car. We were to do the last-minute decorations, make sure everything was ready, and be done early in the afternoon so we could go home, change, and pick up our respective partners.

We decorated, checked tables, made sure the stage was properly set up, and at about three o'clock made the punch. Lots of juice, orange rind, and Vodka, or whatever it was. We were done but could not leave because we were waiting for food, or something to be delivered. We did not all have to stay, but I drove, and my two helpers had no way to get home. We all waited and waited.

Whomever we were waiting on did not show up until about five-thirty. I am sure I called your mother, and they probably phoned someone also to say that we may be a bit late. We were due back at 6:30, I think. Tired of sitting around and inspecting things for the umpteenth time, we decided we should check out the punch. What else would you do? Besides, it made perfect sense to taste it and make sure it was okay. Right? My recollection is that the first glass was okay, but we needed to check it again.

I think the one kid with me was Gwen, who lived in London with her parents, and the other girl was the one who gave me the scoop shovel, if only I could recall her name. Anyway, whomever it was we were waiting for still did not show up. We just kept sampling the punch. I drove them home finally. Gwen did not return.

Your mother and I returned, along with the rest of the gang. I was the Master of Ceremonies. Hula hoops were still in vogue. So, to get one up on Margaret, I had a Hula contest for the supervisors. She did not do well.

A few months later I was transferred to Toronto.

Jane Street TTC Turnaround

The Promotion

Your mother recalls this event, perhaps not fondly, and asked that I clarify the facts. She will proofread this, so know that it is correct. I had been promoted from being one of the "girls" in the Business Office to a rep in the Pay Phone Department in Toronto. A rep in Pay Phone was considered the bottom steppingstone, but what the heck, it was a promotion, more money, and a move to the really big city. Bell paid the shot for everything connected with the move.

I was billeted at the Park Plaza, corner of Bloor Street and Avenue Road. One of the most prestigious corners and hotels in the big city. A night's lodgings probably equaled my week's wages. The lobby was larger than our whole digs and obviously much more luxurious. I took the train from London, leaving your mother with the car, our 1949 Dodge. I had the use of a company car when available, or used the Red Rocket, as the Toronto Transit Commission (TTC) was affectionately called.

The Weekend

Toronto is a large place, and being a complete novice, I thought it would be easier to tour around to look for a place if I had a set of wheels. I called your mother and asked her to drive down on the weekend so she could also check out the real estate. Now, you must realize that asking your mother to drive to Toronto by herself was a stretch, much less asking her to drive into Toronto. I was sure she was capable, but her driving experience was limited, and that was a long jaunt at that time for a kid her age. Not many twenty-one-year-old females drove cars. Not the dark ages, but still the nineteen fifties. She came Friday afternoon.

The office where I worked was at 2150 Bloor Street West, just a stone's throw from Jane Street where the streetcars ended. The streetcars used a turnaround on the south side of Bloor Street. In this maze there were a number of aisles for the buses to drive in and pick up the passengers, disgorged from the Red Rockets. Jane Street ran south from the 401 and dead ended at the TTC turnaround at Bloor Street. Coming south on Jane when you got to Bloor, you either turned left or right, or ended up looking like a bus and driving around one of their pickup circles. Your mother decided to be a bus.

I had given her directions. "Turn south off the 401 at Jane Street, go to where the buses turn around, and I will be waiting." I was waiting but waiting on the sidewalk in front of the turnaround. Wow! Right on time I see your mother at the lights at Jane and Bloor. Well, I saw the car, and assumed your mother was driving. The light turned and I walked to the curb anxiously waiting for her to drive up. Well, no, she wants to be a bus and pick up someone else. My car drives around the first available circle, and people are clamoring with their transfers in hand.

I shield my face lest some of my coworkers are watching. Outside of a hick from some town like London, who would do such a thing? Luckily, it was almost dark, and no witnesses came forward. I ran over and got into the car before those hordes with transfers could fill the backseat. Now, in your mother's defense, she said that she was just following my directions to meet at the TTC turnaround. Is it not strange that one can claim to follow orders, sometimes!

The Hotel

In any event, we bumped along Bloor to my lodgings, and arrived at the Park Plaza. I was obliged to register any guest who shared my room. We went to the desk and I said to the clerk, "I have a visitor for the weekend." The clerk was a bit startled, and your mother was not amused. This was the fifties, and some people just did not seem to have a decent sense of humour. Our room maid, however, was a bit more perceptive.

My room had two beds, twin characters I think, with one pillow each. We moved the pillow from the unused bed and put it on mine, as we slept in the same bed. The next day, the beds were made up with the pillows put back where they belonged. One on each bed. The next morning, unfortunately, the day your mother drove back home, the maid caught on and made up our bed with both pillows on the one bed. We thought it was funny and that the maid was sharp.

Bus Step

How was I to know that you had to step on the step? My office was at 2150 Bloor West, almost at Jane Street. We had found a basement apartment at Bathurst and Lawrence. If you know Toronto at all, you will realize that it was like commuting from North Bay to Winnipeg. I had been to Toronto before. From London, take the train to Union Station, get on the subway to Bloor, walk a block to the hotel for the course, and reverse your path to get back to London. I knew Toronto like I knew downtown Tibet. I was transferred to Toronto from London by the Bell. It was a real step up, and a promotion for me. We located at Bathurst and Lawrence because coworkers recommended this area. I had no idea it was a world away from where I worked.

My first morning to report for work at my new assignment, I was at the bus stop in what seemed like the middle of the night. It was cold, sometime in the winter, dark, about 6:45 in the morning. There were other people waiting at the stop, but no conversation. Take the Bathurst bus to Eglinton, get a transfer, take the Chaplin Crescent bus to Yonge, get on the subway to Bloor, transfer to the Bloor West streetcar, and get off at Jane which was the end of the line. The directions from coworkers who spent their lives in Toronto sounded like a piece of cake. I wrote them on my hand so I would not get lost.

I watched the street signs like a hawk. Not that it mattered in the dark. Most were invisible anyway. I was told it would only take ten minutes and the driver would call out the stop. I anxiously pulled the cord, afraid I would upset the driver by making him stop. He was not the friendliest bus driver I had ever encountered. Shortly the bus bounced to a halt. They don't come to a stop. They bounce and lurch to a stop. Toronto buses are always in a hurry, so they wear out brake pads like we use toilet paper.

I jumped up and waited at the rear door. Nothing. The door did not open. Why is he keeping me captive on this bus? This is my first morning on my new assignment and I do not want to be late. After all, this is a promotion, and I cannot start off with a bad impression. I have never even met my boss. The door stares at me in defiance. Ten seconds pass and people start to wake up from their papers and snoozing, to see what has caused the bus to sit and wait so long.

The silence. People at this time of day going to work do not talk. They read, or pretend to read, try to snooze, or hunker down against the windows to wake up for work. They are used to the routine. When the bus sits for more than a few seconds at any stop, it triggers an automatic panic alarm. What is the problem? The problem is a young guy, probably some out of town hick not familiar with our routine, who is holding up the works. I just want to get off to get the Chaplin Cr. bus. If I miss the next one, I may be late and this is my first day, and oh well, you know....... The silent bus starts to murmur.

I just want the door to open so I can get off. People, who a moment ago were dozing are now looking back at me with disgust and wonder.

The driver is saying something. I have no idea what because the rustle of newspapers and winter coats moving against plastic seats drowns out any rational sound. My face must be red, my mind wonders how great this promotion is that it locks me inside a bus on my first day, and what the heck do I do?

I want out, I want to be invisible. The embarrassment is too much. The driver is now shouting, and those really sleeping are now awake. Why won't he just open the door and let me out? I am not an irresponsible person. I know you do not get out by the front door. That impedes people getting on and there are a lot of people getting on. So, what is the problem? I have my transfer, I paid the full fare, I think. Maybe I have to get off at the front to show my transfer.

I don't know, but it has been twenty seconds or more and the perspiration is showing on my red face. The regulars are getting very impatient. There is nothing to do but face this problem head on. I wend my way down the aisle to the front of the bus. I try to not look at anyone, nor bang into those standing in the aisle. The front door is open, and I just want to bolt, to get some fresh air so I can start to breathe again. I hesitate when I reach the not so friendly driver. "STEP DOWN AND THE DOOR WILL OPEN." Wow, I come from Tecumseh, who ever heard of a bus that would automatically open the door for you? For the next few weeks I made sure I caught a bus that was either a few minutes earlier or later. Big cities and small-town folk don't mix well.

David*

The Neighbourhood

We were Neophytes to Toronto, to finding apartments, and to having a baby. Your mother was twenty-two I think, and I was twenty-four. We were transferred from London and ended up in Toronto, settling into a basement apartment at Fairholme Avenue in North York. Although miles from work, friends suggested North York as a place to live. Fairholme is just below Lawrence and runs West of Bathurst near Yonge. We were a few blocks from Bathurst. It was a typical brick bedroom bungalow, much the same as all the rest that lined the street.

At that time, this area was the residential neighbourhood for the average Jewish family in Toronto, the clan having migrated up from Queen, College, Bloor, and other downtown areas taken over by the Chinese. Irish, English, Poles, Jews, and all others seemed to come in waves to settle in a certain area of the city. As they grew in prosperity they moved north by nationality. Today, in January 2000, you see a different group in the downtown core, and twenty years from now they will inhabit one of the northern suburbs as the next wave moves in.

The Landlords

Our landlords were a great couple, Moisha (Morris) and Pearl Weinberg. They were the best landlords and nicest couple and friends one could want. We were their first tenants in a newly done basement apartment with a living room, kitchen, bath and one bedroom. It was well furnished, and other than the high small windows that are part of most basements, it suited us fine. We were there just under a year when your mother became pregnant.

Moisha and Pearl were overjoyed at our good fortune of having a baby, and one in their house. David was born at Northwestern Hospital in York Township on May 1, 1960. Dr. Barr was a great guy. A young doctor with an office a few blocks away and a person who seemed to actually have time for and an interest in his patients. David came home and slept just outside our bedroom door. This space was part of the entrance at the bottom of the stairs. The bedroom was not large enough to accommodate a crib. Past the spot for the crib and the stairs was the bathroom.

David

Your mother got up during the night when David woke up and wanted to be fed. I did not get up but heard David and was always conscious that his mother rose and fed him. Like most quirts that size, he did not say much and took up little room, but sure had everyone mesmerized by his perfect face and his gaze. We felt that a basement apartment was not a great spot to raise a baby. Sometimes we had water leakage problems. Moisha was as concerned as us and had taken steps to correct it. Nevertheless, we gave our notice, having found an upstairs apartment at 62 Gilgorm Road in Forest Hill. We were to move the next week.

Memory is an amazing part of the mind. In most cases, at least mine, it is selective; selective in weeding out the bad stuff and only having instant recall for the good parts. Funny thing though for me, I guess dates are not good because they just don't stick. I started to write this, got into trouble with the details, and had to confer with your mother. Between us, we pieced this event and details together.

David was six weeks old when we woke the morning of Saturday June 11, 1960, and both realized that your mom had not been up to feed him. If you know anything about new parents, you will know that they are always tired. The endless rounds of changing diapers, feeding, cuddling, and still trying to adhere to your normal work schedule and routine takes its toll. Sleeping is not part of the routine. This particular Saturday morning we woke around quarter to nine. If no hungry kid hollers in the middle of the night, believe me, you can keep on sleeping. An alarm clock set for morning, or any other time, was not necessary.

You want to believe that things are fine, but that feeling, that premonition that something is not right overrides your mind. You ignore it as I did while I got up and went to the bathroom. Not wanting to check on the contents of the crib, I passed right by until I came back from the bathroom. Your mother had gotten up also but went to see David, put her hand on his and feeling it cold, she said, "he's dead!" I said, "I don't think so."

She had already picked him up and quickly dropped him back into his bed. "He is, look at him!" I picked him up. He was as rigid and cold as a plastic doll. He had been lying on his stomach, and as I turned him over, I saw the blue skin. The flat, blue face. I put him back into the crib. David had been a cute, smiley little guy, and now he was just a dinky, rigid body.

The Doctor

We had an appointment that morning to take David to Dr. Barr for a normal inspection. Oil and lube, or whatever happens to new babies when they are still under warranty and the doctor's care. Your mother called him and said, "we can't make the appointment this morning, the baby is dead." When you are in a stupor, beating around the bush is not in order. He asked for our address and said that he would be right there. He arrived within a few minutes, leaving a room full of patients. Your mother recalls that Dr. Barr took David and placed him on our bed to examine him. She knew better but kept thinking that any minute, David would wake up and start to breathe again.

The three of us sat on the chesterfield in the living room and I asked Dr. Barr if he would like a cup of coffee. His response was, "Yes, you both look like you need one." On his advice I called the Morris Funeral Home in Windsor. We had no idea what to do but knew that David should be buried in Windsor. Morris called Turner and Porter in Toronto and shortly a black car pulled up and took David. We gave them a white suit with blue trim to put on him. They would ship the body by train to the funeral home in Windsor. The shipping cost would be sixty dollars, half a week's pay before deductions.

The Phone Calls

We were like a pair of zombies and probably would have agreed to anything except taking the casket ourselves. We are not sure now, but either Dr. Barr or probably the funeral director suggested we could pick David up in his casket later in the day and take him to Windsor ourselves, saving the sixty-dollar shipping cost. After all, a casket that size would easily fit on the backseat. We declined. Just something about carrying your dead baby in the backseat did not appeal to us.

Personal tragedy or not, things must be looked after. I wanted to call someone to tell them that I would not be at work on Monday. However, one of the guys I worked with was getting married out of town and most of the people I knew were going, including my boss. I called and called, and finally got in touch with someone who would tell my boss why I would not be around for a few days. Your mother called Aunt Bessie and asked her to call the relatives in Toronto. We did not call anyone in Windsor. We just packed up our stuff and headed out after David was removed. Neither of us recall telling Pearl, but I know we did, and she was devastated.

The Drive

The 401 was not yet fully completed, and after highway ten, I think, we had to go south to highway five through Paris and eventually back onto the 401. We stopped at a restaurant in Paris for breakfast/lunch. No idea of the time, but I suspect between one and two in the afternoon. We both recall the expression on the face of the waitress, wondering what the heck are these two taking. We were silent and probably looked like we felt. Not sure that we actually ate anything, but I guess we should have told her why we looked and acted like we did. Dead kids can do that to you.

Arriving in Windsor, we went to Grandma Potter's and then to Vera's, according to your mother.

The Transformation

I have no recollection of Windsor at all, other than a few minutes of our time at the funeral home. When we first went to the home to view the kid, I have no idea, I just remember this little, very little white casket. I can't help it but remains, corpse, body or whatever does not sit well in my stomach. He was our kid, and that is how I thought and think of him.

We had given the undertakers pictures and they must have been miracle workers and masters at their jobs. David lay there sleeping, looking as peaceful and natural as any baby. I was overcome by this perfect little child lying in a small, white coffin. This is how I remember David. This was not the thing I had picked up from the crib just a day or two ago. I remembered the sunken head, blue and flat on one side.

Not a pretty sight and not like the angelic child I gazed at now. The only hitch was his outfit. It was on backwards with the little zipper on the back instead of the front. His mother was upset so I asked the undertaker if they could change it. The zipper problem was corrected when we visited later. The rest is a blur. The ceremony was on Monday. We drove home on Tuesday. The weekend was straightforward though. Funerals sometimes are like that.

The Hudson

Edward had Uncle Alex's Hudson. Uncle Alex had left it to him, thinking that with a large family and money being scarce, Edward could use a good car. Ed drove it for a couple of years or so. To him it was just a car, just transportation. It was also old, not exactly common, and parts were not quite available at Canadian Tire. I always wanted the Hudson and told Edward that whatever the condition, and whenever he was ready to get rid of it, call me and I would buy it.

A week, two weeks, or sometime before our funeral weekend, Edward bought another used car and traded the Hudson for $75. Why he never called me, I have no idea. The Hudson was still on the car lot at the bend in Tecumseh Road, by the CPR office. I offered the guy the same amount of money that he had allowed for it and he was glad to take it. Even then there was not a huge market for twenty-year-old cars, Edward had bought a 1937 Plymouth. Go figure.

We drove the Hudson to Edward's house on California Avenue. It had some minor problems, which was the reason he traded it in, but I fixed it so we could drive home. We left for Toronto with me driving the Hudson and your mother following in the MG. She had fun sitting low in the MG and looking up at the Hudson's bumper and trunk for the next five hours or so. We detoured via Kings Corners to go to Dresden and told Auntie Rae our sad news.

You know, I just thought that bringing the Hudson home, with each driving alone in separate cars but depending on one another should one car suffer David's fate, took our minds off the tragedy, and gave us a reason to keep going. I am not for a minute suggesting that a car could replace a lost child, but that activity helped turn two zombies back into human beings.

The New Birth

We got home, trying to forget why we left. Not possible. Our basement apartment was full of David. The entranceway still contained his bed with blankets intact. Dirty diapers still lived in the diaper pail, formula in the fridge, and typical signs of the first child were strewn everywhere you looked. This was Tuesday. We moved to Gilgorm Road on Wednesday. The move was probably a blessing for us, but a shock to the new landlords who were expecting a young couple with their new baby. Life goes on. We survived.

When Steven arrived and was brought home, ask us if we were nervous or checked on him every five minutes when he slept. Tired or not, the slightest sound he made, or not, sent one of us running to make sure he was okay. The tension lowered a bit for the next two kids, but not really. I never felt comfortable being alone with them until they were about five, and that feeling extended to Felicia and Edward. I doubt that it will ever really leave.

Ma Bell Again

Pay Phones

What an experience. From a farm to a small town to a city, to another city (with the year or so on the west coast in between), to Toronto. I was not really prepared for it. I had been to Toronto and lots of times to Detroit, Chicago, Minneapolis and Saint Paul and Vancouver, but had never really lived and worked in a large city. It was different and I guess a real education.

I was assigned to work in Pay Phones at 2150 Bloor West. It was within shouting distance of where Jane Street ended at Bloor. This department was considered the bottom of the sales ladder in the company, but it generated more money than any other area except the Yellow pages. I found it very interesting and challenging.

The Boss

There was a third level in charge. He was a grouchy ex-army officer, cloistered in his private office with the door always closed. People skills - zero. His private secretary sat at a desk just outside his closed door. The Bell ranked supervisors by level. Third level was pretty high and paid well. Fourth or fifth was next to a VP. I think even business office managers were only third level. We also had a second level, Henry, who oversaw only two or three people who called on the city, big business, and the province.

My boss, who towered over about six of us, had the city divided into areas. There were a couple of secretaries and a gang of guys with special trucks who collected the money from the coin boxes. We had a lot of brass for a small number of people. The coin room, where all the boxes were deposited and the coins counted, was part of our office and separated by a glass wall and a locked door. They also had their own second level supervisor. Our little gang also had three green cars at our disposal, and with approval, could go to Tilden and rent one if needed.

The First Day

The bus episode to get to my first day of actual work is another story (see *Bus Step*). When I arrived on Monday morning, I met my boss. I was introduced to my coworkers, assigned a desk, given a tour, and spent the week getting acclimatized. The following Monday I went to work. I went out the front door, briefcase in one hand and a map in the other. I knew where I wanted to go but had no idea where it was or how to get there. Henry and two other people came out at the same time. Henry had been around for a couple of years and looked after the larger accounts. Many days when I needed a car, I had to take the red rocket because they were using the green cars.

Promotion

I was promoted and reported directly to Henry. He treated me as a human being and never questioned my activities. I looked after Maple Leaf Gardens, the subway, Exhibition grounds, the TTC, Eaton's and Simpsons (both very large department stores right downtown), the Island Airport, Pearson Airport, the City of Toronto, and a few others that I cannot recall. It was actually very exciting and interesting. Remember that pay telephones in those areas made a lot of money for the Bell. Most phone coin boxes were emptied monthly, or maybe twice a month in a busy spot. I arranged for some that had to be emptied daily.

I got to wander all around Eaton's and Simpsons, the two largest stores in Canada, and try to find a spot where a pay phone was needed, then try to convince the store management to give us the space. I had the privilege of touring every corner of Maple Leaf Gardens. Take my word for it, that is one interesting and massive old building.

One year I spent every day that the Exhibition was on just touring around the rides and the midway and got tired of the noise and watching the ferris wheel, the roller coaster, and all those other rides. I would roam around and decide where phones were needed and then send in an order to the installation department to have them put one in. I also checked to see if the phone booths were clean and the phones worked. If not I just called repair and asked them to look after the problem. When the event was finished, the phones would come out again. We would look at the revenue, number of calls and number of people who attended the event and decide whether the phones would go back in the same places the next year or locate them in some other spot. It was a neat job but must be changed today with the advent of so many cell phones. It really was a neat job.

Due to my promotion, I ended up in an office at University and Richmond. I liked it and had a good manager. Like me, he did not buy into the system and was much younger than most. We got along well. I called on medium sized businesses all over downtown Toronto. I have already stated how great the training was.

The Course

Well, they developed a new five-week course, and it was to be tried out on people in Large Business Sales. The course was to hold five people for five weeks. Bell was serious about training. Four were picked from various areas around the province, and my boss asked if I could go as the fifth person, although I was not in Large Sales. The course was in Hamilton. We stayed, all five of us and the instructor, in a fancy hotel, everything paid of course, plus our salaries and travelling, as we went home each weekend. Just think of the cost.

The course was held in one of the conference rooms. The other four guys, no females in Bell sales then, were older than me. One dropped out, or rather was sent home partway through. I ate the stuff up and ended up with the highest mark. When I got back to work in Toronto, the training paid off in increased sales, so I guess they knew what they were doing. I did well and ended up being sent up to the office at Eglinton and Yonge. It was also with a rather young guy as manager and things were fine until the department was amalgamated and moved to another Bell office across the street.

The New Boss

My new boss was Anthony and a good friend of Henry. After working with two great guys and all that training, I get another character who likes the system - and when you go with the flow, you do not appreciate anyone who rocks the boat. To this day I think big business and big government still work the same. I guess I had a reputation, albeit short, for not going with the flow and rocking the boat.

Anthony and I did not see eye to eye from the day I stepped into his department. I liked the company, had lots of friends, certainly needed the job, and intended to make a career with the Bell. The pay was getting much better, the stock options were great, and I really liked what I did, but the bureaucracy was making me ill.

I got big red rashes on my hands and part of my arms. Creams, lotions, and other remedies were to no avail. One doctor thought it was psoriasis. I finally went to a specialist. He diagnosed it as caused by nerves. I got some special medication, and between that and realizing what the problem was, it started to disappear and never returned. I decided to keep doing my job; not pull the plug on anyone, but not take any crap either.

The Bell had a yearly personnel review. Every employee got an evaluation form, filled it out and turned it in. The form of course was about your performance. Your manager filled in his or her side and supposedly the two agreed, or they were supposed to help you correct any deficiencies in your performance.

I had worked for Anthony for a few months or so when review time came up. His department seemed to work much like the fiasco in pay phones, so I was not comfortable. We agreed to disagree on my evaluation sheet. You see, both the employee and manager had to sign it, agreeing that the evaluation was correct, and the manager turned the forms into his manager, or third level.

If an employee did not sign in agreement with the manager's evaluation, almost unheard of as a manager, you were in trouble. Most employees were like sheep and signed no matter what it said. Guess they all needed or wanted their jobs badly. I had two little kids, had just built a cottage, really wanted a future at the Bell and needed a job as badly as everyone else. I never heard of anyone else who refused to sign an evaluation report.

I knew that he could not fire me without getting himself in a lot of hot water. Bell did not fire people who were doing their job, especially people they had spent a fortune on in training. I had only been there five years and I bet it would take another five before I would financially contribute to their bottom line, considering the money they spent to train me this far. Besides, I strongly disagreed with his evaluation. I cannot remember his last name, but I can still see me sitting in his office. At the end of our conversation he said, "If you do not change your attitude, one day someone will ask you to leave."

I cannot recall exactly my words of course, but I said something to the effect of "Whenever you feel that I am not doing my job, just tell me and I can clean out my desk very quickly." At that time, you did what

Ma Bell knew was good for you and just followed orders, went along with the system, and got promoted. No one stood up to the system and survived. It seemed too big a mountain for me, and I was not prepared to climb until retirement. A few months later I told Anthony that I was cleaning out my desk. I think he was ecstatic, your mother thought I was crazy, and I think has never forgiven me for abandoning a life of security. I started Funny Services. Funny how life unfolds.

A Car

The Dodge

I never owned a Cadillac, a Mercedes, or a Jaguar, but I did own a BMW. Not just a BMW, but a brand new one. The era that I am talking about, all of those would have been far out of range of the average person. Of course, today, our Saab 9000 fits in very well with most of the above. In 1960 it would have been unthought of for me, had it been around. My BMW was not quite a 760, nor even a 320i, nor a 2002. It was an Isetta. Now if you don't know what an Isetta is, or rather was, then you are, as Sam may say, automobile deprived. Let out the clutch!

We had a 1949 Dodge. They came in two models, a K-car size, and a large job. Ours was a large version with fluid drive. Fluid drive was a neat Chrysler innovation at that time. It had a manual three speed shifter on the column, but you could leave it in third gear at a stop light, not put in the clutch, and it would screech away. When the light turned green, and within a block or so, it could catch the kid on the bike (with training wheels on), who started out beside you. It was a big, comfortable car, reliable, but don't be in a hurry.

The monster ran well, was almost devoid of rust, and looked pretty good. We filled it with everything your mother could think of to pack, and headed for a visit to see mom, dad and Marlene in Victoria, B.C. One of your mother's coworkers, a guy who bought a new car every couple of years, said, "you're not going to drive to B.C. in an eleven-year-old car, are you?" We said, "Well, ya, that happens to be what we own, can afford, and we are going to sell it there and fly back." "Good luck!"

The Dodge did its job admirably well, except for a small body repair that I had done on the tail end, just below the passenger side taillight. It had a rust hole that I filled in with whatever and painted over. I was not and am not a body repair guy. Many days later, the stuff was still fairly tacky in Moosejaw.

Getting off the ferry in Kootenay, B.C, we turned the wrong way, and carooming around the side of a narrow mountain road, the exhaust pipe decided that this trip was just too long. The noise bouncing off the rock wall of the mountain would put a modern rock drummer to shame. Other than that, we made it just fine. We sold the Dodge through an ad in the paper. Cars in B.C. were more expensive, because they were all made in good old Ontario, or somewhere east. Shipping was pricey then. The spot under the taillight had hardened sufficiently that it looked just fine. We flew home carless.

The Chrysler

We lived on Fairholme, by Lawrence and Bathurst. I worked at 2150 Bloor St. West, a hop, skip and a jump from Bloor and Jane. Get out your Toronto map. It's a day's walk just to get there and back home. If you drove, at 41¢ a gallon for gas, it would cost a fortune to drive. We went for six weeks without a car. Yes, the bus was close. Toronto had its subway, but I could not take the bus or the subway cars where and when I wanted.

We bought a 1951 Chrysler Windsor coupe. It ran like a clock, was the size of a grandfather's clock compared to a watch, and actually used gas. I really liked it. It was big, prestigious looking, a step up from the Dodge, fluid drive phony automatic, and never caused a problem that I can recall.

Now we are getting close to my BMW. The Chrysler was getting hard to steer. I was afraid that it may suffer severe heart, lower extremity problems or, God forbid, a car stroke. We decided to sell it and get something else. A friend that I worked with told me about this dealership on Bloor Street, that just started to sell this neat little import that would just about fit in the trunk of the Chrysler, would seat three people, was popular as heck in Europe, and would be great to drive back and forth to work. He did not drive one of these funny little things. But I went and looked anyway.

The BMW Isetta

I thought the Isetta was the cutest little automobile (or reasonable facsimile) that I had laid eyes on. I could stand and lean on its canvas rollback sunroof. Its only door was in the front, the engine was in the back, and the driving wheels were so close together that most people still think the Isetta had only one rear wheel. It was cute as a bug in a rug. I, for who knows why, never cottoned to the standard Fords and Chevrolets of the day. I always leaned towards the Hudsons, Packards and Studebakers. This Isetta thing was right up my alley. I cut a cheque for $1200, I think, and drove off in my shiny, new Isetta.

The VW Beetle became the Bug, but the Isetta looked more like a bug than any other mode of transportation I can think of. The dinky steering wheel was in the middle, attached to the door, so it swung out when the door opened. The four speed (I think) gear shift was a small stick on the left side, just under the window. You operated it by crooking your elbow with your hand pointing upwards to grab this three- or four-inch stick. This little stick moved the widget that moved the chain, which attached the motor to the transmission.

The side window opened, should you want summer air or winter air to keep the cabin ice free, by moving the front half towards the back. No bumper on the back, but it did have two chrome thingamajigs sticking out on either side of the front door. They looked more like two handles than a bumper. They were great to grab onto and pull the car into position if it did not get parked right.

If I recall, I think it did have an excuse for a heater, a VW type heater that worked off the hot air from the engine. Have you ever heard of a one-cylinder engine getting hot enough in a Canadian winter to actually produce warm air? I don't think so. This was a machine for a real he-man, a real outdoors man. Perhaps that is why my fingers cause problems in the winter. You got chilly hands holding onto that steering wheel, even with gloves on. Oh, and the pedals, big shoes could get all three at once if you were not careful. The seat was a thin board, covered in material over an equally thin padding. The battery lived on the seat.

Summer may have been a different story, but we got this can on wheels in the cold weather. Normal cars made a path in the snow. The Isetta did not have the same wheelbase, and the rear wheels kept wanting to slip in and out of the ruts. Winter driving was challenging. It did have its redeeming side though. We filled it up with gas and the most we spent when it was completely dry was $1.13. I think that tank lasted all week. Not bad, eh?

The car was made in England, and the BMW name was put on because they supplied the engine. The same engine was used in one of their motorcycles. A one-cylinder engine may be great to move a bike, but in the Isetta, it was not exactly a machine to gather speeding tickets. Going down a hill I nearly got the speedometer needle to hit 50 mph. Talk about a thrill! The sunroof was a neat feature, except that in winter all it did was add to the lack of warmth. It was canvas, and you just folded it back in its track.

The little bug was more like a bubble, and cold mornings were a real blast. It was parked in the driveway by Moisha's four door Ford. Fords were so wide that year the Ministry of Transportation (MTO) told Ford if they made the next model another inch or so wider, that they would have to put clearance lights on the sides, just like trucks, as they were getting that large. The two cars, or one car and a bubble, made quite the scene together.

I drove it to work so I would go out around 6:30 or so in the morning and start it. We started at eight, so I needed a bit of time. My BMW would fire one little cough and go silent for several seconds. Thinking it had given up, I turned the key again, only to find out that it was still breathing. It only fired every few seconds, giving a strange cough. It would carry on like that for ten or fifteen minutes until it warmed up enough to purr like it should. Purr is being too kind. Single cylinder engines, even from BMW, don't purr. They lurch, rattle, and growl a bit, but no purring. There was just no driving it for several minutes until it warmed up.

So, we lurched, chugged, and bounced. I have no recollection of the stares of other drivers, but did I care? I had a brand new, shiny car, well at least four wheels and a bubble, and it was as long as the hood of the Chrysler we just disposed of. My peers at work were not as enthused. Perhaps though they were more enthused as they had a reason for a daily prank.

The Prank

I came out of the office one afternoon, and my BMW was facing the wrong way. I am sure that four, strong guys could just pick it up and turn it around, which is what they did. Another time, it was missing altogether. Who the heck would steal an Isetta? It was not exactly the most popular getaway car with the bank robbing crowd. Well, it was not far, just around the corner, out of sight. I look back fondly at the joy my little bubble gave all my coworkers.

Cute little car, but it was cold, took forever to warm up, did not track well in the snow, and was noisy and bumpy. Short hops around town were fine, but one would have to have far more beers than I drank then to even consider letting this can near the 401. Just imagine the headline. "Truck runs over strange, slow moving object on 401 between Avenue Road and Bayview." Then the story, "Once the MTO crew have shoveled up the remaining tin, what looks like a bit of gas, and a red substance that perhaps could be blood, the whole lot, about enough scrap to fill a large wheelbarrow, will be taken for the forensic lab for examination."

Sadly, we both agreed, well I think we did, making that a real memorable occasion rarely repeated over the next forty years or so, that the Isetta had to go. My love affair with my BMW was to end after only six short weeks. Sadly, but perhaps not, I bounced and rattled back to the dealer. Ed and Gord were not close enough, and anyway they long ago tired of trying to wean me from my desire to own at least one of every weird vehicle made. In earlier years, just to satisfy them I owned a 1938 Ford and a 1948 Mercury, as well as the Dodge and Chrysler. What I am leading up to is that what I really wanted to replace my blue BMW bubble with, was a Jag. [Editor's note: he never continued the story]

Bell and Funny Services

I always had an entrepreneurial streak and many times wondered how my bosses got to where they were, so I started my own business a couple of times. When my partner, Ron, and I left the Bell and started Funny Services, we were aware that the Bell was embarking on Direct Distance Dialling (DDD). At that time, around 1962/1963, when you wanted to make a long distance call you dialled zero for the operator and told her the city and number you wished to reach. She placed the call for you. All phones were still dial and some manual with no dial at all.

Area codes were just being set up for North America and phone companies in both countries were working on a system of DDD, meaning that the customer would directly dial their own long-distance calls, using 1 to get into the long distance (LD) network and then dial the area code, followed by the local phone number. Long distance was terribly expensive, and this was one way to speed it up and cut down costs by eliminating the need for operators.

Bell, and probably all the companies, were paranoid about a rash of wrong numbers. They were sure that the public was not smart enough to dial that many numbers and not make a ton of mistakes. We approached the local manager at the Bell, who oversaw the conversion in Toronto, to see if there was any business available in training or advertising that we could get involved in. After all, we did know a bit about the company.

Turns out that they had a program in the works to train the management staff in the LD section, the Business Office, and all the other departments, then these people would train their respective staff. The only problem they had was that they had no idea how to do it and were checking outside agencies for help and ideas. Ron and I offered to come up with some ideas and get back to them.

We decided on a flip chart, using a character that Ron thought up and drew called Miss Dialled. On the flip chart she explained the process and all the whys and wherefores of DDD with its advantages and pitfalls. The guys at the Bell liked it and gave the go ahead. We spent days, weeks, I cannot remember, developing the pages and taking them to the Bell to make sure we were covering all their concerns.

Today it would be done on fancy overheads, tapes, VCRs, or computers. None of that stuff was available then. Our flip chart was in a binder that sat on a desk and was moderated by a Bell manager to a small group. We made up a patter to go along with each page.

When the final product was approved, we had umpteen copies made, laminated, and delivered to Bell. I am not sure if they used it throughout the whole company or not. I just recall that it was a coup, and a big job for a small advertising firm run by two guys with no training in advertising or training programs. We charged them what we thought we could justify and what they would pay given our experience. It was a bunch of money then. I bet today that kind of project would run into many thousands of dollars.

I had kept the books and records. Sadly, I turfed most of them as being insignificant and just taking up space as we moved on in life. Not sure if anything at all remains here, save a picture of my original office and perhaps a business card. I often wonder if Ron, who I have not run into for many years, still has our original copy of Miss Dialled. Fortunately, the problems envisaged by the Bell in DDD did not materialize. I wonder if our training package can take credit?

Auntie Rae's Ninetieth*

Aunt Lola and alcohol were like oil and water. They did not mix! She would not allow alcohol anywhere near her house, although in later years as an adult she did allow me, albeit with a sermon attached, the privilege of putting my six pack in her fridge when we went for a weekend visit.

Aunt Lola, or more properly Laura, was the middle child. Auntie Rae was the oldest and my mother the youngest of the three. Those two aunts were very different, but I loved them both, and they also loved one another deeply, although on the surface one would certainly think otherwise. It was the occasion of the ninetieth birthday for Auntie Rae, for which I believe my cousin Helen, Aunt Lola's daughter, had made the arrangements.

The festivities were held in the yard at Lola's. It was a great summer day and lots of friends and relatives showed up. The local paper had also been alerted and a reporter and camera guy were expected. To show their deep concern for one another, Auntie Rae commented that when the photographer arrived, he would probably think Laura was the subject of his mission as she, although being only eighty-five or thereabouts, looked much older.

There was a large table parallel to the big Walnut tree across from the doorway into the house. One item on the table was a large punch bowl full of, I suppose, just whatever an Aunt Lola would put in. Punch. Ed had a mickey of rye. We discussed our aunt's love of booze and sort of challenged one another to a bit of chicanery. I dared Ed to dump the bottle into the punch bowl, and so with her back to the table but not more than a couple of feet away, I engaged my dear aunt in conversation. I should have gotten an acting award as with a straight face I completely ignored the antics behind her back, as my nephew laughed and made faces as the rye sloshed into the punch bowl. My poor unsuspecting and trusting aunt was oblivious to the deception, as a short time later she acknowledged how great the punch tasted.

Ask Ed, but I don't recall anyone else seeing or commenting on this addition to the punch. However, all those in attendance, and there were many including the reporter and camera person, agreed the punch was a hit. However, should you think it is great fun and a hoot to play such tricks on OLD PEOPLE, please think again and don't try it, as I know them all.

Colleen and 401

Lessons not to teach your children. My new three door Saab got smashed by a school bus [see 900 Saab Convertible], and I could not wait for the turbo that was coming, so I settled for a red 1977 Saab five door. You know the one, with the little quarter window behind the back door. A neat machine that I did not like when I first got it, but the longer I had it the more I loved it.

So, my teenage daughter and I (dates and ages are not my forte but she is not old enough to drive) are tooling along 401 just outside of Woodstock. Almost since Toronto there was an annoying Honda with a couple of kids in it, trying to keep up and then passing when traffic allowed. Here was this little tin box doing seventy to eighty miles an hour and keeping pace with me for miles and miles.

What an insult. I wanted to rid myself of this pesky mosquito and planted my foot permanently to the floor, all the time explaining to my daughter that one should not drive like those stupid kids in the Honda. Being older, more experienced and in a much safer vehicle, it was okay for me to drive at ninety miles per hour, weaving in and out of heavy traffic. The Honda was now history.

We crested the hill with the needle just over the 90-mph mark. In today's terminology I think that would be 150 kph. My heart stopped. There on the shoulder was not one but five Ontario Provincial Police (OPP) cruisers, all with roof flashers lighting the sky. Slamming brakes does not cut it in this situation so just release the gas and prepare to take your punishment. I don't use foul language, kids present or not, so not sure what I said to Colleen, but I let up on the gas pedal. And you know what? There is a Saab God. Those five cops had at least two speeders a piece to write up tickets for and they never even noticed me. The shoulder looked like a long parking lot with flashing lights as we flew by.

So, the moral for your kids? Don't speed, don't drive on the 401 near Woodstock, ignore Hondas, forget the above and drive a Saab.

A Trip to The Big City*

It was mid-afternoon, and the traffic gods were in a rare great mood. We never even stopped while merging onto the Don Valley. A little slow, but moving nevertheless. Shockingly it kept right on moving, not always fast, but never completely still, until the Yonge Street exit. From there for the next ten miles or so the only thing missing were parking meters. One can't expect those traffic gods to be benevolent all the time! In any event, I arrived at the pre-described ETA and hung around, drank coffee, and waited for Sam to finish his work duties.

The Chinese take-out, highly recommended by Sam's boss, did not measure up. We sat at one of the four tables, ate from the Styrofoam containers, and used the standard plastic utensils. Way too much food and most not at all edible. I must have made a bad menu choice. The Chinese tea was fine though, and Sam paid, so all was not bad. His rented quarters, just minutes away, while not lavish provided an actual night's sleep until that pesky racket shortly after six a.m.

We were stopped at the light when he explained. "The only problem after we turn left is crossing three lanes to get into the plaza to get to the GO station. Cross the bridge, get your ticket and go up the stairs to platform three, and that will take you right into Union Station." The area was surprisingly calm and devoid of crowds. After a return senior's ticket and then a regular one way, the half-awake young man at the ticket window finally got it right, and for $3.30 I was cleared for a ride right downtown to Union Station.

Aside from two women, one young and one middle age and of Korean origin I think, but perhaps second or third generation Canadians, the platform was empty. A bit windy, damp, and chilly, but no sign or noise of an impending train. I stood next to the little windowed shelter. It had doors at either end and provided a throughway for when the platform became a throng of impenetrable bodies, all wanting to be the first to get on. A young lady entered and stood motionless at the far end of the shelter, only her thumbs moving to create a rhythm on her smartphone. No noise, just a chilly wind, no train and no more people. After all, it was all of 7:30 a.m. on a Friday morning.

Was this what the Exodus looked like from the desert side? Except they had a river or swamp to cross and these people had stairs, but suddenly come they did. Swarms, all shapes and forms of dress, men, and women. They kept coming until the platform was swamped and

176

people rushed through the little shelter and out the far side. I recall from my subway days that regulars get to know which car to get on to be able to get off at the exact spot for their stairs or exit. Those people rushing through the doors knew exactly where to be for the right car and were heading down the platform for the proper spot. Just like Pat from *Wheel of Fortune*, "Okay, this is your spot, stop right here."

A tall, well dressed young lady stationed herself next to me at my post beside the door to the shelter. She remained speechless and motionless, except for her fingers on her Blackberry. Very intense and other than pulling her coat collar up against the wind, all concentration was on that little hunk of plastic and miniature electrical bits.

They kept coming, wave after wave. Soon, passage outside the shelter was impassable. A mob of bodies filled the space from the shelter right to the edge of the platform. I suspect every nation on earth was represented, one of the neat things making Toronto what it is. Like a football line it is hard to break through, so those destined for the far end of the platform had to go through the shelter.

The door was akin to a revolving door, only someone was going to get whacked as it partially closed, and another hand reached to pull it open again. Many hands were full, both for many people, so opening a door became a real challenge. Many, being patriotic Canadians, had one arm full of books, briefcases, and clutched a Tim Hortons cup in the other. Being very close to the door and with it opening towards me, I became a door man. Sort of unique I thought, a GO train door man. I liked my new job.

The tips were numerous, being many smiles and thank yous from every race, creed and colour. And this is cold, heartless Toronto. Only one exception, and that was from an obvious really newcomer to Canada. I don't think he was ungrateful or whatever, just unused to and awed by someone who would hold a door for a perfect stranger.

Stick in Toronto long enough and they will learn that friendliness is the rule rather than the exception. Being known for our politeness is a great thing, I think. Don't you? And people think Toronto is cold, callous, and unfriendly. What a misconception, and this observation comes from a person who does not live there and never was a real Torontonian so has no drum to beat.

A surprising twist took place on my short journey. I sat on an aisle seat on the top level. Across the aisle sat two obvious friends and business acquaintances, along with another gentleman and a young lady. All were deeply engaged in their separate world of smartphones. No conversation from them, nor anyone else, until some chatter breaking the silence rang up from the seats by the bulkhead at the stairway. Immediately, one of the fellows across the aisle popped up and turned his head to the source of the chatter. He was a stern looking person to start with, so his reprimand was not completely surprising. "Please be quiet, don't you see the sign? This is a quiet car." The chatter ceased, he sat down and returned to his tiny screen and miniature keyboard.

Wow! Who knew? But there, posted clearly just above the head of the guilty party, was a sign signifying that this was indeed a "Silent Car", from Monday to Friday, 6:00 a.m. until 9:30 a.m., and again in the afternoon. I sat while the workers jostled for position to hurry off the train. The admonisher, passing the noisy culprits, exchanged unfriendly words. Across the aisle, to everyone and no one, another female voice offered, "they always talk."

The walk from Front Street up Bay to Queen was considerably further than I remembered. I think I had forgotten about having to pass Wellington and maybe even Adelaide. At the corner of Bay and Queen a man was lying on the grate, covered in newspapers. People walked around his shape, both he and the crowds oblivious to one another, as if this was a normal fixture during the morning rush. As friendly and helpful as most Torontonians are, this sight seemed like a cruel reminder of why I was heading to the Ontario Non-Profit Housing Conference, just a couple of sleeping bags away from his corner.

900 Saab Convertible*

[Modified with permission from Alex's story *Deal of a Lifetime* published in the December-January 2018 issue of *Our Canada*]

The words of Mother St. Leo from grade 7 still stick in my mind. "If you spend as much time on your schoolwork as you do drawing cars, you will be better off!" Despite that admonition, I was still top of the class. At some point I did stop drawing cars, but I never lost my interest in them. As a young man, however, I was never interested in the ordinary offerings from the "big three" automakers, like my older brothers were. As opposed to Ford, General Motors, and Chrysler, my choices were Studebaker, Hudson, and later MGs-style Fiats. For a short time, I even had a BMW Isetta live in my driveway, but Saab has been the manufacturer nearest and dearest to my heart for quite a long while now.

For some reason the technology, strange design and quirky features really attracted me, so when Saab first hit here, 1976 or 1977 I think, I bought one. After a test drive, I was hooked and in deep trouble, as I had never spent that much money on a car before. Did I mention that I drove it home before telling my wife I bought it? Not smart, I admit.

Too bad Saab was not better understood, as they were billed by *Road & Track* magazine, pretty much the Bible of car enthusiasts, as the best winter car in the world, until the rest of the pack caught up. The company probably innovated more bits and pieces now found on most cars today than any other recent manufacturer. Unfortunately, they never boasted about their accomplishments, nor took full advantage of all their innovations. Since my first Saab I have owned seven or eight, can't recall, but they have all been great cars.

Saab has also been noted many times as also the safest car in the world. I can vouch for that, having been involved in a collision during one of those strange, late-spring blizzards. I could barely make out the vehicle ahead, spinning its wheels, trying in vain to get up a hill. I was having no trouble but did not want to chance passing in such lousy conditions. I backed up to give him room to back down and turn off onto a side road. He was having a real hard time, so I pulled over, lights and flashers on, and helped him maneuver through the slush. Once done, I returned to my car and was just putting on my seat belt when I glanced in the mirror and all I could see was bright yellow. A school bus rammed me from behind. It was travelling at a brisk clip as the driver tried to get up the hill and ended up putting my car into the guardrail. Thankfully, other than being a bit shook up, the bus driver and the students were unhurt. My Saab did exactly what it was designed to do upon impact - fold like an accordion but keep the cabin intact. Unlike my poor car, which was a write-off, I came out without a scratch.

I loved that car, so when the 900T convertible came out in 1986, I wanted one. I had never owned a convertible before, but the price for that beautiful 900T was simply out of my league. Besides, the very small handful allocated for Canada were gone in a blink of an eye.

Fast-forward to 2016, when my youngest kid Sam, an even nuttier Saab guy than me, told me about a recent find that he said could not be passed up. It was one of those mythical deals you always hear about, but never actually happen to you. The car in question was a 1988 Saab Classic 900 Turbo convertible. Part of an estate sale, it had been stored for years, had low mileage, and was in great condition. Long story short, Sam and I are now its proud co-owners.

This model is one of the few vehicles that I think will appreciate over the years, so I took the purchase price from my investment account. After all, I had to satisfy my wife Shirley that it was not only a sensible purchase, but an investment. It is also registered with movie companies and event planners, so Sam and I can make a few extra bucks and demonstrate to Shirley that our purchase really was a smart move. Although the Saab is extremely reliable, you can't avoid normal wear and tear on a vehicle, but we keep maintenance costs low as I do much of the work myself.

Being an optimist, I think one day Shirley will admit it was a great deal. It truly is a beautiful car - it's in tremendous shape, handles better than many sports cars, is fun to drive, goes fast and is very safe. I can't wait until spring to get it out of hiding and put the top down again. It's a wonderful, wind-in-your-hair machine!

PICTURES FROM ALEX' STORIES

Alex on the farm

Muggs

Alex and Uncle Alex

*Alex at Cadets (front middle). In typical Alex style,
he's the odd one out with his hat tipped back.*

Alex in his Funny Services office

Laura, Rachel, and Flowilla at Auntie Rae's 90th birthday

Saab Convertible

QUOTES ABOUT DREAMING

I don't think it is true that if you tell someone about your dreams or wishes that they will not come true. Don't think it makes any difference. Lots of times we share secrets with friends, or family. Wishes & dreams are just secrets that we want to come true. Other people have no control over the outcome; only you & God. Others can influence them, agree with them, or ridicule you for having them, but they cannot change your dreams or wishes. I don't see any problem with changing wishes. Kids change their dreams & wishes almost weekly. As you get older your dreams and wishes change. Sometimes we wish for something that is not good for us, or impossible to attain, so we should not be upset if it does not happen. Unfortunately, we all wish for things sometimes that are silly, or impossible. Only as we gain maturity does it finally dawn on us. Sometimes maturity comes at an early age and sometimes not at all, but no matter how old we get, we should never quit wishing and dreaming. (1998)

Regarding a dream keeper necklace he gave Felicia: Dream keepers are great little characters. It gives you a place to store your secrets in. Like confiding in a friend who will tell no one else, but if you change your wish, you can replace it and your friend will forget all about the first one. Does that make sense? (1998)

I went by the store today where I got your little dream holder and I wondered if it still has something in it. Dreams are great things that we have but they are usually passive, like wishes. We dream about things we think we want but really take no pains to get them. As you get older dreams turn into goals. When one is old enough everyone should have goals in life. Goals are like dreams except you really work on getting there and most other things are set aside until that goal or dream is achieved. Most of us really do not know what our goals are until we get older and then sometimes our dreams turn into goals, or we get new dreams that become our goals. Anyway, keep something to dream about in that little holder and if you really want it, keep working on it, thinking about it, and one day it will not be just a dream, but reality. That's my philosophy lesson for today. (2000)

I have concluded that I am a dreamer. I am great at envisioning things. I can see things in the future, in my mind, and imagine the outcome. Does not always happen but, in the end, life seems to work out just fine. For some reason, my mind is always busy. It just seems to race from one thing to the next with ideas popping up all over the place. Does yours work like that? Trying to stay focussed on one thing at a time is a problem. I will be concentrating on fixing this little wooden guy on wheels, and out of the blue, a great idea for the church jumps into my head. I have to stop and write it down, and then I start to develop that idea and my concentration on fixing the car is out the window. Now I never took psychology, but both your parents did and when I think about things that I have done in the past, and the course my life has taken, I now know why. Wish I had known long ago how my mind works. It may have prevented some mistakes but never would have stopped me from dreaming. When you read this, you will probably think, what a crack pot gramps is, must be getting old. But someday you may say, wow "he really knew what he was talking about." Well, maybe not, but time will tell. (2001)

I read something the other day that made me think of you, so I am passing it along. You will like it. From Proverbs: "without a vision, the people perish". In my mind a vision is just a dream. And from something from Walt Disney, "If you don't have a dream, how are you going to have a dream come true?" Neat, eh? (2001)

QUOTES ABOUT GOAL SETTING

One way to really get these things on the go is to set goals, write them down, and stick to them. I think the secret is to bite off a little at a time. (I will set aside 15 minutes each day to write. Fifteen minutes is just over 1% of the available time we have each twenty-four hours) sounds achievable, and over a year that is over 90 hours, or about a dozen eight-hour days, without even a coffee break. If it were only as easy as doing the calculation. However, for some people it does work. (1998)

Time sure goes, and unless one sets goals and works to achieve them, nothing seems to get done. (2004)

MEMORIES OF IMMEDIATE FAMILY MEMBERS

Shirley Jackson, wife

The Date

I had been planning on going to a square dance at a church with my girlfriend, which was about twenty minutes outside of Windsor. Unfortunately, our ride to get there was no longer available, but I found out I could get a ride with Alex in his car. I wasn't overly keen with this arrangement as I had only met him once before. Meanwhile, Alex had been working late that day and didn't really want to go to the dance, but as I found out later, he did want to go on a date with me, so we went. At the end of the evening, I accidentally dropped my gloves in his car and left them behind. In order to get my gloves back, I agreed to go on another date with Alex. The rest is history, and that history lasted more than sixty years.

Hotel

We had been married for six months and Alex was doing his stint in the business office for Ma Bell in London, ON. On his birthday, March 17, 1958, I had a meeting to attend and Alex went out with some guys from work to celebrate, and to drink some green beer. He was to phone me around 10 p.m. to pick him up, but no call came then. I don't remember when he finally phoned, but it was probably near midnight. We both had to go to work in the morning.

I asked him where he had been, and he said "furst of all we went to the totel." I started laughing and asked him where he was then. I don't recall if someone drove him home or I picked him up. The next day he did not feel the best but went to work anyway, and the girls in the business office felt sorry for him and covered some of his calls. I don't think he went to the 'totel' again while we were in London.

MG Rust

Our '58 MG was a great car except the body was subject to rust. Alex decided to fix the front fenders and we put the car in the basement for a few days. We had a large opening which consisted of three wooden doors. One was all by itself where we entered and exited the basement. The other two were attached together with hinges, and when all were opened was large enough to drive a car through.

Anyway, the front fenders behind the headlights were in bad shape and Alex repaired them. I can't remember exactly what he used, but probably plaster or something similar. When they were sanded and painted the car looked super, but unfortunately the fenders did not withstand rain. They were repaired again, this time with proper material. The smoothing of the work was a lot harder than the first time, but at least they didn't deteriorate in the rain.

MG Holes

In February 1975 Sam was just a year old. Back then cops would pull over older vehicles to check for floorboards with holes in them. I was coming home from bowling and I saw a police car behind me going down George Street. I made a quick left on Romaine hoping by the time I got to Lansdowne and Lock Streets, he would have had to wait for the light at George and Lansdowne. I was not lucky, and he pulled me over just east of Lock Street. Of course, there were holes in the floor. I explained to him that I was going away for two weeks, for Sam and me to visit Alex's mother in Victoria, B.C., and my husband would fix the problem while I was away.

He said this would be okay, and to bring the car to the police station after my return and someone would check it out. This was done, but Alex's mother decided to come back with me, and she was sitting in the front passenger seat with Sam on her lap (*you could do this back then*). A police officer came out and checked the driver's side floor and everything was okay. I told Alex he didn't bother to check the passenger side, mainly because it was occupied by an elderly lady. Alex said, "you mean there were holes there too?" He fixed them also and I was never stopped again.

Pool

We purchased our twenty-four-foot circular pool in 1971. In 1980 we needed a new liner and decided to move the pool closer to the house, with part of it in the ground rather than have it all above. There are sixteen curved pieces which sit on the bottom, and the steel pool sides fit into a groove, and the railing is then put on the top. The side is in one continuous piece with a blue side and a white side. We had had the blue side out and decided to put the white one out as the house was green and the white would look better. Anyway, I guess we both (Alex and I) figured if these sixteen pieces fit together you would have a round pool. Not so as we found out when we tried to put the liner in. We measured it and it was about twenty-two feet one way and twenty-six the other.

Someone told Alex that if there was some water in the pool, the liner would be easier to manipulate. We started to fill it and as it was dished in the middle, we had about two and a half feet of water in the centre, and about a foot at the edges. A man told Alex that he would come over about 7:30 a.m. to see if he could make it rounder, but the water had to be removed first. Alex rented a submersible pump and put it in, only to find out the pump would not work, so he entered the pool to retrieve the pump.

Because water had been sitting for about two weeks the bottom was pretty slimy, and Alex could not move from the middle, and the water was not deep enough to swim to the side. He said it took him about half an hour to reach the side by taking his hand and rubbing the bottom to get rid of the slime, and then putting his foot there and gradually made it to the side. The pool was never really round after that but better than it had been. Colleen was taking an extra credit in high school at the time and Sam, Steven and I had gone to Victoria to help Alex's mother get settled after she had moved, so no one was home to witness this event. We've had lots of laughs about it though.

Steve Jackson, son

Dad was always great for giving out advice and helped Sandra and I with projects around the house, including building a shed five years ago. My dad's stories were the best; he had many to tell and had a special knack for writing them. Several years ago, he gave Colleen, Sam, and me a book of them which we will treasure. Nicholas is looking forward to reading them.

Workbench

When I was young my dad built me a workbench next to his, as I loved doing many of the same things that dad did. We were always fixing things around the house and the car. I learned a lot from him. Occasionally things weren't as expected. I remember that we had a brake that was stuck on a car that had been sitting, and we needed to remove the drum. We cut it off with a torch only to find out that it was held on with a nut we hadn't seen!

Patio

When I was twelve, I was proud to be entrusted with the task of mixing the cement for the backyard patio. Before I had my driver's license, I was also given the responsibility of driving our station wagon around the backyard carrying loads to dad.

Spending Time

When I was about fifteen, I belonged to the rocket model club. My dad helped me make several rockets, and we spent many fond hours launching the rockets and sometimes looking for them. I also remember morning runs to Burnham's Woods. Those runs were fun; it makes me think of the bike rides I do with Nicholas.

Driving

For some reason, I was the first person in the family to drive dad's brand new 1977 Saab. I felt privileged. I ended up with that car when he was done with it and had it for many years.

Working

My father had a business. I remember helping him fix cash registers and worked with him on one of my Co-op terms in university. I spent many hours in the backyard at my parents' house building, fixing things and doing landscaping.

Tinkering

Dad was always a tinkerer. I don't recall him building anything large for Colleen and me, no doubt due to time constraints. He put a lot of effort into things for the grandkids, such as Felicia's schoolhouse and a rocking horse for Nicholas.

Canoeing

A little before Nicholas was around, Sandra and I invited our dads on a canoe trip. My father had done that sort of thing before, and Sandra's dad hadn't, but he was fairly active. Unfortunately. his limited canoeing experience showed when they got in the canoe, and they tipped while still at the dock! What a start to the trip, all soaking wet.

My father-in-law was uncomfortable sitting up on the seat, so he spent most of the time sitting on the bottom of the canoe, with my dad doing the bulk of paddling. I will never forget that trip.

Colleen Ketcheson, daughter

My dad was an extremely modest man who believed in fairness, honesty, being proper and never swearing. He was a dreamer, yet he rarely acted on those dreams because he had a family. He volunteered extensively and helped people in various capacities, especially the underdogs of the world. His disarming smile and sense of humour made him very popular. I will miss his endless stories, his advice, and our talks. I could talk to my father about anything, and he listened without judging, and he always believed in me. He never played favourites with my siblings; he knew we were all different and loved us equally. My dad and my husband Dwain got along wonderfully, and he loved his grandchildren Felicia and Edward so much, and always wished to have many more grandchildren. He was special to many people, and I feel so privileged to be his daughter.

Workbench

When I was a kid. I loved spending time in the basement with my dad, while he worked on various projects. Some were necessary and others were fun and relaxing, I am sure. He had a nice, long workbench and I loved it. My brother Steve and I got our very own workbenches on either side of my dad's, and we were in heaven. Now, I know I never really did much there except some crafts and play with my rocks and bottle cap collection. My dad I am sure knew that it was a waste of his time, but he did it anyway. Over the years he made me other things, such as a stool and an outside bike rack.

Presents

Most Christmas presents were purchased by my mom, but I did get some just from my dad. As a child I loved colouring, and his pet name for me was Doodle. So, one Christmas he bought me Doodleart. It was all the rage at the time and came in a canister with markers and four posters. The posters were a bit bigger than the normal size of paper. I loved colouring the intricate pictures, and they were all different. Another gift came when I was fifteen. It was a calculator, but not just any calculator. This was in the shape of a six-inch ruler and came in a cool slide case. Not the typical gift for a female. Another non-traditional gift was a bike repair kit. I was really thrilled with that as I loved riding my bike everywhere.

Any time my dad was away, either for business or visiting my grandma and aunt in Victoria, he always brought me home a gift. Because my name isn't overly common, one gift I received was a pack of yellow *Colleen* stickers, in various shapes and sizes. I also used daily until it fell apart, a canvas bag with pictures of cats on it. I loved it and carried it everywhere for years.

Alligator Pie

When I was twelve years old my dad took me to Trent University to hear Dennis Lee read from his new children's book, *Alligator Pie*. I was a bit older than the other kids who came with their parents, but I didn't care. I was thrilled that my dad loved me enough to take me, as he knew how much I loved poems. Not that my dad was cheap, but with three kids and his own business we were just surviving, but he still purchased a signed copy of *Alligator Pie* for me. I still have the book.

Stuffed Animals

This isn't something that was made for me, but it was laborious and very creative. I was in school and working part-time, and my dad had his own business and was quite busy, so this was one way for him to show me he was thinking of me. Many nights, from 1982-1983, I would come in late, and he had set up my stuffed animals into various scenarios in my bedroom. Some of these were quite creative and would have involved a lot of time. It always made me smile, especially if I had been having a bad day.

Selling

I loved spending time with my dad, and because he was busy with his own business, I took the opportunity whenever it presented itself. On a snow day from school when I was in grade ten, I went with my dad to Toronto and back. The roads were essentially okay, but the school bus I took had to traverse some slippery roads, hence my bus was cancelled. He owned his own cash register business at the time.

On 115 hwy on the way home we stopped at a new restaurant that was opening, and while I was right there at the table, my dad and the restaurant owner talked. We weren't there all that long, and before we left the owner had purchased a cash register system from my father. Back at the car I asked my dad how long he had known the man, and he said he had never met him before. That made me realize how good of a salesman my dad was, that I could be right there and not know that he had just made a cold call.

Driving

What better way to spend time with your dad, than having him teach you how to drive? Like everything he did, he was thorough and started at the beginning, which was for me to learn how a car worked, before I got behind the wheel. I learned to drive a standard vehicle in the middle of winter and had the most patient teacher ever. He had me practice moves that were challenging to a beginner. He wasn't at all nervous, at least on the outside.

Canoe Race

My dad and I did the yearly canoe race from Young's Point to Little Lake, which was almost twenty-six kilometers long, with several portages, including going around the Peterborough Liftlocks. We were entered in the mixed category, which meant a male and a female together, and there were dozens of canoes at the starting line from various categories. The first year we came in third place which was so impressive, until we noticed there were only three entries in our particular group.

Sewing Box

When I was in my late teens, I took up sewing. I had purchased many items that I needed, but one thing I didn't have was a sewing box. I never even considered getting one, which is a good thing, because for Christmas my dad made me a wooden sewing box. It had the words *Sew What* etched on the lid. It had a nice, heavy duty lid that had an inside slot for the current pattern I was working on. In the main section there was a top tray with a large glass knob to help with the lifting. There were many dowels to hold spools of thread. If you lifted out that tray, underneath there were three separate compartments. The middle section was empty, and the outer two had more dowels for thread spools. I used it for years, and about ten years ago I pulled out the dowels and now I use it for my embroidery box. The main reason for the switch was that not every spool of thread is the same size, so I couldn't fit in as much as I wanted!

Talks

When I was a teenager working part-time. I would come home later at night when the household was asleep, except for my dad. We would stay up late talking about a variety of issues, like current events, his business, school, or friends. Sometimes we would discuss my future opportunities, and he always made me feel like I could do anything that I wanted.

Smuckie

While we were dating, Dwain bought me a beautiful black, half Persian kitten, which charmed his way into my dad's heart. Because of his farm background he thought that cats belonged in a barn, and even though he once saved Smuckie from choking, he always seemed to just barely tolerate him. One day I was walking by a bedroom he was in, and heard him talking to Smuckie, and I knew his aloof behaviour was just an act. I never did tell him I knew he secretly liked my cat.

Creative Alex

My dad had a bathroom put in the basement, and constructed an outhouse around it, complete with a moon shape cut out on the door. In the backyard he created rock gardens, flower beds, stairs, and a fountain. In the kitchen he made a china cabinet for my mom. She was running out of space for her jewellery, so he made her a unique box. He also made a stable for her knitted nativity set. We bought a dwarf rabbit, and my dad made a wooden cage for her that was made for easy cleaning, as one end slid up.

Saint Theresa Medal

This is the note my dad gave me two days before my wedding. I put the charm on an unbreakable chain.

"Colleen, this is not much of a special wedding present if one only thinks in dollars. I dug through stores, but new glistening things did not seem to mean much. I wanted you to have something that was important and meant something to me. You are supposed to have something old, anyway.

When I was fifteen, and near death in the hospital, a neighbour had this medal blessed, and gave it to my mother for me. Catholics put a lot of faith in medals blessed by the priest. Did it help? I'm here, so I guess it did not hurt. Anyway, I don't remember it, but my mom sent it to me some fifteen years ago. It seemed to be the only thing I could find that you might like and appreciate. Just pop it into your purse or wear it on a chain like everyone else did then. Don't lose it or my mom will give me heck."

197

Speech for Colleen and Dwain's Wedding

This is an excerpt from Alex's speech to Dwain and me at our wedding reception.

"*Well, Colleen, tradition says that this is the most exciting and happiest day of your life, and Dwain, women's lib or not, society has not caught up to giving the groom equal billing in the wedding ceremony. But I imagine you may also be just a bit excited too. You have to understand, though, that I am a father, and while I share your happiness, I also have other emotions running around inside. You see no matter how old you may be Colleen, you are still dad's little girl.*

I can look back on all the times we shared, both good and bad. I don't look back with sadness, though, nor should you. I look back with happiness, thankfulness, and even some pride I guess, that you and I did share in so many of life's little adventures. I can even remember some fond memories of our canoe races that you and I participated in, even if someone [my dad] did dump the canoe into the Trent Canal. The day we passed the five OPP officers when we were going over ninety miles per hour sort of sticks in my mind. Probably not one of my better lessons.

When we packed the car to the roof and deposited you at Waterloo kind of stands out. I spend a lot of time driving by myself, but that was the loneliest ride home I can remember. You used to come home late from working at Ponderosa and everyone else was in bed, except me. You will remember that was the period that we were experiencing lots of problems holding the business together. We had many conversations, and you will not know how sustaining they were to me.

As I said earlier, I am not offering any advice. Both of you were brought up in Christian families. You experienced the workings of fathers and mothers, sisters, and brothers. I am sure you will both accept those good things you remember from your own family life, and you will use those while rejecting any of the bad parts. I am also sure you will both continue to treat one another with love and respect and can face your new life knowing that God's light will continue to shine on you. My one wish for your happiness would be, that if you are lucky enough to have a little girl, that she be just like the one we have."

Sam Jackson, son

I was very close to my dad. We spent a lot of time together, either when I was young, or now as an adult. Everyone seemed to know him. I loved going on road trips with him, and we would go to fairs, car shows, events, go for coffee with mutual friends, or just anywhere to get out of the house. We also went for a lot of walks in the woods. We even shared a love for a certain kind of car, and bought a classic convertible together, much to my mom's annoyance. I will always cherish the car. Of course, we spend hours working on our cars. He was always the one I went to if there was anything to do with cars, whether it was repair or purchasing advice.

I didn't quite know the reason I moved back to Peterborough, until my dad got sick. Now, I know. My dad taught me so many things, for which I will always be grateful. I am going to miss him. Thank you, dad.

Seatbelt

I spent a lot of time with my dad when I was younger, going to work, events and going on road trips. This was my favourite thing to do. Well, on this particular day I don't remember where we were going, but I was about three years old, I believe. We were driving on the 401 heading into Toronto.

My dad had some sort of contraption that enabled me to stand on the passenger seat, and I was belted in with my seatbelt on. It was apparently legal to use and was great as I could stand on the seat and see out the windows. Well, we were flying along at my dad's customary racing speed, when an OPP officer spied us. Dad was actually trying to beat him as we were in the express lanes, and he was in the collectors. We got pulled over anyway. The officer was not as concerned about the speed as he was about me standing on the seat. I proudly showed him I had my belt on.

For some reason I was wearing a baseball cap with some team logo on it, and I rarely ever wore them. The nice officer noticed and asked me if I played baseball, and even though I didn't play or care for baseball, I wisely said, "yes." He then asked me if I had a bat to go with my cap and I said "no." My dad was told if he bought me a bat, he would not be given a ticket. We breathed a sigh of relief and went on our way. A few years later I got my bat.

Fountain

Dad, Steve, and a friend were in our boat on Little Lake one morning, fishing near the fountain. I made mention that I thought the fountain came on around the time we were sitting out there. Well, they dismissed me, as I was a kid at the time. Not too long after we felt and heard a great rumble. It was the fountain of course coming to life! We were pretty close, and we were getting drenched. Do you think dad could get the motor started??? Of course, he had trouble with it then. We eventually got it started, but not before I had to bail with the tiny plastic bottle we had, every few seconds. It was a bit of a panic. But we laughed pretty hard after!

Locked Out

I have a friend who did something dumb. He got locked out of his apartment building in the middle of the night, and broke a main entrance window to get in. This had some consequences and ended in his being evicted. My dad, knowing everyone in town, including the property owners, talked to them and got the decision overturned. He was pretty smooth in his talk, and I think he was amazing.

Children's Story

My dad was always jealous of the many props that Rev. Don Nicholson and Rev. Brad Weeks used at George Street United Church. Well, dad wanted to top them both, and suggested he could do the children's story one Sunday, and he would bring a real prop! He went to Sears' warehouse and got the biggest box he could that would fit in their car, which was a full-size fridge box. My dad proudly showed the box to Don and Brad on the Sunday before the service. Dad started his children's story, I dragged out the box, and the kids eagerly stared at it.

My dad asked the kids, "What do you think is in the box? Is God in the box?" Then he asked the kids, "where do you think God is?" Of course, the point he was making is, God is EVERYWHERE. While he was asking his questions, a couple of kids knocked over the box to see what exactly what was inside it. Well, that started the kids becoming more interested in the box than in the story. At this point, dad was motioning Don and Brad for help. They both looked at each other, shrugged as if to say, you're on your own, you got yourself into the mess, you get yourself out. Well, by this time all the kids were in the box, laughing and giggling, and not paying attention to dad, forgetting his story and his point. I remember getting kids out of the box, which was getting destroyed. It was quite a sight, and very funny. Interestingly, I don't think dad was asked to do another children's story.

Parking Space

My dad had his own personal, free, and secure parking garage just off of the 401 at Yonge Street in Toronto, at his previous work headquarters. Even after he retired, he still managed to talk the parking attendant into letting him park there. They always let him. He told me that if you act like you belong somewhere and have confidence and authority, you can get almost any request you want.

Auto Show

One of the things my dad and I did was spend time going to events about cars, as we had a mutual love of vehicles. Not too many years ago we made our almost annual trip to the Toronto Auto Show. After we left our car at his favorite free parking garage in Toronto, we hopped on the subway for the convention center. We ran into a huge crowd of people waiting in line to show their tickets.

My dad took one look at the line, and said, "I am not standing in line half the day to get into this place. I'm going home." I pleaded with him, "dad, we spent two hours to get here, we can't just go home. We have new versions of our favorite cars to check out. It won't be too long, let's just wait." Well, we had waited in line for a couple of minutes, when dad announced he was going to go through another line that had hardly anyone one in, marked VIP, I believe. "Dad," I pleaded, "we are not VIPs this year, we can't get through that line." "Watch me", he says.

I had little choice but to follow him. We made it through the first two or three security points, until we were finally stopped. We were told we could not go through that way and would have to go all the way back. My dad just told the security guard that he was old and didn't know what line he was supposed to be in, and he was here now. Guess what? It worked.

As we walked through the VIP area, I could feel all the people in the other line staring at us and wondering why we were so special. Dad turned to me and said something to the effect, "see, this is what happens when you do things a little different." That was dad. He acted aloof and innocent, but he wasn't. He knew EXACTLY what he was doing!

Advice

One of my favorite things to do was go to work with my dad, whether it was when he had his business of Jackson Business Systems LTD, or later with the Canadian Federation of Independent Business (CFIB). This memory is from his time at CFIB, and I was his chauffeur for the day.

Towards the end of the day, he always took a coffee break. This time it was in a little restaurant outside of Lindsay. After we had just about finished our time there, I decided to visit the restroom. When I came back, there was a woman talking to dad, asking what she should do about her pregnant, teenage daughter. I caught the tail end of the conversation. Being dad, I am sure he dispensed sound advice. As we left, I asked if this was someone he knew. Apparently, she was a complete stranger, and the woman had been waiting for me to go so she could talk to dad. That was dad, always ready to lend an ear, and help dispense advice to whomever needed him.

Dwain Ketcheson, son-in-law

My father-in-law and I, over the thirty-five plus years that I had the pleasure of knowing him, had the most wonderful conversations on a variety of imaginable and not so imaginable topics. He also shared the most wonderful stories from his life which were usually both humorous and informative.

Faith

Alex was a man who had a very deep and active Christian faith. He put his faith into action by volunteering his time and considerable gifts to help others, on a personal level as well as in the community. His faith was also active regarding exploring it further. I remember him always having a variety of books on the go reflecting his varied interests, and that always included a faith related book. As a result, after reading a book, exploring, and even calling into question certain aspects of faith, he would talk to me about it, which in turn would cause me to go deeper.

Preaching

Alex preached and led many worship services over the years. He was an excellent public speaker, and preaching gave him the opportunity to explore faith in a manner that many in the field of preaching would dare not go. I remember the focus of one of his sermons being on the question of, "Why does the Bible say that Jesus was poor?" Alex said along the lines of, "Jesus was a carpenter. The trades people that I know are all doing very well financially. Was Jesus poor because he was a lousy carpenter?" As I recall, Alex concluded that if indeed Jesus was poor, it was because money to him was something to be shared with those less fortunate. In my experience, money was also not important to Alex. For him, living a life of faithfulness to God, with love, integrity and devotion to family and friends was what mattered.

Humour

Alex was also a man who had a very witty sense of humour. A couple of weeks before I was to be ordained into ministry and sent to Saskatchewan to serve in my first pastoral charge, I left my black dress shoes at the Jackson's home. My father-in-law returned them to me in time for me to wear them at my ordination. As part of the service of ordination, the person being ordained kneels. I did not realize until after the fact, that Alex had painted large white letters in such a way that those behind me could see on the bottom of my left shoe GO, and on the bottom of my right shoe SASK. I still have the shoes.

Integrity

Alex one day bought a new pair of pants and after returning home, he hung them up in his closet. A couple of days later he went to put them on when he noticed that the cuffs of the pants were frayed. So, he went back to the store with the pants, asked to see the manager and in his polite way asked for his money back, which he received. A day or so later Alex was in his closet, when he discovered and realized to his horror, that the pants he returned and got his money back for were an old pair that were identical to the new pair still hanging in the closet. I tell this story not just because it is humorous, but because of what happened next. Alex's integrity was more important to him than his pride, or accidentally getting a new pair of pants for free. So, with embarrassment he went back to the store, explained what had happened to the manager, tried to pay for them, but the manager said not to worry about it.

Wisdom

I did not know that my last conversation with Alex would be the last, as he passed away suddenly only a few days later. I phoned him not to talk about some deep theological issue, but to seek his wisdom about something mundane. After exchanging niceties and enquiring about his most recent health tests I said to him, "As you know my interlocking driveway has been slowly sinking over the years, and now it is to the point that I can't get the car in the garage. I have a few quotes and the lowest one is X." He replied, "Wow that's a lot of money!" Then after a pause he went on to say, "I know that the driveway has been a sore point for some time. If you have the money I say go for it." Shortly after his passing I took his advice, and I continue to do so.

Sandra Romanauskas, daughter-in-law

Alex gave this letter to Steve and me on our wedding day, and it (as well as the hunk of barn board he refers to), holds a place of honour on our mantle. When I read it, I can see him tinkering with bits from his "really good pile of stuff," and can hear his voice and see his smile when I read his words of wisdom: from solid beginnings, look to the future; light - and talk - in a marriage are good; and listening is better.

He was a wonderful man; one I am so fortunate to have had in my life.

Letter to Sandra and Steve from Alex

You will recognize the hunk of brass, or not. It came from the lock set on your old front door. I asked Sandra if she wanted to keep it for some craft or whatever, and she did not, so I brought it home, and stashed it with the other pile of really good stuff. It was pretty sad looking, but a bit of polish and rubbing does wonders. I knew one day I would find a use for it.

Well, what it turned into seemed like a perfect fit. I dug through my wood box for a piece of hardwood to make a nice square frame for it, with fancy routed edges and an insert to mount it on. Well, that was not to be had, but low and behold, a remnant of a 150-year-old barn board was in my hand. It was left over from building our little barn. Why the shape, I have no idea, but to me it fit perfectly with what I had in mind. Like the brass, it was pretty yucky, so I sanded it, oiled it with Murphy Oil to seal the dust inside, (I did not have clear varnish) and drilled a hole for the picture, and voila!

I thought it was a real neat piece of barn board with no changes needed, other than a cleanup, and a hole for the picture. The pointed top says, look to the future, and the solid base that it will stand on testifies to your beginning. It is pretty sturdy, although the shape is a bit irregular, but that sturdiness testifies to your commitment to a future together.

The picture is from an email from Sandra's dad from Easter 2003. Change it if you wish. You may have a better one, as my printer did not do wonders for it. The brass plate is just glued on so a knife will pry it off, that is if the glue holds, and it does not fall off anyway from Newton's Law. The hole is drilled all the way through, so if you have light behind it the picture brightens. Light in a marriage is good. The kind of light that keeps the lines of communication open. Talk is good, but listening is better. I considered routing out a spot on the back and putting in a LED for lighting, and a switch, but a 150-year-old barn board and an old brass fixture is not very high tech, so that did not seem appropriate. Just hold it up to the light.

So, it can hang, stand, have a new picture, or be dismantled and get turfed into the various recycling bins, and the wood will burn in the fireplace. Sort of like a lot of wedding presents, that you gotta wonder, what the heck do we do with this! So, do with it as you wish, and I will not be offended.

Felicia Ketcheson, granddaughter

Ya-Ya

When I was an infant, I referred to myself as Ya-Ya and this became grandpa's nickname for me. He called me Ya-Ya almost exclusively in person and in his letters (except when he wanted to be "formal" and addressed his letters to Felicia). As I got older, he started calling me and addressing letters to Felicia more and more. However, he said I'll always be Ya-Ya to him.

Creativity

My grandpa was a very creative person. He had a sizable workshop and spent lots of time there, as when Edward and I were young he made us many different things, all of which we still have. He made me a pink and purple highchair for my Cabbage Patch doll, a truck and trailer with working headlights, and a scooter. He made both of us growth charts. He also designed and made a go kart which could seat one of us and be pushed from the back. It has a windshield, an adjustable seat, a license plate, spare tire, bumpers, lights, a box to put 'junk', and a CB radio. A few years later, he made a wooden schoolhouse for my Playmobil school kids. It is a replica of the one-room schoolhouse he attended with a flagpole, bell, stove, real chalkboards, and an outhouse.

Mustache and Hair

When I was young, I really liked my grandpa's mustache and would rub it with my finger. It became a tradition for me to do this whenever I said goodbye to him, including the last time I saw him (I try not to think of how weird it probably looked when I did this as an adult!).

Unlike his mustache, he didn't like his hair being touched, but one day when I was eleven, I persisted in wanting to touch it. He finally gave in and let me put his hair in a Mohawk. Despite not wanting me to touch his hair, he was very tolerant and patient as he was in all things.

Going against the Grain

When my family and I moved to St. Catharines in 2001, grandma and grandpa took Edward and I for a drive. One of the bridges along the Welland Canal was going up just as we approached it which meant traffic had to wait for the ship to go past the bridge. Instead of waiting with the other cars, he pulled off the road to a side street. We got out of the car, he bought Edward and I peaches at a roadside stand, and we ate peaches watching the ship go by. My grandpa certainly wasn't the type to do what everyone else did and this was just one of numerous times he went against the grain.

Letters

When my family and I moved to Saskatchewan in 1997, grandpa started writing weekly individual letters to Edward and me. I rarely wrote back but this was not a deterrent to him. Come 2013, we both wrote to each other once per month. Sometimes his letters would contain words of wisdom (philosophy lessons he called them) and this is where most of this book's quotes are from. Most of his letters included stickers and a hand-drawn snake comic, once I got my snake. His last letter was dated April 23, 2018 and found by grandma unsent and in an envelope after he passed away. It's likely the last thing he ever wrote, which is of special meaning to me, given that we corresponded for 20 years and shared a love of writing. The hundreds of letters he wrote are a window into who he was and hold a special place in my heart.

Technology

My grandpa was technologically savvy and often ahead of the game in the technology realm. Not only was he the first person I ever emailed, but he was also the first person I knew to have email! He also convinced George Street United Church they needed to have a website years before this was commonplace as he knew he was the way of the future. He taught himself HTML to look after it.

Dreaming

My grandpa was a dreamer and encouraged me to be one, too. For my 9th birthday, he bought me a wish keeper necklace. I was to write down my dreams on paper, put it in the necklace, and wear it so they come true. I used it well into high school. After he passed away, I couldn't find it. Of course, I found it after I purchased a replacement! The wish keeper he bought me is now kept safe at home while I wear the replacement every day, as a reminder of how my grandpa wanted me to follow my dreams.

Ever since I was eleven, I've wanted to be a novelist. Grandpa always encouraged me to publish my novels. He always had faith in my abilities, telling me to not be afraid of rejection. When I was a teenager, he gave me a stuffed Snoopy. Snoopy is wearing a backpack which is actually a small book. Grandpa told me that if Snoopy can publish a book, I can too. Snoopy now sits on my desk, beside a picture of grandpa, reminding me what grandpa taught me and of how he believed in my abilities. Thanks to grandpa, I'm finally working on publishing my novels.

After Dinner

As evidenced by this book, he had a seemingly unlimited number of stories to tell. I have countless fond memories of him regaling us with story after story around the dinner table. I could (and did) listen to his stories for hours. Another dinner table memory is playing games. There is one game our family enjoys called *The Game of What*. In this game, you're asked a situational question or something such as "What would Alex do if he ruled the world". Someone reads everyone's answers, chooses their favourite, and everyone guesses who said it. Almost without fail, my grandpa and I would have an identical answer to at least one question out of the 15 in the game. This always humoured me, especially given the generational gap!

Snoozes

Grandpa trained himself to power nap years ago and would take a quick "snooze" for 30 minutes or so in the late afternoon, amidst the action going on in the house. You'd often find him snoozing on the couch or curled up on the living room floor in front of the fireplace.

Vitality

In 2014, my parents, grandparents, Edward, Uncle Sam, and I went to the Canadian National Exhibition. As people tend to think I'm younger than I am, we thought I should go to one of those 'guess your age' booths. Everyone agreed I should take grandpa with me, because I may be seen as a younger girl with my grandpa. My grandpa told the man at the booth that if he guessed my age correctly, he could guess his. The man guessed my age correctly. He guessed my grandpa's age to be 69 and was floored to learn grandpa was 79.

This man hasn't been the only one shocked by my grandpa's age. Two people who attended his funeral expressed their surprise he wasn't 60-something years old! I know it wasn't just because he looked younger than his age. It was because he was always healthy, busy, and active. His letters always spoke about people he had helped, boards he was on, church activities he was involved with, volunteer work he was doing. He purchased a bike in 2014 and rode it into late 2017 before the snow hit the ground, did his own car repairs, loved to walk, and enjoyed hiking in the "bush". In June 2017, at age 82 he was able to keep up to my dad and Uncle Sam while they walked around a car show all day (when they returned to my place, he immediately curled up on my living room floor for a snooze). Due to his vitality, I truly never considered him to be 'old'.

Grandpa: I always admired you for keeping so busy and for helping others. The world needs more people like you. You have been such an inspiration to me. I only wish I acted on your words of wisdom sooner in my life. Thank you for everything.

Edward Ketcheson, grandson

My perception of my grandpa has grown and evolved over time, so I've written this in a way to describe who he was to me through various stages of my life.

Making Stuff

When I was a kid, I saw him as someone who could make or fix just about anything. He had a huge work area in the basement with all sorts of tools, and over the years he made a lot of different things for both me and my sister. The most memorable was a wooden house with all sorts of amazing details, including an electric garage door that really worked. And as a testament to his love of cars, the garage took up well over half the space in the house.

He also wrote letters to me on a regular basis throughout much of my childhood. I always looked forward to receiving them, even if I was less than diligent in replying. I especially enjoyed his use of amusing stickers, drawings, and cartoons.

Unconventional

As I got older, I began to notice some of his other traits, including his curiosity, humour, and, most of all, his willingness to not be afraid to defy standard conventions. When I was about 10, I remember having popcorn at my grandparents' place and one of the kernels didn't pop. My grandpa decided he wanted to try and make it pop, but rather than simply putting it into the microwave he decided upon a more unconventional method – using a blow torch. Needless to say, all that resulted was a burnt kernel, but that didn't stop him from trying. On another occasion we were in the backyard celebrating my grandma's birthday, eating cake off crystal plates. Now, most people would just gather up the plates afterwards, and take them inside to be washed, right? My grandpa decided it would make more sense to lay the crystal plates on the grass and spray them off with the garden hose. The plates survived this just fine, incidentally.

His way of dressing also sticks out in my mind as being uniquely his, including his cowboy hat, plaid shirts, and walking stick, and of course his pipe and moustache.

Opinions

As I reached university age, I started to really enjoy talking to my grandpa about current events, technology, politics, or really anything. He was a great person to talk to as he was very smart, and always had strong opinions that often ran counter to convention. But despite these strong opinions, he was always respectful and non-judgmental, so I was never afraid to express my own opinions with him. For example, he was well aware that I have no real desire to ever own a car. While he might not have fully understood my reasons, he never judged or tried to persuade me otherwise. Rather, I think he found it amusing, considering the family I come from.

He also told the best stories – not only were they always interesting, but he told them in a way that really drew you in. Even if it was a story I had heard before, I never grew bored of listening. The fact that he had so many interesting stories to tell is, to me at least, an indication of a life well lived.

CFIB

A few years ago, I worked as a summer intern at the Canadian Federation of Independent Business (CFIB), where my grandpa had spent many years working. Now I always knew he was good at his job, but I didn't realize the full extent until I worked there. It turns out he has an almost legendary status, even though he had at that point been retired for a few years. Grandpa had apparently let several people know I was coming, and so I received a very warm welcome when I was taken around to meet everyone on my first day. I think all of this is a real testament not only to his dedication, but also the level of impact he had on everyone he met.

Outlook on Life

More recently, I've realized he was a person who didn't wait for life to happen. He took action. My last conversation with him was over the phone on his birthday. I mentioned I had a list of places I wanted to travel to in Ontario and B.C., to visit various friends and family, but for some reason kept putting it off. The last thing he told me was that I need to start crossing some of those places off my list. Some of you reading this may recall that during my speech at his funeral, I made a promise to visit all of those places within a year. Although it ended up taking me slightly longer than a year, I have managed to visit every location.

Thanks grandpa, for helping me take action in my own life, and for all of your wonderful lessons and stories.

Nicholas Jackson, grandson

The Train Set

Just in case you didn't know, grandpa had a train set. Sometimes when I came to visit him and grandma, he would have already set it up so that we could play right away, instead of having to put it together. For me at that age, it was really hard to put it together. I really liked playing with the train set with grandpa. I remember once when we tried to put it together, we did it the wrong way, so we had to take it apart and rebuild it the right way. It was always really hard to put the tracks together because we had to find the right piece of track to match with the other one. The train set was really fun to play with him, and he even let me play with it when the box said 14+ (I was around five years old). When we played with the train set the track broke at least once every time we played with it. When we were done playing with the train set it was always a hassle to put it back in the box.

Soccer with Grandpa

Once when grandma and grandpa were looking after me, grandpa and I played soccer. When we were playing soccer, I got a bit thirsty, so I went inside to get some water, and then I came back outside. When I was done drinking the water, I got thirsty again. So, I asked grandpa if I could have some Gatorade if there was any, and he said "yes." I was lucky there was still a bottle left because I would be mad if there wasn't. After I snuck inside, I opened the fridge as quietly as I could, grabbed the Gatorade and snuck back outside. After I had a drink of the Gatorade, I dropped the bottle on the cone that we were using as a post, so that grandpa could take more shots on me and get a lot more goals. The next time I went to get a drink I took a slug of it and my hands were all sticky. I realized that it was the Gatorade that seemed to be leaking out of the bottle. The next thing I knew I was covered in Gatorade.

213

PICTURES FROM MEMORIES
OF IMMEDIATE FAMILY

Shirley and Alex's wedding (1957)

Alex and Colleen's canoe race

Alex and his outhouse in the basement

Dwain's ordination shoes

Go Kart

Wooden schoolhouse

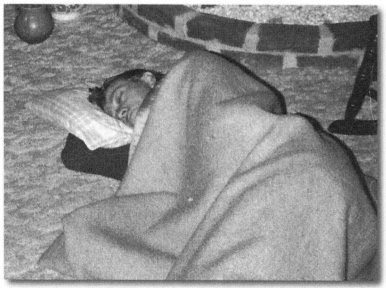

Alex sleeping on the floor in 1981

Alex sleeping on the floor in 2017

Wooden house with garage

QUOTES OF ALEX BEING ALEX

Do you suppose God thought it would be funny to watch us fight with weeds that grow twice as fast and umpteen times as numerous as our flowers and vegetables? I don't find it funny when my green onions are puny, the radishes look anemic, the carrots are almost afraid to show their leaves above ground, and weeds have no conception of birth control, and their kids dine on fast food, so they are all over the place and all overweight. (date unknown)

[Saskatchewan] is probably the most interesting and diverse hunk of land in Canada. (date unknown)

[I] pulled weeds, fixed the fence, moved rocks, shovelled dirt, got my hands dirty and enjoyed the things that make you achy, but feel closer to God. (date unknown)

After his 63rd birthday: I do not need any more birthdays. I have had lots. Guess that bad news comes when I do not have anymore. That's a long time yet. (1998)

I don't know about you, but my brain just won't stop thinking; it keeps putting these thoughts in my head and right now it is thinking about two little kids in Saskatchewan. (1998)

He sure was snarly. (1998)

You write very well for a squiggly little kid. (1998)

As you get older, you will realize the importance of New Year's Eve to most people. We used to party. But as an old geezer I do not like crowded rooms, full of smoke, loud music, and loud people. I like things nice and quiet and serene. I have had my share and contributed to the celebrations. (1999)

After several items broke in a short period of time: Seems everything around here is suffering from age deprecation all at the same time. Your mother is fine but everything else is busted. (1999)

Make sure the kids don't get uptight about answering letters. I like to get their letters, but I know they have lots to do, and they can write whenever they feel like it or get time. (1999, to Colleen)

I see this keyboard and I want to write even when I have nothing to say. (1999)

I don't know why I am writing to you again so soon, but I have had a busy, exasperating day and I need a nice kid to talk to. (1999)

I am sure the band-aids will come in handy, although I have not needed one for about two weeks. I am glad you sent some good decorative ones, since I like them much better than the plain ones. I am sure shortly Sam will ask me to fix something on his car, and guess what, I'll probably need a band-aid. (2000)

Your mother told us your marks this afternoon when we spoke on the phone. Pretty awesome. I think it must be the gramps factor coming out. (2000)

I went to the [Peterborough] Examiner this morning, at their request, and had my picture taken. I sent a letter to the editor and they called me yesterday and said they want to use it for their Sunday editorial, and like a picture to go with it. CFIB says that I am not allowed to write such stuff, but hopefully they will not see it....oh well, I have been in trouble before. (2000)

Got work to do but I am tired of shuffling papers. (2000)

It is always relaxing for me to write to you. I hope you like my letters, even with all the nonsense in them. Guess old guys like granddaughters and nonsense. (2001)

Glad you like to write. I enjoy it and thought of writing a book a few times, but never did. (2001)

I only like to shop for necessary things: like cars, tools, fishing equipment, etc. Even then, most times I find it a pain. If I want something, I go and buy it. Can't take the hassle of running up and down aisles checking out junk I don't need nor care about. If you need it, go buy it. If you think the price is too high, don't buy it. Do without, don't waste time looking at stuff you don't need. That's today's shopping channel lesson. Oh! Very important, if you can buy it from a local independent store, preferably a CFIB member, even if it costs more, get it there, rather than a large chain. Keeping a community intact is more important than saving a few dollars on a purchase. (2001)

I have not told anyone, so keep it under your hat, but I have started to write a book. Since you are an aspiring writer, I thought I would share this secret with you. I have the outline ready, and a couple of chapters done. Been doing a lot of research and have pages of scribbled notes all over my desk. I think that some publisher may be interested in it. (2002)

The grandmother and Steve went to the hockey game and I stayed in Steve's apt. and read a book. I only went out on the balcony once and lit my pipe. The balcony is big enough to hold a party, and it is interesting to watch the traffic on the roads a mile away, especially at night. It was nice, just the way I like it, quiet, no radio, and no TV. And no noise from the neighbours. (2002)

I detest getting the runaround from bureaucracy and that is what is happening. They will find out that they are dealing with the grandpa & he does not take kindly to their crap. (2002)

After that, we stopped at Sears and I got a couple of shirts. Needed some long sleeve ones for winter. Not really what I wanted, but they were on sale, and I dislike paying fifty bucks for a shirt. I especially will not pay that, nor any amount, for a shirt with the manufacturer's name on the front. I don't want to walk around and be a billboard for Tommy whatever, or anyone else. They can pay me if they want their name on my clothes. This crap, of putting the name on garments, was a great way to suck people in, especially kids, who need to be part of the crowd and want to belong by wearing the latest fashions seen on TV. I hope you don't succumb to this money grab by big business! Well, I guess that is my soap box for today. (2002)

The trees were just something out of a movie or painting. Drive around a bend, down a hill and you were met with a blanket of colour. Some crimson red, tons of shades of yellow, interspersed with a bit of light purple. It was a great scene and went on for miles. You could see hills just brilliant red, with the odd green pine in the middle, and next a green forest of pine and spruce, with a shot of bright red or orange sticking through. Some of the trees and colours were reflected in the water if it was calm. It was worth going to work just to see the scenery. What a great spot in the world we live in and still we nater about things that don't matter. (2002)

Oh. Listen kid, I can put up with a lot, but when you get into high school, please don't follow that crowd of nose rings or lip whatever, or tongue studs, or any of that stuff. They may think it cool, but it just looks stupid and, in some cases, poses health risks. Not even Sunday & you get a sermon. Well at least it is short. (2003)

My letter that I mailed on Tuesday came back. No stamp. Wouldn't you think after all the letters that I mail, that post office would send one little letter to St. Catharines without a stamp on it? No way, just return it! What a way to treat a good customer. (2003)

"Just singing in the rain" yesterday, today, and sounds like tomorrow too. Rain is good though, or nothing would grow, and we would eventually all look like a piece of straw. (2004)

Some people seem to be able to keep a nice neat clean desk, but I have notes on little scraps all over. I got scraps for my book, articles that I want to check out, and who knows what else. Is your desk like that? Or perhaps you are a neat, tidy, organized kid. I have tried all kinds of other methods, including keeping everything in the computer, but scraps of paperwork best for me. (2004)

This summer is going so fast, I am not sure what is happening. Just seems to be a lot to do constantly, or someplace to go, and no time to sit and read, do nothing, or just contemplate. One needs to just sit and meditate sometimes. I have a couple of friends who do that each morning. I could never get into the habit for some reason, but it is probably good for you. (2004)

After Felicia got a snake: I guess that is one good thing about a snake, you won't get bucked off. (2004)

After Felicia got a snake and he started drawing a snake comic on every letter: Riding around on a little tractor is very relaxing and allows one time to think and contemplate, so I started to think about good uses for snakes. I made a list but will just divulge one at a time so if you put them to use you won't wear out your poor pet. The first one is on the bottom of this letter. (2004)

What the heck happens to all the time? I suspect if my memory is right, that time passes rather slowly for you, especially if there is a major event coming up. For me, it just whizzes by. Guess that happens when one gets a bit older, however I know old geysers, or at least retired people, who sit around and think that time has stopped, and they just wait for the next mealtime. I suspect they worked in boring jobs, never had hobbies, and never did any volunteering. I have so many things to keep me busy

223

that I won't ever get caught up and have nothing to do, even if I lived to be a hundred. (2004)

Something must be wrong with me because lately I don't mind browsing through all the stores looking for presents. Shopping has never been my bag, unless it is for something important like a boat, car, or tractor. (2004)

I am not much of a reader of fiction, but I got another free book from Reader's Digest a few days ago and read two of the four stories. Maybe I don't read much of that stuff because, depending on the stories, I get too emotionally involved and it is difficult when you wear glasses. Reading the two stories that I did, my eyes want to water and mess up my glasses so I am constantly cleaning them off so I can see. What a pain. (2004)

You know, this being old and retired, or at least partially, is not what it is cracked up to be for providing spare time. Anyway, I don't feel old or think of being old, but I am busy and wonder how to get everything done some days. (2005)

I just mailed a letter, and I am starting over already. Do you get that urge, or need, to write? You know, you just feel like telling people things, expressing ideas, and putting things down on paper, I guess. (2005)

I hate to see stuff go into the garbage that can be recycled. (2005, to Edward)

It is very satisfying, if that is a good term, that my kids get along and like one another, which is not always the case in families. (2005, to Marlene)

You know, sometimes things just get to you, so you have to say or do something. Do you get like that? You hear, see, or read something that seems so stupid, or harmful, or just plain wrong, that if you don't vent your concern, then you are in agreement and as guilty as the person who said it. (2006)

I am thinking of keeping the boat and using it to run up and down the river and to fish. The grandmother will think that I am nuts of course, but then she does not fish and can't start the motor anyway. So, I am hoping that no one wants to buy it, and perhaps I may take the listing off the Internet, but forget to tell your grandmother, of course. (2006)

Regarding a car show: I hate crowds - I remember saying I would not go to one again. What a dummy. (2006, to Edward)

Everyone needs a little John Deere tractor with a snow blower on it for winter. How else do you have fun? (2006, to Edward)

I am impressed, and for me to be impressed with anything the government does, well that is really something. (2006, to Edward)

I read as I want to know where we came from, how and why, who God is and all those questions that one cannot find answers for, but I keep looking anyway. (2006, to Marlene)

For an old, retired guy I sure seem to have lots to do instead of just going fishing and other sensible activities. (2013)

I never had an interest in health nor medicine and hate hospitals and don't really have a lot of faith in the medical community. A happy and grateful attitude have proven to be a big contributor to a healthy life. Another study some years ago found that those who attend church regularly are healthier and live longer than those who don't. Now that church attendance is fading fast, I have no idea what will happen to that stat. You know, one serious concern I have is that churches do an awful lot for society and their local community, and as they disappear their good works go as well. I don't think any level of government is able and willing to pick up that slack, and I doubt they even realize. Another noticeable stat is that church goers are the biggest volunteers and donate the most dollars to charity. Ok, so much for the soapbox. (2013)

Might be a sickness or compulsion, this need to write. (2014)

People sometimes ask, "what do you do when you are retired?" Obviously, they are not [retired], as often there does not seem to be sufficient time or days for meetings, errands, repairs and fix it jobs for widows and of course funerals. (2014)

Most [bureaucracies] are so protected by rules and regulations that their lair is almost impenetrable, even by some other government departments...if one has a dispute and is right, you just have to stand your ground and be patient. Really patient. (2015)

I don't think most realize what a great place Canada is with such diverse scenery & climate. (2015)

Don't know about you but sometimes I just don't feel like writing, letters, reports, etc., but when the bug hits the words come faster than the fingers can put them on the screen. (2016)

You must be doing a good job. I just tell people that you take after your grandfather! (2016)

I have a list of errands for tomorrow. I have not been out [of the apartment] since Saturday except for a short walk yesterday so am actually looking forward to it...Since I was out every day for fifty years when I worked, and usually out of town, I still feel that urge to spend money on gas, and weather makes no difference unless it is really really bad. (2017)

After Felicia got two rats and he added rats to his snake comics: Hope you realize this transition from one snake to two rats is causing me some problems! (2017)

We had a little plastic garbage can in the [church] auditorium to collect batteries and when it got full, I took them to the recycling. I brought it home, cleaned it up, made a sign and a lid and put in a motion sensor wired to a chip that plays bird songs for a few seconds, so when you dump in your batteries a bird chirps. (2017)

Have not ridden my bike much this summer as for some reason my knees and legs complain. (2017, at the age of 82)

Telephone calls are great and people text and email for no reason, but it is not the same as receiving a letter; I think anyway. A letter takes a bit of time and thought and the cost of a stamp of course, and the trouble to find a mailbox. (2017)

I too dislike crowds and always said if my closest neighbour was a mile away it would be just fine. (2017)

I have tried various methods [to organize notes for various activities]. I don't think there's one solution that fits all, but I think we look after the problem as it best fits us! Now, if one is not involved in more than one activity, or not at all, then there is no problem. Unfortunately, I have never had that experience and normally have five or six different strings to pull, plus their offshoots to dangle at the same time, so I have always had the pile of unruly notes and papers on my desk. (2017)

HUMOUROUS QUOTES

Must be warm to wear shorts. I do not like shorts. All the girls whistle at my legs. (1998)

I have been working on material for the web page for the church. It is going to be neat. I looked at some others tonight and they are pretty borrrring. (1998)

After attending two church services: When you go to church two times on one Sunday, it must mean you are really good or really bad. (1998)

Now that you have my life story for the last two days, how are things in your world? If you keep [these letters] when you are old (like your mother, not old, just older) you can read them and think "boy my grandpa was a real nut case, but he was ok". (1999)

I think we are having liver and onions. Bet you would like that. Most kids do not like it, but I am not sure why. It is good for you. It will help you live to be a grandmother someday. (2000)

Enough of this sissy e-mail stuff. It's time for a real letter. (2000)

The TV station called on Monday to see if I would do an interview for the ceiling [of the church]. Of course, I was not here so I was glad that your grandmother gave them another name. I do not have to be on TV, besides my hair may have been messed up and it would not be good for my image. (2000)

The black flies were as bad as getting a moose in the face. Every time I got out of the car hundreds of them said, "c'mon guys here is an old guy we can bite to pieces". They did. (2000)

It just started to rain. Not hard, just a very soft gentle shower, which is great, as everything is dry as poop (that's really dry). (2001)

Yesterday afternoon I trimmed the front hedge and never cut the cord once. I was pretty proud of myself. (2001)

Regarding only having gum product stickers to put on Felicia's letter: Sorry, but things are tough & I have had to resort to paid advertising again. But I still don't think people should chew gum in public! It looks yucky. (2002)

For days, it has been cold as poop here. Sam says that is a silly expression, since poop is normally warm! Well, ya, unless it lives in Peterborough this past week, and gets frozen in two seconds outside. You should have lived on a farm with an outhouse, and then you would realize what cold as poop really means. I guess that is my information for today. (2003)

Little tractors do not like to be dirty; they feel self-conscious. (2004)

Sort of like trying to hold onto a snake that has been well buttered and wants to go. (2005, to Edward)

It is raining, almost like snow. It is a good thing my body is waterproof. (2009, to Edward)

It's like that social media website Myface. (2011, to the family, when he meant to say either Facebook or Myspace)

QUOTES ABOUT CARS

A fellow is coming tomorrow afternoon to look at Steve's Austin. I think he will buy it since he has been here to look at it three times already. He wants it but his wife does not want him to spend the money for it. He has two already. I have not met her but boy she must be a grouch. The poor guy only has two and she does not want him to get another one?????? Geeze, I have always had two or three cars, so what's her problem??? (1999)

Going to tune up the grandmother's car tomorrow. I don't mind doing that. It is pretty easy and more fun than taking things apart and trying to fix them. At least I will not get all full of grease and have to use three bandaids to cover the scratches. If I could have collected all the blood I have lost from cuts and scratches from fixing cars over the years, and donated it to the blood bank, there would never be a blood shortage again. (2001)

One day I may be just too old to bend and twist to fix cars. I don't think I will like that. (2013)

MEMORIES OF FAMILY MEMBERS

Barrie Jackson, nephew

When I was sixteen years old Uncle Alex was going to take me duck hunting, so I went to Canadian Tire and bought a shotgun. We sat in the boat freezing and we didn't see a duck, so when we were going home, I said not until I fired my gun. I stood up and fired into the air, and it had such a kick it almost tore off my shoulder. I almost fell into the river. After Uncle Alex quit laughing, I told him this was not fun, and you can have my shotgun.

Another time, Uncle Alex and Aunt Shirley bought a cottage, and I went to help put up the footings so that we could start putting the cottage up the next time that we went there. We ended up having to knock the footing down because they were crooked. I guess we used too much beer to hold the footings together.

Cousin Brian

There are many memories I have as a child spending time with my cousins in Peterborough. It was always a great visit being able to sit in a bumper car on the rear patio, being able to have a Pop Shoppe soda from the basement as a treat or swimming in the backyard pool. Every time I went to visit, I had fun and exciting adventures.

A lot of my memories revolve around the vehicles that were being driven by the family and what new cars Alex had purchased between visits. Alex always had a taste for different styles of vehicles and buying cars outside the norm. From the Hudson parked in the basement garage to Colleen's sleek and sporty Puma, it was always intriguing to see the vehicles that came and went.

One of my favorites was driving in the Subaru Brat. The truck was designed as a two-seater pick up that had two seats welded into the cargo bed facing backwards. This was a legal option on the Subaru Brat and allowed the company to skirt the light duty pickup truck tax imposed during that time, as they were able to bring the truck into America as a passenger vehicle to avoid the tax. When you are ten years old and not only allowed, but have to, sit in the bed of a pickup to get places, you do it. Even as an adult, I would be happy to do the same.

It was one of the fondest memories I have. With Alex driving, Shirley in the passenger seat and Sam and I strapped in the back of the Subaru we went to places all over the area. It must have been confusing for the drivers as they pulled up behind us. There were two young kids facing the wrong way while waving frantically at everyone that was around us. We tried hard to make everyone wave back and were pretty successful if I remember correctly. It was one of the many memories of my visits and I am thankful that Alex and family were part of them.

Dave Bourne, cousin

Some of my earliest memories of my cousin Alex involved exploring the outdoors in and around Peterborough - which for a kid from the city seemed like another world. I remember a trip to Warsaw Caves when I was about eight years old, and I can recall Cousin Alex showing me how to squeeze through a tiny opening to find a cavern that was cold enough to maintain ice year-round. There was no way he was going to join me, but he wanted me to experience it for myself.

He was perhaps a little more comfortable on the open water, and I'm pretty sure the first time I ever got to paddle a canoe was with cousin Alex. In the winter months it was tobogganing, and I remember some great times barrelling down the hills not far from the Jackson home.

And when we weren't outside, I will always remember being impressed by his collection of electronics and early computers. I have vivid memories of entering BASIC computer code on a glowing green monitor, and learning what programming was all about. Nobody had home computers in those days, so for a geeky kid, this was incredible! It would be another three or four years before I had my first computer at home.

I didn't see cousin Alex nearly as much as I got older, but when I did, I was always struck by how he never seemed to change...same moustache, same grin, and same quiet sense of humour. He will be missed!

Dave Davis, cousin and friend

R. Alex Jackson, a man unto himself. I met Alex in the late sixties, and as time went by, we became good friends. I learned to respect the man because of his attitudes and beliefs. The following is just one of many examples of what makes him tick.

It was a warm day in July, and Alex and I were walking down a main street in Peterborough, looking for a pub to quench our thirst, when a group of young men approached us. One was eating a chocolate bar and he dropped the wrapper on the sidewalk. Alex went up to him and told him to pick up the wrapper and put it in the trash barrel attached to the light standard. To my surprise, he did it as his friends clapped their approval! I was both shocked and amazed...I feared the worst, which was getting the crap knocked out of us. WRONG. This is the man I came to enjoy and respect. I could give you several more examples, but I think this about sums it up. Wouldn't it be nice if we all shared his attitude!!!! Thanks Alex.

Gail, cousin

I recall Alex with his pipe in hand, leaning back with one leg over the other knee. He was always happy and smiley and looked to the positive side. Even when he was irritated, he didn't appear so, as he was so easy going.

Lenore Jackson, niece

Alex was a terrific man and a great father. There was always time for his kids, he made sure of that. I suppose they had to make time for him!

We always had good times with Alex and Shirley, especially with your dad. The first winter we were married (1967), we went to Peterborough on the bus to go skidooing. Alex and I were on the skidoo and I had never been on one before that night, and there was a little wine to warm us up. He told me to head for a little tree nearby, so I did, and because I had never driven one before we ended up stuck on the sapling. It took us time to dislodge the sled from the tree due to laughter. He told me to head for the tree, but he didn't tell me not to hit it.

The day of the boat and motor on the lake, we were out for a fun ride and the motor fell in the water, still attached to the boat by its chain. Alex and I must have sat in the boat and laughed for ten minutes, because every time he went to pull the motor up, we got laughing so hard he would drop it again.

Cousin Sue

Now, I am aware this story is to be about my cousin, Alex Jackson. Well, he is the reason as an adult I finally have a sister. Years ago, Alex and Shirley held quite a few family reunions at their home in Peterborough. My mother Helen Stacey, my brothers Fred and his family, and Dick and I attended. We booked a large room each year at the motel at the end of the lane, leading to the Jackson home.

One year, early on, we talked to the lady who ran the motel about the family reunion. She looked at me and stated, "I know who you are, you're Shirley's sister." Well, that did it...I went to Shirley and she agreed, we were sisters. That day, all those years ago (as an adult), I finally had a sister! It was something I had always wanted, especially growing up with three brothers on a farm.

This story is not specifically about Alex, but it was due to him. You know what I mean; all the small pieces of life have to fit together in order for wonderful events to happen, like becoming a sister! So, I have always credited Alex with giving me a sister!

Tracy Jackson-Wiley, niece

Uncle Alex was my favourite uncle. For me as a young child, it was always exciting to come and visit him in the summers. We also wrote to each other via snail mail. When I did a school project on the Peterborough Liftlocks, he took me through the locks in his boat. I will remember his pipe and his love of Saabs. He was always such a kind, gentle soul who was deeply loved and will forever be remembered.

Valerie and Tarah Rivington, cousins

Our best memories are his smile, as he always had a great smile, and his love for family and extended family. He loved telling jokes. I remember as a young child going to his place to swim, and he always made sure I had fun, and he would take me around on his shoulders. I also remember the love he had for his pipe, and I loved the smell. Alex and Shirley were great cousins. I never understood why we all called each other cousin in front of the names, but once I got older my mom told me why. Out of all the cousins I had the most fun with Alex and Shirley.

Wendy King, niece

Uncle Alex is my favourite uncle. He was the smartest man I ever met. He wasn't just smart, but a good listener, funny, patient and understanding. When he and Aunt Shirley would visit and stay at our place we would talk for hours. The next day we would go to the cemetery in Comber. I learned a lot from him, especially about our family.

QUOTES ABOUT PUBLIC SPEAKING

A couple years after Felicia joined Toastmasters: Probably Toastmasters is one of the best decisions you could have made. The ability to put interesting words on paper that others want to read and also to stand up in front of a crowd, big or small, and actually hold the audience's attention are rare gifts only a few people really possess. (2015)

Regarding his presentations at the Zoo board meetings: [My presentations are] pretty short and although my five minutes is no big deal, I want to make sure it is done professionally, so I have been making notes, scribbling, and rewriting. I won't read my little report but take my notes anyway just in case a blank pops up, and as one gets older, blanks do happen. I guess what I want to say is it does not matter that one has made many, many speeches and presentations, one still has to prepare if you want to present yourself and your information properly. Impromptus are a different matter. (2016)

Too bad not more people are involved with Toastmasters. You know that we are supposedly all born with a fear of heights...but as we grow the fear of public speaking seems to top the list. No idea why but I do have friends who would get physically ill just at the thought of speaking to a crowd. Never a problem and I won the speaking contests all through school as well as always topped the class for writing. Composition it was called then...I used to practice in front of a mirror so I could monitor posture, hand gestures, make sure the tie was right and nothing else was amiss with clothes, hair, etc., that people could focus on instead of paying attention. (2017)

I really think the biggest, most important asset for public speaking, is confidence that you can do it. (2017)

QUOTES ABOUT TECHNOLOGY

Regarding frustration at using a new computer program: And this is supposed to be the new easy, user friendly version. What on earth would it do if it was unfriendly? (1998)

Be back in a minute, going to check if I can get on the net yet; so much for that, I was only gone three minutes and this gadget says "Disconnected by remote computer" whoever that is. I WANT MY MONEY BACK!! Is it any wonder grandpas get grouchy when these stupid bits of plastic, wire, a few volts of electricity, and a drop or two of silicone try to tell you what to do and rule your life? I may just turn the hose on it and its printer and monitor and watch them squirm and sputter and shoot sparks as they disintegrate. Guess that would teach this hunk of STUFF TO SMARTEN UP?...... I am getting tired of this thing trying to run my life. I have real people that do that. (1998)

I check my email every day, I have two here, so I have to check both. Some days, like today, there are none, and yesterday there were four. It is kind of neat and exciting to turn on your computer and there is a message for you, just like getting a letter in the mailbox. (1998)

Regarding spellcheck: I don't use it because I hate a machine telling me that I do not spell correctly. Bad enough that grandma tells me. At least I can talk back to her (under my breath). (1998)

Regarding his computer: Glad you do important things like homework on the computer. They can sure take up your time, like this stupid character who seems to think it knows more than me. I keep telling it that without me pushing its buttons it could do nothing and it still acts as if it really knows what is going on. (2000)

Regarding computer problems: If these things were any more annoying it would be like having your worst nightmares all day long. Nobody said life is easy, especially using a hunk of wiring in a box, along with software that a rocket scientist could not figure out!!!! (2004)

CDs won't play if they are put in upside down. (2005, to Edward)

I have used email since its inception, but I still regard it as very impersonal and for short notes only. (2008, to his nephew)

I am just amazed at the technology I have witnessed and have been involved in, but I think it is petty cash compared to what you are going to witness. If I can sneak a USB stick in my will and leave you the password, perhaps you can update it and ship it back to me, wherever: hey, WIFI works most everywhere. Anyway, your generation is in for a great ride, like it or not, with the technology advancing like an unstoppable horde of locusts streaming across Saskatchewan wheat fields. There will certainly be a few bumps along the way, but the stuff already in the pipeline is either scary or fascinating, depending on your outlook. (2014)

You see my brain works on the KISS system and I get really ticked off at some websites that are so cluttered you can't find what you need. (2016)

I had email and used a computer before most people even knew what email was. (2017)

MEMORIES OF FRIENDS

Ada Lee, friend

Alex was the best friend I ever had. I miss that friendship. He helped me with anything I asked him to, it didn't matter what the task was, he was just helpful in every way. Once he introduced my choir and that meant a lot to me. He did so much, but I don't think he was appreciated at the church for all his hard work and dedication. His intelligence was his kindness. People thought highly of him as he was so out front, honest, and straight ahead good. He was one of a kind and I really miss him.

Allan Paton, friend

Here are some random thoughts about my friend Alec/Alex (I heard both of these so often that I never did get it straight in my mind which was correct, so from now on I will refer to him as Alex, for the sake of consistency if not correctness). I will not concentrate on the things that Alex valued most, such as family, friendship, honesty, standing up for justice and those needing help. I think those values will come through indirectly. To give this writing some focus I will put in some subheadings for apparent order.

Beginning George Street United Church

I think that Alex and family, and I and my family, probably first met at an after-service coffee/social time at church in the mid-1980s, shortly after we had moved (back, in my case) to Peterborough from Windsor. It was the time of Robin Sharp as Minister and Dr. Kewley as assistant Minister. Alex and Shirley sat near the front on the north side, just in from the centre aisle, and we typically sat a few pews behind them. There were lots of good times there as our children grew older around us. In mid 1990s I had been away for a time, and when I returned to Peterborough Alex was acting as the lay opener of the service, greeting the congregation, and making some announcements, all typical of his ongoing involvement at George Street. In more recent times of continuing difficulty (in most mainstream churches), Alex was a respectful opponent of some actions taken in the ongoing problem of downsizing, due to declining membership.

CFIB (Canadian Federation of Independent Business)

Through many of the years that I knew Alex, he was a member's representative for this association, and he was the main one that helped me become hired when I returned to (Peterborough) from teaching abroad and needed a job (approximately 1998). I came back to Canada that year on May 24 weekend and thanks to Alex, (mainly providing me with information about the CFIB way of doing things before I returned to Canada,) I started working at CFIB right away. It was a great job for me, and I was able to consult with Alex whenever something arose, when I didn't quite know the best way to proceed. For my time at CFIB we went to the annual meeting/dinner at least twice with Alex and Shirley and enjoyed their company very much.

Saabs

I was always an enthusiast of cars in general, and I knew something about the relatively obscure and rare Saab, but it was Alex (also his son Sam) who expanded my knowledge and experience with Saabs. Firstly, as far as I observed or could ascertain, Alex and his family were the only owners of Saabs in Peterborough. Therefore, whenever I saw one around town, I could assume that some member of the Jackson family was out and about. One of the peculiarities I learned and observed during my years with CFIB was that Rob Wilson, Regional Manager of Alex's and my district, was also a Saab owner and enthusiast. I at first wondered if Saab ownership was some sort of informal requirement for a successful career at CFIB, but eventually met and heard of others who did not drive a Saab but seemed to get along okay in the organization.

Scott-Atwater outboard motor

I'm prepared to bet that most of you, unless you happened to know Alex quite well, never heard of this brand of outboard motor. I knew something about Scott-Atwater, from studying and drooling over brochures and articles about boats and outboard motors in my younger years. Except for Alex, I never knew an actual owner of a Scott-Atwater. His had approximately 15 horsepower. It was certainly not a mainstream outboard, like Saabs are not a mainstream car, (you can infer something about Alex from that) but were generally regarded as quite original (if not exotic) in engineering and design (like Saabs). Some of you may swear you have never seen one, but if you have seen Hitchcock's movie *The Birds* then YOU REALLY HAVE SEEN ONE. It's the motor on the boat that Tippi Hedren's character takes across the bay to meet Rod Taylor's character.

Business mentor

During my friendship with Alex, I came to realize that he was a good mentor on various business matters from his approach to life, his personal experience as a small business owner, and also as a CFIB representative (which exposed both of us to the experience and knowledge of small businesspeople literally, every day). One of the times when Alex's role as business mentor was especially helpful was when I established a small business in Oshawa (wine store owner). As is typical of many businesses the first years were particularly lean moneywise, and I took great comfort from the following story from Alex's early years as a computer service business owner.

At that time Alex's finances were so lean that on a certain Friday afternoon he had to take the drastic step of pawning the collector gun given to him by his grandfather in order to have enough cash for Shirley's Friday grocery shopping. How immediate and critical is that for a shortage of cash! Well, he got past that lean period and was able to redeem the gun from the pawnbroker. If Alex could survive that kind of cash shortage, I should be able to as well. I found remembering that pawnbroker story quite helpful when I had my own lean periods in business.

Volunteer/Unofficial Advocate

Alex and I met every few months for coffee, especially during my years when I was working in Oshawa and was in Peterborough only on the weekends. In many of our conversations Alex had a story in which he had written and appeared in some other way to have helped out someone who needed an advocate. This could have been an issue with a landlord, where Alex and various other tenants had an issue that needed advocacy, issues at George Street Church, where strong principled presentation was required, issues involving a housing project where Alex was involved, and his representation on behalf of some important principle was required.

End?

Not quite. We all know we have attended a memorial service for Alex, but there are too many good memories to speak of and think of in terms of *an end*.

Angus Tulloch, friend of the family

I always felt like I was part of the family, and Alex treated me like I was another son.

AOTS (As One that Serves) President

Although Alex came to AOTS later in life, he made up for it very quickly and was instrumental in many areas and tasks for AOTS. He was President of George Street United Church's AOTS in Peterborough a couple times, stepping up when others could not. He personally wrote to Angie in Honduras, who is the young girl the club sponsors. He always came up with offbeat fundraising ideas, including the first ever Tool Sale Fundraiser. He assisted in the annual clean-up of Camp Quin-Mo-Lac. He led many devotions and group discussions at club meetings, delivered Sunday Sermons on AOTS Laity Sunday, and was involved in the Central Region AOTS planning.

He was known on a National level as well. He wrote several devotions on the National AOTS website. In fact, right up until his death he was planning a group discussion at our Annual Roundup weekend. He was also heavily involved in AOTS Community Homes, as he had been acting chairman and treasurer. He saved the organization several thousand dollars by cutting out unnecessary expenses. In short, AOTS greatly benefited from his wisdom and tireless devotion. He will be forever greatly missed.

Bill Gilbert, friend

Personally, I found Alex Jackson to be a great leader and friend in volunteering his spare time to the church and community. He was a board member of AOTS Community Homes for 2016 and 2017, and he was chair of the Board for 2018 until his passing. Alex was also chair of George Street United Church AOTS Men's Club for many years. He was a member of George Street United Church Trustees and chaired the committee.

Alex was always looking for new projects around the church and started the Loonie Fund for Mission and Outreach, and the collecting of used batteries for recycling. He was always able to give us guidance and training in any projects, with new ideas of how to do things better.

He was there to help when there was work to be done. Alex was always very hard working and focused on the task at hand.

Brigitte Wellershausen, friend

Alex and I were on the Board of Trustees together at George St. United Church. He was well respected and very honourable. If something was wrong, he said so, and would do something about it. He didn't succumb to pressure. He was great to work with and the most caring man I ever met in my life.

Rev Gai Burns, friend

When I think of Alex Jackson, I think of a man who cared deeply, and a man who spoke his truth. People didn't always seem to want to hear it, but he had an integrity and intellect that I admired. He could be counted on to consider a situation, do the research and offer advice worth listening to. He was one of the wise ones I knew I could turn to, and George Street United was the richer and blessed by having him on board. I think Alex was the one who insisted, woman or not, that as the minister of the church I was part of AOTS and should attend their dinner meetings. Yup, those were the days!

Alex had a light spirit and ability to care. I remember one time a friend of his had gone off to be a hermit for a year with his beloved lab, and Alex was concerned about him, and so we visited this man together out at his cottage. Alex cared enough and was worried enough about this old friend to take his minister to check out how he was doing. When we look back at people we've known, there are always a few that stand out as real characters, and Alex was one of those. I'm glad that our paths crossed.

Graham Hart, friend

Alex was one of those genuine people who never seem to feel the need to be someone they aren't. His inventive mind could always stimulate broad ranging conversation, and that, sprinkled with his dry sense of humour and unassuming and generous nature, always made it a pleasure to be in his company.

Jessie Stockton, friend

During the years I worked at George Street United Church, Alex was the chair of Christian Education. He was a joy to work with, was upbeat and had a keen sense of humour. He was a great encourager! I could always count on Alex's support on my adventures in Christian Education and Outreach.

We had an active youth group. One week they decided they wanted to camp overnight in the church. I had planned to be the adult supervision as the youth work was part of my portfolio. I think it was only a few days since the youth group had been on a retreat, and I was exhausted trying to keep up with the kids. Alex remarked that I looked tired. He said, "You are not going to sleep over with the youth group. I am. You go home and sleep. You're exhausted."

I sure did appreciate his help, knowing that the youth group were well supervised, and I could recuperate! I think Alex found another adult and together provided chaperons for the youth group sleepover at the church. As chair of Christian Education Alex went above and beyond! (*On a side note, the other adults Alex found were his daughter, Colleen, and his future son-in-law Dwain!*)

Alex and Shirley and others from the church hosted a party at the Bay of Quinte Conference on the day of my Ordination May 1991. Alex's generosity, sense of humour, and his care for youth made him an excellent chair of CE. He was a great encourager and energizer. I know there were many more events when Alex's generosity of spirit, and gift of encouragement gave support to the work of the church.

Hospitality at the Jackson home is also a great memory. Alex will be greatly missed. I am sure glad both Alex and Shirley were at my 80th birthday party.

As a friend of Alex, I need to tell you how very dear his kids and grandchildren were to him! That came through loud and clear.

Jim Moloney, manager and curator of Riverview Park and Zoo

I appreciate the opportunity to make a contribution as I really enjoyed working with Alex. He was a dedicated, passionate, and very creative person, and he brought new energy and vitality to the Committee. I really enjoyed his creativity. Following our meetings, he would regularly spend time developing a strategy to address a raised issue or concern. His solutions were always "original" as he was very comfortable thinking *way* outside the box. He sometimes didn't seem overly concerned about the practicalities or constraints of a given situation. Here are a few I remember:

1. We were having trouble with night security and vandalism. Alex suggested that we could have automated drones (remote-controlled helicopters) with night-vision cameras patrolling the park and zoo. In spite of my less than enthusiastic response to the idea, he continued to research it. In the end he found out that current regulations do not permit automated drone operation (there has to be an operator), and that they cannot be operated after dark.

2. We spent a fair bit of time working on ideas for fundraising and revenue generation. Alex had a bag full of ideas, but one of his favourites was a massive tomato fight event (like La Tomatina in Italy). We would set up hordes of students (after selling them tickets) in the lower picnic area, with massive amounts of tomatoes and let them have at it. He was convinced that this would be hugely popular and a great fundraiser. All I could

think about was the liability and the giant mess left to clean up. He never was able to convince me to proceed... :)

3. My favourite of his ideas related to our planned replacement of the miniature train engine and cars. As part of our capital campaign, he suggested that we could get a Lego kit that would allow us to build a large replica of the train engine, and that we could sell visitors Lego blocks that they would then put together, helping to build the engine. I love this idea and we will do our best to find a sponsor to help us make this happen.

Judy (Masters) Stephenson, friend and neighbour

I have known Alex for over fifty years, and he always considered people's lives to be just as important as his own. When I think of him, I remember how punctual he was, all the time, because he never wanted to be the person holding up others. He was on many committees with my husband Dave, from Home & School where they took turns being President for six years, to many, many church committees, and was always a very willing worker, and never said no when asked to help. He even carried furniture out of our basement with my husband when we had a flood. Alex and I spent a lot of time sharing emails and chatting on the phone, and I always valued his input. *I think of him often and miss his wisdom and our chats.*

Rev Julie van Haaften, minister and friend

Alex loved life. He was interested in everything and enjoyed learning something new. We had many great conversations about theology, Biblical interpretation, and what it means to be a Christian. It was okay with both of us that we didn't always agree, as there was tremendous mutual respect, and that's what mattered. Alex seemed to be able to find common ground and a shared interest with almost anyone he talked to. If a shared interest wasn't apparent, he was simply keen to learn what made that particular individual 'tick'.

Alex loved family. His devotion to Shirley, his children and grandchildren was exemplary. He cared about the people he met and interacted with, and was always asking after my own family, wondering what subjects my husband was teaching, how my children were making out at school, and how my ministry was going. And he made time to listen. It was an honour to know him.

Kathy Bertrand, friend of the family

I met Alex about thirty years ago when I came to George Street United Church, and met him and his wonderful family, Shirley, Sam, and Colleen (Steven was out west at this time). Right away I liked them all. They dove right into many things including our 'amazing' slow pitch team. That was a lot of fun! Alex became the announcements person every Sunday. He would get up to the front and deliver the announcements like a boss! He never looked nervous. He had a great sense of humour and knew how to deliver a joke. He always seemed to have a twinkle in his eye.

I would run into Alex and Shirley off and on throughout the years when we were out and about. Alex always had a smile for me. I wish I could remember the stories he would tell me. Alex never seemed to change the whole time I knew him. He always looked the same, that same kind of smiling, sneaky expression I thought he had.

The second last time I saw Alex was last November at Chapters waiting in a long line to see Red Green. He sure looked happy to be meeting him. The next time I saw Alex was at my mom's funeral in December, although I don't remember seeing him or anyone else really. Alex and my mom were fast friends. My mom loved Alex. In later years they would give each other funny birthday cards, loving to tease each other. We all had lots of fun at church picnics together. I look back on those years and always smile, remembering the good times, and Alex is always a big part of those memories.

Katherine (Kathy) Blackwood, Director of Housing KPP

The first time I met Alex I was afraid of him. Alex was the Treasurer of AOTS Community Homes. The city had placed this organization under a supervisory agreement, because of poor performance by their previous property management company. As the new Property Manager, I was keen to show I knew my stuff, and it was apparent the Treasurer of the Board was very passionate about the work that AOTS Community Homes was doing. It was also very apparent that he knew his stuff and was very serious about the work they were doing. I didn't want to mess up in front of him.

I learned very quickly that I had nothing to fear. Alex was genuinely concerned about the work he and his board colleagues were doing, in providing housing for families and youth on low incomes. He was passionate about ensuring the housing was good quality, with excellent services.

I sincerely enjoyed working with Alex. I respected his knowledge and enjoyed his sense of humour. His concern for the less fortunate was obvious, and he was always willing to step up to support people who couldn't advocate for themselves. He seemed to enjoy making things right for people. He was a friend and colleague, and I honestly miss him.

Laurie Lowes, friend of the family

Alex treated me like family, and I looked to him as an adopted father. Alex always had a story to tell, and so many times he was there for my family, and I loved how our two families always spent time together at each other's homes. One great memory is Alex and my mom using the crosscut saw in his backyard, after one of the baseball end-of-season parties. They were showing the youngsters how to use one. I fondly remember Alex performing the eulogy and sharing memories of my mom at her funeral.

Morris Cox, friend

I was thinking back to when your father worked at Brant, and one thing stands out in my mind. It was his pipe that he loved to smoke, and now, there are not many buildings where you can light a pipe. But he got a lot of enjoyment out of the pipe, and I believe there were times that it was not even lit.

N. Jackson, friend of Felicia

He was among the nicest people I've met; he felt comfortable to be around which is a very rare experience for me. I feel privileged to have met him.

Patti Shaw, friend of the family

My memories of Alex always have him wearing an apron. We spent many July 1st holidays at Alex and Shirley's house, and Alex always had his barbecue apron on, while he cooked up the hamburgers for everyone. At church, Alex was always wearing his apron and cooking up pancakes, sausages, and eggs for the sunrise breakfast at Easter, Shrove Tuesday dinners and AOTS fundraiser meals. At church picnics he wore his apron cooking up hot dogs and hamburgers. I can still see him waving the barbecue lifter in the air while he cheered on the kids in their various races. I also remember him and Sam taking part in a few of those races too. Alex was always at the heart of the activities at George Street United Church, and his loss is deeply felt.

Penny Carson, friend of the family and church friend

I have known Alex and Shirley Jackson for close to forty years, as friends at George Street United Church. Over the years, they and their children, Steve, Colleen and Sam, have played an active role in the life of our church. That applies more to Sam, because Steve and Colleen started careers, then marriages that took them away from Peterborough.

When Colleen needed a place for Felicia, her daughter, to live when she was on semester work placements in Peterborough, Colleen asked if Felicia could stay with me. Shirley had said that Colleen and Felicia wanted a place where she would have room and board provided and based on that I thought my house would not be of interest, because my cooking ability leaves a lot to be desired. When Colleen came with Felicia to look at my house, Colleen explained that it would do Felicia no harm at all to have to do her own cooking. Based on that, I was happy to have Felicia stay at my home, and we got along just fine.

Sam was working out of town but often came home on weekends. The way our paths crossed even more was the time when Alex and Shirley moved from their home to an apartment, and that meant that Sam needed a place for his many items related to his love of cars. As it happened, I had managed to clear some space in my basement, and I was very pleased about that. With my permission Sam proceeded to fill that space with his car paraphernalia, as well as using half of my double garage for his out-of-season car. Sam came by his love of cars honestly, from Alex. Sam also filled one of my bedrooms with his things, although in all the time his things have been here, Sam has only slept in his bed here once, because he has a room at his parents' apartment.

The deal was that, in return for using space at my house, Alex would be my handyman. True to his word, every time I needed something done at my house, Alex knew how to fix it for me, promptly and quite creatively sometimes. I would tell Alex the problem and he always came up with a good solution for me. I look around me now and see so many things that Alex has worked on at my house, and I smile and sometimes I cry too, because I miss him. I remember asking Alex how Shirley felt about him spending time at my house, and Alex said that Shirley had learned very early on in their marriage to trust him, because in those years he worked at Bell Canada, where he was the only man working with many women. I spent my whole working career at Bell Canada, so I knew exactly what he meant.

Alex was a true gentleman and working with Alex was always a pleasure. Any time he offered a solution to a problem, when I wondered why he thought something was a good idea, he explained the merits of his idea in a very clear fashion. He had me thinking, and sometimes saying, "You are right." Surely those three words are three of the nicest words in the English language...*you are right*, almost as good as *I love you*!

Alex had a sense of humour, and *The Late Miss Penny Carson* is a title Alex gave me many years ago, to tease me and to impress upon me the importance of being on time, with varying degrees of success on my part! It showed that he cared enough to find a solution for me to erase a bad habit. That's just further evidence that Alex is a very caring person. I use the present tense because he is still alive in a very different way in heaven, and that is the very best trip any Christian will take. Ever.

Alex and I also worked together on the Board of Directors of Chemong Village. Alex was chair and I was (and still am) secretary, and we worked well together as part of the team to keep this rent geared to income housing project running smoothly. When Alex didn't have the energy to continue, we were taken off guard because Alex had always been so active and full of energy.

An illustration of how dedicated Alex was in keeping my house in good repair, early in the week that he died, he was at my house to replace the spigot on my rain barrel. Shirley drove him over here because Alex wasn't steady enough on his feet to come alone. Thank you, Alex, I will never forget you. I see some of Alex in Sam, and his presence here from time to time does comfort me. I believe that this world is a better place because Alex Jackson was in it.

Rob Wilson, former General Manager, CFIB

Alex was a very special person, in so many ways. I am heartened that I have so many wonderful memories. I always cherish those days I spent with Alex making calls, talking politics, and sharing mutual interests. His love of Saabs was infectious. We caught that bug and bought a couple of Saabs. The pipe was ever present, and part of his charm. He always had that wonderful smile, and genuine interest and caring for others.

I initially recruited Alex to join CFIB, and the contribution he made to our region was profound, both in membership growth, and impact on colleagues and their understanding of the important role the organization plays in the life of a business owner. He drew on his personal experience extensively, and I'm sure there are many business owners throughout Peterborough and beyond who have fond memories of their meetings with him. He was a valuable colleague, and our relationship grew to become good friends. If I could have only cloned Alex...

Sylvia Whan, friend

Alex was a great neighbour. We had lots of fun and laughs with our families. One time he got out his megaphone and called out to a woman across the road who was cutting her grass in her work boots. He could do this as he was part of a close neighbourhood and everyone got along. I will always remember the good times.

Tanya, sister-in-law to Colleen

I know Alex was a wonderful man, father, and husband. I wish I had known him better.

Tom Deas, friend of the family

I have known Alex for over thirty years. I found Alex willing to help anyone who needed help. He worked fixing breakfast for school children, for kids who could not afford it. He was also president of our men's club and chairman of Chemong Village Board. He was a trustee at church and chairperson of Christian Education Committee. Also, he looked after the church funds as treasurer. He helped with many beef suppers and pancake breakfasts. When asked he helped with making meat pies. On many occasions he served communion. Alex loved his family and grandchildren, and he loved his wife Shirley very much. He was a good friend. Rest in peace Alex.

Tom Harding, friend

Alex was a great friend. We had lots of good fun and always had great conversations. We had coffee together, usually in a group, but once it was just the two of us. At AOTS I found Alex to be smart, and I always learned something different from him. He seemed to know something about everything and was enjoyable to be around.

QUOTES ABOUT WORKING AND VOLUNTEERING

Regarding frequently volunteering at church: Anyway, what would I do if I did not have to run around and prepare for things like that. (Maybe have some time to read or do things that are on my list). (1998)

Started out early this morning or tried to. Just before I left, I called a fellow who called me yesterday. He has a problem and I had to take time to send faxes and email to head office. It was 9:30 before I left. Jeeze! Do these people think I am Ann Landers or somebody? Everyday someone calls with problems. (1998)

I wrote an article yesterday for the [Peterborough] Examiner to let people know that George Street [United Church] has a web page. Just have to get the minister to approve what I said. Well, I really do not need her approval, but I thought it would be polite to let her read it first and pass comment. If she wants anything changed and I do not like the changes I won't do them anyway; but just thought I should be polite and offer. (1998)

I just got home, it was really hot today, and have some abominable paperwork to do. They always want me to do paperwork. I HATE PAPERWORK AND REPORTS. I think the government should pass a law making it illegal to fill out forms and do reports if you are a grandpa. (1998)

Regarding his CFIB resignation: I did not think I made that much of an impact, but I got a letter from one vice-president, a handwritten card from another one and a letter from [the president], all telling me what a great contribution I made, etc. It is nice and sort of humbling. (1999)

Sunday is our annual meeting. I just love them, so I offered to look after the kids. Smart idea, eh? I will have to go into the meeting for the trustee report, but that is ok because it will be near the end. I spent hours doing that thing. Because of the ceiling I sold stocks and moved money around, and now I have to account for how and why. No one will understand it anyway, but someone will ask dumb questions, so I am making sure that I have the answers. (2001)

One day, perhaps next year at this time, I will have none of this stuff to do and I can run around in my little boat, fish, and do sensible things like that. Time will tell. I could not just sit around and watch TV or whatever. I guess all my life I have been doing things and have no desire to stop now and do nothing. Some people ask why I donate so much time to the church, [Youth Career Counselling], etc. when I could be just bumming around. Well, it's pretty simple. Society has been good to me and donating my experience and time is one way of contributing or paying back. I enjoy it also, or I would not do it. (2002)

A few months back I gave my resignation letter to the executive director, but she is a good friend and she and the other two ladies that keep this place going are so dedicated that I can't leave and let them down until I get some people who will take over and do things. UGH!!!!! (2004)

Can't figure out why a guy who is retired is always so busy - has a long list like a roll of toilet paper. (2008, to Edward)

Your grandmother thinks I am involved in too many things, but so far been able to stay on top. (2014)

Regarding having resigned from one volunteer position and still having 6 other volunteering commitments: Your grandmother keeps yapping that I have too many jobs & some days I think she is right. (2014)

Almost every meeting I have some hair-brained scheme, usually turned down of course. (2016)

Most other members did not think much of my last proposal but have not kicked me off the committee yet, so will see what happens with this [proposal]. (2016)

Gotta quit doing this [volunteering] stuff…getting too old. Like the song says, "I just wanna have fun." (2016)

Your grandmother…would like me to quit some of the…obligations I am involved in…but [I] don't really mind [that] stuff…I have no desire yet to just sit and watch TV or whatever most old geysers in our building do. One wanted to know if I got paid. Did not seem to realize that volunteers don't get paid; just pay. (2017)

Regarding the card and money received from tenants whom he advocated for by getting back-rent for botched building upgrades: I suspected a few bucks as they talked about a collection a few days ago, but this was not expected. I did not do it to get rewarded. Some years ago, I had a sales trainer whose motto was 'cast your bread upon the water and it will come back cake'. He was referring to how to treat customers and you know what, it works in every facet of life. (2017)

Getting tired of these commitments but then wonder what will I do if I opt out? (2017)

Kiddingly, regarding seniors asking for assistance on a frequent basis: Guess I gotta start charging or just plead ignorance and tell them to check with their kids. (2018)

QUOTES THAT SHOW WISDOM

Regarding not wanting his daughter to suffer financial hardships: Marry first for money, you can always marry for love later. (circa 1984)

Regarding celebrating another birthday: Forget the age, it is only a number, and not everyone is good at math, so it means nothing. (1999)

If you have little trinkets that you really attach special moments to, treat them nice and keep track of them. (1999)

Regarding a car accident in which a 16-year-old purposely drove into the car Colleen, Felicia, and Edward were in: Guess you had an exciting time last week. It is sure something you will remember to tell your kids one day. It is unfortunate that there are people in our world like the young man who was driving the car but do not be too harsh on him. I suspect he was not fortunate to have parents like you have, and probably has a hard time as a kid and was just doing things he thought he had to do to survive without any thought of the harm to other people. Perhaps he will get some help & counselling in jail. (2000)

Your two choices in life, I have read, are to lead or be led. (2000)

Regarding a five-year-old asking Alex to help her over a fence again and again: Well, Ya Ya, she made me think. I thought of what is important in life, because when I was running a business, I did not always recognize or have time to realize. This little squirty kid made me think of things that I remember that really mean something. Things like "Alex Jackson, Top Salesman of the Month", "Alex Jackson, all expenses paid trip to Mexico", "Alex Jackson, Diamond Award winner, Jackson Business

Systems, Top Dealer in Canada for...., etc. And then the really important moments in life came to mind. "Push me! Can you play cars?? Pick me up. Grandpa, chase me! I want to sit with my dad. I need to sit next to grandpa. Can we do that again? Can I go too? Dad...gramps can you... dad can you check this for me...ask dad...I like the stickers..." (2000)

So, your mind keeps you busy eh! Lots of people get weird ideas when they are sleeping, so they keep a pad & pencil and a flashlight by the bed. If you wake up you can jot it down before you forget, or if you get up in the morning, you can scribble a note right away while you still remember. (2001)

Regarding having had no water for a day: Ya know be without water for a day, and you realize how important it is, and how, as a society, we just take it for granted. We should be much nicer to our air and water. (2001)

I know how hard it is when you are a kid to sit down and write a letter. My mother wrote to me every week. Some of her letters are in my dresser drawer, and some day, you may even read them. I was not a kid then, but still found it hard to find the time to write to her. To me, she was a Saint, and I should have written...You write when you get the time or feel like it, but don't feel obligated to do so. (2002)

Sure, keeps me from getting bored. Like I would ever get bored with life! So much to do and so little time. Did you ever hear that phrase before? Six years old, or sixty, we all get the same number of hours, minutes, and seconds, each day. We can't trade them, they can't be stored for tomorrow, they don't return, their good before date is now so they are more precious than gold. Most of us don't realize, until we have used most of them up, how important each moment in time is. I bet you do. (2002)

I cut out the newspaper article for you, so here's your chance to try out your writing skills. Read it and ship them something. If it does not get

259

published right away, just keep sending stuff. Rejection is just part of writing and getting things published. (2003)

Regarding an 87-year-old woman he drove to appointments: She is old: even old enough to be my mother, but I really, really like her. She has constant aches and pains, shuffles along as the feet and legs don't do what they are asked to, and she remembers less than I do, which is pretty bad, but she does not complain. She is funny, laughs at herself and her ailments and just seems to love life and put up with the stuff it throws at her and makes the best of it. What a world if we could all live with her attitude! (2005)

Spring is a great time of renewal and rebirth, but it is such a short time span that if you don't do it now (raking, planting, cleaning up, etc.) tomorrow will be too late. I sometimes think the spring rush is a good lesson for doing other things in life. (2005)

If your stories are like your letter writing skills then they must be OK, dark characters or not. So, keep it up, hone your skills and send your stories to magazines, publishers, and wherever. Don't be afraid of rejections, I have a few. If you don't have any, it only means that you have not tried. You won't get any "NOs" if you don't send stuff in. Most successful writers will tell you that their rejection slips (NOs) could paper every wall in their house, and then one day a "YES". There is a litany of Abraham Lincoln's life and the rejections he encountered and yet he is revered among American presidents. You escape failure if you don't try, and you also escape winning. Losing is not a sin, not competing is. (2005)

Life can be a pain sometimes and it really gets in the way of, well, just daily living. (2005)

How's [your first job] going? In any event you will learn a whole lot about people and their behaviour, and I guess the possibility exists that we were all created equal, but we sure do not stay that way. But you will learn all that and a bunch more. Should be an interesting summer and on top of the free life lessons you will get paid. What a deal. (2005)

Remember, education, things you learn, can never be taken away. We can be robbed or lose all kinds of material possessions, but knowledge cannot be taken from you. (2005, to Edward)

Regarding a spider making a large web: Anything that smart should be left alone. (2005, to Edward)

Every job no matter how small or yucky, is important to the whole. (2006, to Edward)

What would you like to do after university, assuming you are going that route? There are many many more jobs out there than people to fill them, so finding something will not be a problem. The other solution of course is to marry some rich dude and stay at home. That would be my choice. (2006)

Life is full of adventures and surprises so make sure you always try to enjoy the journey wherever it takes you. (2007)

Yep, when I was your age, I think I thought someone seventy-years-old was ancient. Now I think your health dictates your age, or at least what you do and how you act. Luckily, I still dig in the garden and do all the things I normally do. Well, I don't jog for a mile or that kind of stuff, but I still crawl under the car to fix things and change the oil and climb the TV tower to get onto the roof to clean the eavestrough and check things out. And yes, once you get to be an adult, a ten- or fifteen-year span in ages seems to matter not. One thing you do realize, at least I am pretty sure most people would agree, is the importance of friends and family. At a certain age we are pretty independent, cocky and sure of eternal survival. We may miss them, but we can live without our family and real friends as there are always new people coming in and out of our lives. Someday however, reality hits and being alone is no fun. Cultivating real friends is one of the most important assets a person can have. You just never know when you will need them, or more importantly, when they need you. (2007)

Your mother and Uncle Steve were in public school when the Cold War was in full swing. The papers made daily reference to the fact that both Russia and the US had atomic bombs and one of them may make a mistake and push the button, blowing up half the world. A scary thought, especially to a kid I thought. My advice to those two kids was to not worry about the Cold War...rather, their concern should be whether they would have clean air to breathe and water to drink when they grew up. And sometimes our predictors are right. Water quality, and in some areas, quantity as well, is a real concern. Air is pretty yucky in most areas of the world...Governments take the easy route and put pressure on cars and light bulbs because they are very visible and popular to regulate. The biggest problem is that we want stuff, whether we need it or not. In most cases we don't need it, and when you get to be an old geyser like some of us, you will realize that most of that stuff is no guarantee of happiness, and we would be better off not having it. (2007)

I am pretty sure the dictionary would define progress as going forward, and I don't agree that people having more stuff is always growth. I think rather that it is just change in society, not growth, and not always good change....as you progress through [university] I look forward to some interesting discussions. Not arguments, just discussions. (2007)

Time has a way of disappearing. (2007, to Edward)

I don't know about you but most people, me included, keep things that we will need someday, or get to tomorrow, or read when we have time, or maybe, find a use for, etc. A good rule is if you have not used, needed, or thought about it for the last two years, get rid of it. I got rid of a ton and am still sorting. As I sift through stuff I wonder when I am no longer here, but the stuff is, will the kids, maybe you included, sort through it and save some or just turf everything! Ya gotta think about these things when you get older, and you see friends passing on and know that one day people will be reading your name in that certain column in the paper. (2008)

One thing we need to learn early in life is how to handle disappointment and that there are many more "no's" than "yesses". (2008)

After Felicia moved to Halifax for graduate school: By the way, Saskatchewan rules still apply. I can only imagine the pressures of your [program], especially since I can barely pronounce the name of it, so if you have the time and desire to write, that's great, but do not feel obligated to answer every letter. Grandpa will continue to write anyway. (2013)

This journey through life is pretty interesting. You know, sometimes we natter and complain about little things, very little things it turns out when compared to real problems some people seem to encounter. (2014)

I think of religions and I believe that 'do as I say' stinks, but actions are everything. I try to live as I believe. (date unknown)

If you keep breathing kid, one day you will be old. (date unknown)

CONCLUSION

What is there left to say about our dad and grandpa, Richard Alexander Jackson? Most people that met him liked him right away, as he had a very disarming personality, and immediately put people at ease. He was the calm presence for family and friends over the years and was relied on to diffuse many tricky situations. He had a great collection of stored up advice, but rarely gave it out to those who didn't ask first. Alex had his own opinions and didn't mind that others around him didn't share the same. His convictions were his alone, and he knew that not everyone shared the same views.

Whether he was at work, with his family or volunteering, he was fully attentive. He knew that any activity or job was worth doing correctly; to him it didn't matter if it was a trivial task or something important. Along the way he tried to have fun and bring his own specific aspect to the situation. Some of the ways he lightened circumstances were apparent in his way of talking, as he was so unique in his phrasing of everyday sayings.

Like I care was spoken when he figured that others wouldn't share his views. Another favourite along the same lines was *I don't give a hoot*. He loved listening to music that he liked, but was unable to read music well, and referred to the notes as *black squiggles*. Throughout his life he was always busy doing his *little jobs*, as he referred to them. This could be something for the church or a project at home. If he was trimming a bush, he would use what he called a *chainsaw on a stick*. While driving he might mention being in a *traffic snarl*, as opposed to a traffic jam.

He loved to say a *nickel past five*, instead of five past five to refer to the time. Speaking of time, as he got older, he called people younger than him *kids,* but this could mean a five-year-old, twenty-five-year-old or a great-grandmother. Conversely, he would mention *old geysers* for people sometimes not much older than himself, never caring that he himself was one.

If he knew someone who talked non-stop, he would say they were *yapping.* Alex preferred to say *holler* instead of yell, as in *holler at your brother to come in here. Stomach* meant a person who ate a lot, usually a family member who was in a growth spurt. Nobody would just go by, they *scooted.*

Alex scooted by in life all too fast. Many personal projects remained incomplete, and his community volunteering was left with a void to fill. Friends were saddened and a family devastated. Life does continue, and for those who have read this book we hope you carry some of Alex's spirit with you.

– Colleen and Felicia Ketcheson

APPENDIX 1

R. Alex Jackson's Life History

<u>Select Work History</u>
- 1957 - Bell Canada
- 1963 - founded Funny Services, an Advertising/Marketing Agency
- 1964 - sales for Smith Corona Marchant (SCM)
- 1967 - transferred to Peterborough to work as a Sales Manager for SCM
- 1975 - founded Jackson Business Systems Ltd., a cash register sales and service franchise with Data Terminal Systems
- 1985 - sales representative for Canadian Federation of Independent Business; stayed on as a fill-in representative after retiring in 2000
- 2005 - Employment Insurance Appeal Board Tribunal

<u>Volunteer History (chronological)</u>
- Forest Hill United Church
  - Youth leader (three years)
- George Street United Church
  - Board of Trustees (many years)
  - Delivered the announcements (eleven years)
  - Wrote and delivered several sermons
  - President of the men's club As One that Serves (AOTS) (seven years)
  - President of the Bay of Quinte for AOTS (two years)

- St. James United Church
  - o Secretary of men's club (two years)
- Boards and committees
  - o Otonabee Township Planning Board Member (eight years)
  - o Peterborough Public School Board Trustee (four years)
  - o Sir Sandford Fleming College Electronics Advisory Committee Member (ten years)
  - o Chaired the Youth Career Counselling board (three years)
  - o Chemong Village Housing Development Board Chair (on and off for four years)
  - o Riverview Park and Zoo Board Chair (four years) and member; headed a committee to come up with fundraising ideas and was responsible for getting sponsors for the 2017 Father's Day car show
- Other
  - o Taught a course when Sir Sandford Fleming College opened and helped develop the computer program curriculum
  - o Sold cookbooks for the International Plowing Match (two years)
  - o Keith Wightman Public School Breakfast Program helper (five years)
  - o Got back-rent for tenants in his apartment building after botched building upgrades (one year)
  - o Organized barbeque for his apartment building (two years)

APPENDIX 2

Tractor Story

This unfinished story was written by Alex in June 2004 as an example to Felicia of the type of story they could co-write.

I still remember the day that I saw the Sun. It was a bright spring day when the large door opened, and I was carefully driven out into that big yard where my siblings were.

A while earlier I was pushed off the end of the assembly line. A nice man in white coveralls dusted off my hood, fenders, and seat. My engine had already been checked and I was full of nice, clean oil. I sparkled all over. The nice man checked me over once more, from tires to steering wheel, then put a bit of gas in my tank.

When the key turned, my engine buzzed a few times, and then settled into a nice tractor-like purr. The exhaust noise was like music. I was ecstatic as I rolled out the door and the Sun glistened off my hood. We toured the test track. I went slow. I went fast. I backed up and did everything that a little green & yellow tractor was supposed to do. My transmission shifted in all the right gears, my brake worked just fine and my variator made me go slow and then really fast. The wind in my grill was a feeling that I had not experienced bumping along the assembly line. What a thrill.

The ride was over, and I was parked by # 145629, had a tag wired to my steering wheel and one on my key. The man left and I was alone to bask in my accomplishments and share stories with # 145629 who emerged an hour before me.

That night two more men came. They packed me up in a big wooden crate along with a shiny lawn mower deck, a snowblower, sparkling chains for my rear tires, and a set of very heavy looking weights to attach to them. It was then that I knew that I was a real tractor. A small tractor perhaps, but a real one just the same. I was not just one of those riding lawn mowers. Oh, I knew I could cut grass, but I could also throw snow, I could run a tiller, push dirt with my blade and do all kinds of things that my big brothers could do. Yes, I was a real honest to goodness tractor, and green and yellow to boot. A plastic bag of little thin books was stored in the crate with me. These books were about my history, my feed and care, proper oil, the proper spark plug, and waxing to keep me looking new were all part of the contents of those books. What a great companion I would make for somebody who appreciates and loves little tractors. As my crate was loaded onto the truck, I prayed to the great green tractor god who ran and worked forever in that big field of grass and snow and had endless piles of gravel to move. I never thought of the day that I would finally join him, I just prayed for a nice green lawn to look after, lots of gravel to push around and haul in my trailer, and of course tons of snow to play in during those long winter months. But most of all, I prayed for a really nice owner who was obsessive about keeping me in my nice new condition and would treat me with respect.

The truck pulled out of the gate and I felt sorry to be leaving # 145629 sitting all by himself in that big yard. I wanted so badly to toot at him, but they never gave me a horn so all I could do was wiggle my front wheels, but I knew he could not see me locked up tight in that big wooden crate. I was off to a new adventure, off to do all the things that little tractors do, but where?

As we rumbled on and Moline, Illinois disappeared into the distance, I thought about a nice home in Abaline, or maybe somewhere in Colorado, or even some lush acreage to look after for a famous star in Hollywood. Ending up in a dealer's showroom in Texas seemed exciting, or maybe Detroit where I could work in Greenfield Village and show those little Ford guys what a real tractor could do. With my blower attachment strapped to the pallet in front of me, even a home in Alaska was not impossible. Wow, being a little tractor had endless possibilities. With this future enfolding, I wondered what # 145629 was thinking, sitting there along in that big lot, and where he would end up. We were buddies but after all he was only a 210 and I was 214. Maybe cutting grass for a convent was his destination or, heaven forbid, being driven around some little park in downtown Chicago. I wondered if we would ever meet again, and swap stories about our owners, about cutting knee-high grass without a whimper, about throwing snow over high farm fences, or, or... The rumble of the truck wheels lolled me to sleep, and I drifted off thinking of all the adventures to come.

The sun again. Little slivers of sunlight coming through the cracks in the crate were bouncing off my hood. People were talking.

"Yep, got a 214 and some other stuff to take up to Canada. Going through the Soo, down #17 along the lake and into the tip of southern Ontario. Nice country. Been there once before."

"Good machines, those little 214s," came another voice.

That was me they were talking about. My engine and frame swelled with pride. I felt happy all over, except southern Ontario was not Texas, nor California, nor...I had no idea of my fate. Where was I going and who would be looking after me? Suddenly life as a little green tractor was not so exciting. My tires started to shake.

The truck rumbled on, and on, and on. More stops, more anxiety about my future. I even started to wish that I was just a lawn mower to cut grass in Nevada, Florida, or somewhere that I knew. But I was a little tractor and destined to work wherever someone needed and wanted me. My fate was not mine to determine, and I almost wished that I was still sitting in that big lot beside # 145629. Would I ever really cut grass and throw snow and be taken care of?

The noise was deafening. Crowbars chewing off the corner of my crate, cutters biting through the straps, and someone pulling on the sides. And there I was, in the sunlight again, with three men staring at me, and looking admiringly at the mower deck and snowblower that had shared my space.

"First 214 we got in. Pretty cute eh! Looks like a real tractor, just a bit smaller, a whole lot smaller. Bet Joe will really like this one when he comes to pick it up."